The Origins of SDI, 1944-1983

Modern War Studies

THE ORIGINS OF SDI, 1944–1983

Donald R. Baucom

 University Press of Kansas

Published by the University Press of Kansas (Lawrence, Kansas
66049), which was organized by the Kansas Board of Regents and is
operated and funded by Emporia State University, Fort Hays State
University, Kansas State University, Pittsburg State University,
the University of Kansas, and Wichita State University

Library of Congress Cataloging-in-Publication Data

Baucom, Donald R.
   The origins of SDI, 1944–1983 / Donald R. Baucom.
     p. cm. — (Modern war studies)
   Includes bibliographical references and index.
   ISBN 0-7006-0531-2
   1. Strategic Defense Initiative—History. I. Title. II. Series.
UG743.B42 1992
359.1′74′09—dc20   92-5922

British Library Cataloguing in Publication Data is available.

Printed in the United States of America
10 9 8 7 6 5 4 3 2 1

The paper used in this publication meets the minimum requirements of
the American National Standard for Permanence of Paper for Printed
Library Materials Z39.48-1984.

FOR "POP"
RALPH FRANCIS BAUCOM
18 November 1910–6 September 1987

> Integer vitae scelerisque purus
> Non eget Mauris jaculis neque arcu.
> —*Horace,* Odes, *I, 22, 1*

In any case, the whole ABM question touched off so intense and emotional a debate in this country as to be virtually without precedent on any issue of weaponry. . . .

We shall not attempt here the impossible task, impossible especially in a few brief pages, of weighing the case on its merits. Highly knowledgeable and specifically informed people could be found on both sides of the argument. Scientists, engineers, and others disagreed with each other about the reliability or basic workability of the system. The amount of obvious bias on each side was often wondrous to behold.

—*Bernard Brodie and Fawn Brodie,* From Crossbow to H-Bomb, *rev. and enl. ed. (Bloomington: Indiana University Press, 1973), pp. 305–6*

CONTENTS

ILLUSTRATIONS

We were all sea-swallow'd, though some cast again;
And, by that, destined to perform an act,
Whereof what's past is prologue; what to come,
In yours and my discharge.
　　　　　　　　　　　　—Shakespeare, The Tempest, *II, 1*

　　　　In May 1987 I joined the Strategic Defense Initiative Organization (SDIO) as its staff historian.* On the second Saturday morning after my arrival, Lieutenant General James A. Abrahamson, the first director of SDIO, asked me to meet him in the agency's offices, which had just been constructed in the old bus tunnel under the Pentagon's concourse. After explaining SDIO's mission and how he was attempting to accomplish it, he described for me how the program had gotten started. He understood that his own information was incomplete, but he knew enough to recognize that much of what was being written about the program's origins was inaccurate. As a result, he suggested that my first project should be a study of President Ronald Reagan's decision to launch the Strategic Defense Initiative (SDI). Since he realized that much of what had happened was still locked in the minds of those who had contributed to the decision, he recommended that I begin this study by interviewing the key participants and indicated that he would help me secure these interviews.
　　As my interviews and research progressed, I came to recognize that

*This book is a significantly revised version of the study I completed in 1989 for SDIO and presents my own, rather than any official, positions and interpretations.

not even the participants themselves were aware of all the factors that contributed to the president's decision. Nor was a complete written account available. Judging from the first round of assessments of the Reagan presidency, such an account is still lacking. The most glaring omission is a full and accurate account of the role of Karl R. Bendetsen's High Frontier Panel and its relationship to the widely known High Frontier organization led by Lieutenant General Daniel O. Graham, U.S. Army (Ret.).

Additionally, my research indicated clearly that one could not properly understand the SDI decision apart from its broad historical context. Yet I discovered that published accounts generally gloss over the three and a half decades of strategic, technical, and political developments that are the prologue to Reagan's March 1983 speech. This point was driven home to me during an interview with Maxwell W. Hunter II in the fall of 1987.

Hunter had recently retired from his position as a senior aerospace engineer with Lockheed Corporation. He had spent much of his long career working on ballistic missile defenses, having first become involved in this endeavor in the 1950s. Thirty years later, he attended a briefing given by a member of the Fletcher Committee, which was investigating technologies that had potential for missile defenses. At one point, the briefer remarked: You may not believe this, but after you think about missile defenses for a few months they begin to make sense. Hunter could not restrain himself and blurted out: "For Christ's sake, Harry! Some of us have been thinking about this for twelve years. How do you think you got your chance to spend three months on it?"[1]

My aim in this book is to provide a reasonably complete account of President Reagan's decision that is firmly rooted in the political, technological, and strategic framework that did much to drive the decision. In the first part, I treat the dawn of the missile age, covering events from the first V-2 attacks on London in 1944 through early U.S. efforts to develop ballistic missile defenses to the decision in 1969 to field the SAFEGUARD system. During this early period, the American missile defense program was guided more or less by the idea that no offensive weapon should be left unopposed by defensive countermeasures.

In Part II, I discuss arms control negotiations in the 1970s and address how the agreements produced by these talks institutionalized offensive nuclear deterrence by making it impossible for the superpowers to field operationally effective missile defenses. In a strategic world dominated by concerns about assured destruction of enemy targets, defensive systems could no longer be considered intrinsically good; defenses could not be pursued without evaluating their possible impact on the delicate balance of nuclear terror that had come to exist between the Soviet Union and the United States.

In the third part, I describe how the SALT agreements contributed to the demise of SAFEGUARD in 1976 and explain that the post-SAFEGUARD ABM program was transformed into a research-only program that was to provide a hedge against a technological breakthrough by the Soviets. After 1976 U.S. missile defense work focused on the technologies that promised to eliminate SAFEGUARD's shortcomings. The success of this effort, combined with American concern about increasing Soviet strategic power, had sparked renewed interest in missile defenses by the time Ronald Wilson Reagan became the fortieth president of the United States.

In the final two chapters, I cover events that occurred during the first two years of Reagan's presidency, giving an account of the activities of Bendetsen and Graham and an explanation of how a crisis in Reagan's strategic modernization program led the Joint Chiefs of Staff (JCS) and key members of the National Security Council (NCS) to recommend a new strategic initiative—the pursuit of ballistic missile defenses and their incorporation into national strategy for the deterrence of nuclear war.

Virtually all of the events described in this book have occurred within my lifetime. For centuries, historians have known the pitfalls of writing about their own times. Almost four hundred years ago, Sir Walter Raleigh wrote his famous *History of the World* (1614) while confined to the Tower of London under a death sentence after being implicated in several efforts to overthrow James I, king of England. Not surprisingly, Raleigh took some comfort in the fact that his book ended with the era of Imperial Rome, which was separated from his own time by more than a thousand years; he warned the historian who might write about the events of his own day that if he followed "truth too near the heels, it may haply strike out his teeth. There is no mistress or guide that hath led her followers and servants into greater miseries."[2]

In writing this book, I make no claim to the dispassionate objectivity that Raleigh's thousand-year perspective allowed. Nevertheless, I have tried to follow truth as closely as possible in my efforts to produce an account of Ronald Reagan's SDI decision that is set firmly within its historical context. To the extent I succeeded, this book my serve as a starting point for future historians who will have the advantages of additional sources and a fuller knowledge of the consequences of this decision.

Like everyone who completes a major research project, I owe a tremendous debt to a number of people. As already noted, General Abrahamson suggested this study and actively supported my research and writing for almost two years. Once my efforts were under way, I received steady encouragement from Alfred Goldberg, the historian for the Office of the Secretary of Defense, and Richard Kohn, who until recently was the chief of Air Force History.

Although all of the people I interviewed were very generous in sharing their time and providing important insights into the SDI decision, Admiral James D. Watkins, former chief of naval operations, was especially helpful. Not only did he grant me a lengthy interview, but he also provided me a written summary of his activities during the period immediately preceding the president's decision. He also read parts of the manuscript and met with me for brief discussions on two other occasions.

I am deeply indebted to Gladys Bendetsen, widow of Karl R. Bendetsen, for graciously allowing me full access to her husband's papers on the activities of the High Frontier Panel. I was assisted in going through these papers by Ms. Geraldine Pugh, Mr. Bendetsen's personal secretary.

I also deeply appreciate the detailed criticisms of my manuscript that were provided by Drs. David MacIsaac and David R. Mets; Stephen J. Cimbala, professor of political science at the University of Pennsylvania, Delaware County Campus; and Dr. Gregg Herken, chairman of the Space History Department at the National Air and Space Museum, Washington, D.C.

I also owe Mr. Arnold Kramish a debt of gratitude for his assistance with the chapter on the High Frontier. Maxwell Hunter helped me understand the significance of a number of important breakthroughs in missile defense technology and provided valuable information on Senator Malcolm Wallop's activities on behalf of missile defenses. Dr. Martin Anderson, who played a key role in advocating ballistic missile defenses as a member of Reagan's immediate staff, helped considerably with insights into activities in the White House.

Other people who helped considerably are Ms. Nancy Stenger and Ms. Deborah Miller, who prepared numerous interview transcripts. Mrs. Bobbie L. Stephens of the army's Pentagon Library provided assistance by helping me secure many of the secondary works I used in completing this study.

Finally, I want to thank my wife, Peggy, for her patience and understanding during the many nights and weekends when this book totally absorbed my attention and energies.

ABM	antiballistic missile
ACDA	Arms Control and Disarmament Agency
ARPA	Advanced Research Projects Agency (changed to DARPA in 1970)
ASAT	antisatellite
ASCF	American Security Council Foundation
ATP	advanced technology program
BAMBI	ballistic missile boost intercept
BMD	ballistic missile defense
BMEWS	ballistic missile early warning system
C³	command, control, and communications
CDC	Control Data Corporation
CEP	CNO's Executive Panel; circular error probable
CIA	Central Intelligence Agency
CNO	chief of naval operations
CPA	continuous patrol aircraft
CW	continuous wave
DARPA	Defense Advanced Research Projects Agency (formerly ARPA)
DDR&E	director of defense research and engineering
DEW	directed energy weapon
DOD	Department of Defense
DOT	designating optical tracker
DSB	Defense Science Board
DUB	deep underground basing
EIS	environmental impact statement

FASS	forward acquisition sensor system
FBS	forward-based systems
GBMD	global ballistic missile defense
GDL	gas dynamic laser
GLIPAR	Guidelines Identification Program for Antimissile Research
GPALS	Global Protecion Against Limited Strikes
HOE	homing overlay experiment
ICBM	intercontinental ballistic missile
IDA	Institute for Defense Analyses
IFPA	Institute for Foreign Policy Analysis
INF	Intermediate-range Nuclear Forces Treaty (December 1987)
INSATRAC	interception by satellite tracking
IOC	initial operational capability
IRBM	intermediate range ballistic missile
JCS	Joint Chiefs of Staff
KKV	kinetic kill vehicle
laser	light amplification through stimulated emission of radiation
LLNL	Lawrence Livermore National Laboratory
LoADS	low-altitude defense system (becomes SENTRY)
LODE	large optics demonstration experiment
MAD	mutual assured destruction
maser	microwave amplification through stimulated emission of radiation
MIPS	million instructions per second
MIRV	multiple independently targeted reentry vehicle
MPS	multiple protective shelter
MSR	missile site radar
NASA	National Aeronautics and Space Administration
NATO	North Atlantic Treaty Organization
NCA	national command authorities
NCCB	National Conference of Catholic Bishops
NORAD	North American Air Defense Command
NSC	National Security Council
ONR	Office of Naval Research
OP-65	Theater and Strategic Nuclear Welfare Division, Headquarters, U.S. Navy
PAR	perimeter acquisition radar
PEPE	parallel element processing ensemble

RBIG	Reentry Body Identification Group
RV	reentry vehicle
R&D	research and development
SAB	Scientific Advisory Board
SAC	Strategic Air Command
SAG	Scientific Advisory Group
SALT	strategic arms limitation talks
SANE	[an antinuclear group]
SDI	Strategic Defense Initiative
SDIO	Strategic Defense Initiative Organization
SLBM	submarine-launched ballistic missile
SPAD	space patrol active defense
SPS	solar power satellite
STP	systems technology program
TOW	tube-launched, optically tracked, wire-guided

Part One
Dawn of the Missile Age

The image of squadrons of bombers lumbering over the Arctic Circle with frightened and fallible young men in their cockpits somehow seemed quaint and manageable compared to the specter of a barrage of inanimate but precisely guided metal cones hurtling through space toward targets in the United States.
—*Strobe Talbott, 1988*[1]

World War II ushered in the era of strategic bombing, as thousands of U.S. and British bombers dropped tons of bombs on targets in Nazi Germany. As the war was ending, the Nazis initiated the missile age when they launched the first V-2 ballistic missile against London in September 1944. This attack sparked a quest for defenses against ballistic missiles that has continued to this day. As the war ended, technical experts in the United States realized that it was only a matter of time before the United States would be threatened by nuclear-tipped missiles and began calling for the initiation of a research and development (R&D) program to develop missile defenses. Not surprisingly, within a year of the Japanese surrender in the Pacific, the U.S. Army Air Forces (AAF) had begun two formal studies of the ballistic missile defense problem.

In addition to the efforts of the air force, the U.S. Army launched its own missile defense program. Both programs continued until 1958, when they were merged and placed under the control of the army. By the early 1960s, the army had successfully tested its NIKE-ZEUS antiballistic missile (ABM) and was pushing to begin deployment of an operational system.

As the 1960s progressed, the army's ABM program became enmeshed in the emerging body of thought about strategic nuclear deterrence. At the beginning of the missile age, there was little doubt that developing defenses against ballistic missiles was the appropriate course of action. However, as the Soviet Union developed strategic nuclear forces comparable to those of the United States, the central concern became establishing and maintaining a stable state of deterrence between the superpowers. Now development and deployment of missile defenses had to be viewed in the context of how they would affect the "delicate balance of terror." Deterrence doctrine notwithstanding, as the decade of the 1960s was ending, a divided U.S. leadership decided that it was appropriate for the nation to field a missile defense system.

CHAPTER ONE

The Origins of Missile Defenses: From V-2 to NIKE-X

There is a rough rule-of-thumb principle that no enemy vehicle of attack must be permitted to have "a free ride." The enemy should not be relieved of uncertainty with respect to any avenue of attack which it is feasible for him to use. The main value of ballistic missiles over aircraft to the attacker is precisely their high probability of successful penetration per unit, at least under present techniques of defense.

—Bernard Brodie, 1959[1]

On the evening of 8 September 1944, as residents of London sat down to dinner, they were shaken by a terrific explosion followed by the sound of a "heavy body rushing through the air." Sixteen seconds later, a similar event occurred near Epping. What had caused these mysterious effects? British scientists had the answer. In July 1944 the Swedes had shipped to them the debris of a large German rocket that had gone astray and crashed in Sweden during a June test. Using the debris, the British had constructed a rather accurate picture of the size and performance of this large new German missile, which they concluded would probably carry a warhead of about 1 ton. After examining pieces of wreckage from the sites of the 8 September explosions and listening to descriptions of the attacks, British scientists knew that England had been struck for the first time by German V-2 ballistic missiles traveling so fast that the sound of their approach was not heard until after their warheads had exploded.[2]

Within a month of the first attack, specially adapted radar units were detecting V-2s once they rose above 5,000 feet. Soon radar data were being used to compute the time and point of impact of attacking missiles. The availability of this information gave rise to a scheme of defense. Using the predicted target and time of arrival, batteries of antiaircraft artillery would fire a heavy barrage in front of the incoming missile. The exploding artillery shells would create a barrier of shrapnel that would destroy the missile. Although this idea was seriously considered, it was abandoned as impractical. A barrage of 320,000 shells would be required to produce a likely kill. Of these shells, about 2 percent would be duds that would fall undetonated on London, causing more damage and casualties than a V-2. In the end, the Allies could not find a means of defeating a V-2 once it had been launched; the only effective defensive measures were attacking the V-2 factories and launching sites or capturing the territory from which the missiles could be launched.[3] The origins of the U.S. antiballistic missile program may be traced to these efforts to stop the German V-2s.

Following the war, analyses of the German missile program produced some sobering findings. As the war ended, the Germans were developing a large two-stage rocket that might have become the world's first intercontinental ballistic missile (ICBM). The initial stage of this missile was the A-10, a large booster with 200 tons of thrust. It would have accelerated a second missile, the A-9, to a speed of 1,500 miles per hour, at which point the A-9 would have fired and accelerated to a velocity of 3,360 miles per hour. This velocity would have given the A-9 a range of 3,500 miles. Had the war continued into 1946, the Germans might well have made good their plans to bombard New York City.[4]

German plans for an ICBM and other wartime developments indicated clearly that the near-absolute security Americans had enjoyed during the war was becoming a thing of the past. As a result, several studies recommended immediate efforts to develop a means of defending the United States against attacks by aircraft and ballistic missiles. On 4 July 1945 a group of officers sent to Europe to study the Allied efforts to counter the V-2 recommended the initiation of a research and development program aimed at developing defenses against missiles like the V-2. Five months later, a report of the AAF's Scientific Advisory Group (SAG) discussed the use of homing rockets armed with nuclear explosives and some form of energy beam to defend against attacking missiles.[5]

In May 1946 the report of the War Department Equipment Board, which had been headed by General Joseph W. Stilwell, was completed. Among its more prescient statements was this one:

A German V-2 is apparently being readied for firing in this photograph taken from a German prisoner of war on 13 April 1945. (Photo SC-232839, National Archives)

Guided missiles, winged or nonwinged, traveling at extreme altitudes and at velocities in excess of supersonic speed, are inevita-
ble. Intercontinental ranges of over 3,000 miles and pay load [sic]
sufficient to carry atomic explosive [sic] are to be expected. Re-
motely controlled, and equipped with homing devices designed to
be attracted to sound, metal, or heat, such missiles would be incapable of interception with any existing equipment such as fighter
aircraft and antiaircraft fire. Guided interceptor missiles, dispatched in accordance with electronically computed data obtained
from radar detection stations, will be required.

The report recommended that "the development of defensive measures
against atomic weapons be accorded priority over all other National
Defense projects."[6]

THE QUEST FOR MISSILE DEFENSES BEGINS

Given the revelations about the German missiles and the work of the
Scientific Advisory Group, it is not surprising that the Army Air Forces
had developed military characteristics for antimissile missiles by the
middle of February 1946 and let contracts for two missile defense projects on 4 March 1946. Project WIZARD (MX-794) was a series of studies
to be completed by the University of Michigan, where the project chairman was Professor E. W. Conlon. WIZARD was to provide the basis for
developing a missile that could destroy a vehicle traveling up to 4,000
miles per hour at altitudes between 60,000 and 500,000 feet.[7]

The second contract established Project THUMPER (MX-795), which
was to explore the interception of "rocket-powered ballistic and glide
missiles and supersonic ram-jets." This project involved several test
flights using the two-stage BUMPER missile, which used a rocket similar to the German V-2 for its first stage and the WAC Corporal for its second stage. Like WIZARD, the THUMPER concept involved intercepting
targets traveling at 4,000 miles per hour at altitudes up to 500,000
feet.[8]

Although THUMPER was canceled in March 1948, WIZARD survived
until 1958 when it was merged with the army's NIKE-ZEUS antiballistic
missile system. This had evolved out of the earlier NIKE program,
which aimed to develop a missile defense against bombers and air-
breathing missiles.[9]

The first NIKE missile was the AJAX, which had been deployed around U.S. cities and air bases in the early 1950s to protect them from attacks by bombers. Before the end of the decade, the army added the nuclear-tipped NIKE-HERCULES to its air defense arsenal and began serious consideration of what would be needed to defend the country in the next decade.[10]

This consideration took the form of the NIKE II study, which was initiated in March 1955 when the army contracted with Bell Laboratories for an eighteen-month review of air defense requirements in the 1960s. While Bell was directed to concentrate on the air-breathing threat, it was also to consider defense against ballistic missiles. In June, prompted by intelligence reports that the Soviets would soon have an ICBM capability, the army shifted the emphasis of the Bell study toward antimissile defenses. Five months after this change in focus, Bell also secured an air force contract to complete a complementary study on ABMs.[11]

In its first report of 2 December 1955, Bell identified many of the basic challenges posed by ballistic missile defense (BMD). These included such things as determining the optimum point in the ICBM's flight for interception and detailing the role required of an effective ABM command and control system that had to include the difficult task of distinguishing decoys from warheads. Soon after the submission of this original report, Bell also recognized that the development of a "long-range, high-data-rate acquisition radar" was a critical factor in missile defenses and should be undertaken immediately.[12]

While completing these studies for the army and air force, Bell accomplished one of the first technical milestones in the effort to develop an antimissile system. At this time, the scientific community generally believed it was impossible to intercept an ICBM because of its extremely high velocity—24,000 feet per second. Intercepting a target moving at such a speed, several scientists thought, was tantamount to hitting a bullet with another bullet. During its examination of ballistic missile defenses, Bell used analog simulations to run 50,000 intercepts of ballistic missile targets. The results indicated that it was possible to intercept an ICBM.[13]

From the NIKE-II study, a new missile emerged. NIKE-ZEUS was a three-staged, solid-propellant missile designed to carry a nuclear warhead of 400 pounds. In addition to this missile, the ZEUS system was to include advanced radar equipment and communications links to tie the subsystems together.[14]

THE ARMY BECOMES THE CHAMPION
OF BALLISTIC MISSILE DEFENSES

As the Bell study was being completed, two interrelated concepts increasingly dominated U.S. strategic thinking: deterrence and containment. At first, American defense policy was concerned with restraining the massive conventional force the Soviets kept under arms after World War II. In the United States, there was no support for maintaining the large conventional military force that would have been required to accomplish this goal. Therefore, the cornerstone of our defense policy became the deterrence of Soviet aggression by the threat of nuclear air attack against the Soviet homeland, a policy more bellicosely termed "massive retaliation" during the Eisenhower years. At first the nuclear-armed manned bomber was the mainspring of deterrence, and the air force became the dominant military service. As the Soviet nuclear arsenal grew and ICBMs replaced bombers as the backbone of the U.S. deterrent force, the dominance of the air force continued until the advent of submarine-launched ballistic missiles (SLBMs) gave the navy a major role in deterring nuclear war.[15]

This situation placed the army at a disadvantage in the annual budget competition and led the army's leaders to energetically pursue a strategic mission that would ensure it a larger piece of the budget pie. Thus the army began to push the development of its JUPITER intermediate-range ballistic missile (IRBM), which was equivalent to the air force THOR, and to work diligently on the development of its ZEUS ABM system.[16] Not surprisingly, this competition for missions and scarce defense dollars intensified the rivalry between the air force and the army.

As the end of 1956 approached, the feud between these two services over the development of the IRBM had begun to upset President Dwight Eisenhower, who also wondered why the army needed a missile with a range of 1,500 miles. Furthermore, the time had arrived for Secretary of Defense Charles Wilson to choose between THOR and JUPITER. To this point, the secretary had permitted each service to develop its own missile in the belief that overall missile technology would be advanced by having two projects, even though there would be some overlap in efforts and one project would end up being canceled.[17]

Wilson's decision on the IRBM and his adjudication of the associated roles-and-missions dispute that surrounded missile development and acquisition were disappointing for the army. In a memorandum of 26 November 1956, he gave the air force responsibility for land-based IRBMs. Where the air defense mission was concerned, he divided it, giving the army responsibility for terminal defense and the air force control over area defense.[18] Generally, this meant the army was responsible for developing a missile defense system that could be based near a vital potential target such as a city and be capable of striking an attacking missile or bomber at a horizontal range of 100 nautical miles. Left undecided in the Wilson ruling was which service would have overall responsibility for the operation of the air defense system. This undecided issue gave the army hope that it might be able to lay claim to a strategic mission by eventually gaining control of the nation's air defenses. A strong push by the army into this small strategic niche ensured that the rivalry between the army and the air force would continue.[19]

The year after Wilson issued his memorandum, the army spent between 10 and 15 percent of its budget on air defense and was beginning to talk about the role of defense in strategic deterrence. Such talk was sure to aggravate the army's conflict with the air force, since it threatened the air service's dominance of strategic nuclear deterrence. In November 1957, the air force presented general arguments against air defense and specifically criticized the ZEUS system that the army was developing for the point defense mission. To begin with, the air force argued, the key to deterrence was offensive capability. Moreover, the ZEUS system itself was flawed. It could be fooled by decoys and easily overwhelmed if the Soviets simply added to their attack force. Since ZEUS could not be operational until 1961, it would not even help with the missile gap the United States supposedly would face over the next few years. Somewhat inconsistently, given its arguments, the air force continued to support its own WIZARD BMD program.[20]

The army's answer to the air force charges stressed the value of an ABM system in defending vital U.S. targets and protecting American bombers, which were still the backbone of the U.S. deterrent force. Such a defensive system would also support nuclear deterrence by complicating possible Soviet plans for a first strike. Additionally, the army pointed out that the ZEUS system possessed potential for growth in response to a Soviet threat of increasing size and complexity.[21]

The Gaither Report, which was completed on 7 November 1957, lent credence to the air force position. The committee that completed this report had been appointed by President Eisenhower to study civil defense and was named after its chairman, H. Rowan Gaither, Jr. The committee's charge was expanded to include an examination of the vulnerability of Strategic Air Command's (SAC) bombers to a surprise attack by the Soviets. The Gaither report stated that it would be after

An early model of the NIKE-ZEUS missile is shown here in a test flight at the White Sands Missile Range on 23 May 1960. (Photo SC-572795, National Archives)

1962 before the United States achieved even a limited defensive capability against Soviet forces. In the meantime, the best defense was the deterrence of nuclear war by SAC bomber forces, and the committee recommended measures to improve the survivability of those forces. Where the development of missile defenses was concerned, the committee held that the United States should begin by deploying systems with limited capabilities around SAC bases in 1959 and improve these defenses as possible in the years beyond that time. Concerning the defense of populations, the Gaither Report stated that "the importance of providing active defense of cities or other critical areas demands the development and installation of the basic elements of a [missile defense] system at an early date. Such a system initially may have only a relatively low-altitude intercept capability, but would provide the framework on which to add improvements brought forth by the research and test programs."[22]

By the beginning of 1958, the continued bickering between the air force and the army over ballistic missile defenses reached the point at which the secretary of defense, now Neil H. McElroy, felt compelled to intercede. Since the army's ZEUS missile was well along in the development stage and the air force had no missile suitable for the ABM mission other than those being studied under the WIZARD program, McElroy decided on 16 January that the army would have primary responsibility for developing the ABM system. However, he directed the air force to continue working on the radar systems and the command and control electronics under development in the WIZARD project, since the air force had gained considerable experience in this area from working with its ballistic missile early warning system (BMEWS). McElroy ordered the air force to see that the equipment it developed was compatible with the army's ZEUS missile.[23]

McElroy's decision was promulgated while the House Armed Services Committee was holding hearings into the Department of Defense's (DOD) guided missile program. As these proceedings continued into February, the air force expressed its disagreement with McElroy's decision through Lieutenant General Donald L. Putt, deputy chief of staff for research and development, who appeared before the committee on 18, 19, and 20 February. In his opening statement, Putt noted that the air force had been working on ballistic missile defenses for ten years and stated that both RAND and the air force Scientific Advisory Board (SAB) had conducted studies of missile defenses. He also described the McElroy decision in a matter-of-fact fashion and then explained the work the air force was doing on a system to give early warning of a missile attack.[24]

Later, under questioning by the committee chairman, Carl Vinson (D-Ga.), and the committee chief counsel, Robert W. Smart, Putt admitted that he had reservations about a NIKE-ZEUS system that was expected to provide coverage of the United States for about $6 billion. According to Putt: "We have in the Air Force grave concern as to the capability, for the cost involved. I think we must get on with something, but I don't believe we are convinced that this is the best approach." He went on to say that "if the Air Force had the operational responsibility and the development responsibility, it would not develop the Nike-Zeus system, for immediate operational employment." When asked by Representative Mendel Rivers (D-S.C.) if the same thing applied to the air force's WIZARD program, Putt said: "no." Putt then explained that the air force had not yet settled on a missile design for its defense system, as the air service wanted to be sure its system would be able to deal with possible Soviet responses to the deployment of U.S. defenses. If the air force had responsibility for missile defenses, it would pursue development of one of three proposals for interceptors that contractor teams had submitted under the WIZARD program.[25]

The committee continued to question Putt on this matter during the second day of his testimony to be sure he and the air force did not think NIKE-ZEUS was the best missile for use against ballistic missiles. It also wanted to clarify the relationship between WIZARD and NIKE-ZEUS, which was done for the committee by the assistant secretary of the air force for research and development, Richard E. Horner, who stressed the complementary nature of the parts of the ABM program as it had been divided by Secretary McElroy. Putt qualified his position from the previous day by noting that he supported proceeding with the NIKE-ZEUS program but not with attempting to produce a missile at that time. Under further questioning, Putt advised the committee that the air force had spent about $34 million on WIZARD between 1946 and 17 January 1958 when the program was ended in response to the McElroy memorandum of 16 January. This money, Putt indicated, had not been wasted, for the WIZARD program had produced important advances in radar, including the Millstone Hill radar, which could pick up an ICBM warhead at 3,000 miles. Such a radar would play a key role in any missile defense system the country might develop, Putt said.[26]

Later, Representative William H. Bates (R-Mass.) asked Putt bluntly which was better, WIZARD or ZEUS. Putt again referred to the fact that Project WIZARD involved three contractor designs. One design was done by the team of Bell Laboratories and Douglas Aircraft Corporation and was "almost identical" to the ZEUS missile. Putt said that he believed both of the other designs, one by a contractor team composed of the Lockheed and Raytheon companies and the other by a second team of the Convair and RCA companies, had greater promise than the first design. However, the air force was still not ready to choose between these designs when McElroy made his decision to restrict WIZARD to the development of only electronics components.[27]

The SAB study mentioned by Putt in his testimony was really a confluence of several studies that were in various stages as Putt was appearing before the House Armed Services Committee. In May 1957, prompted by concerns about military missions in the cislunar realm, Putt directed SAB to establish an ad hoc committee to examine issues related to advanced weapons technology. This panel was chaired by H. Guyford Stevers and included among its members Drs. Clark B. Millikan and Simon Ramo. Since studies being done by RAND, Ramo-Wooldrige, and air force organizations indicated that vehicles capable of operating in space would soon be available, Putt asked the group for an assessment of the current state of space flight technology. On 9 October, five days after the launching of Sputnik I, this committee submitted a report to the air force chief of staff, General Thomas D. White, recommending a high-priority basic research program that would prepare the air force for exploratory and logistical operations in space.[28]

Another part of the SAB study activities was the work of a group chaired by Dr. Edward Teller, a member of SAB's Nuclear Panel. This group was composed of SAB members, representatives of industry, and technical advisers from the air force's Air Research and Development Command. It met on 21 and 22 October 1957 and submitted a report on 28 October that recommended consolidating missile and space programs in DOD and assigning them a top national priority.[29]

About six weeks later, members of Stevers's committee and those of Teller's group came together at a full meeting of SAB in Arizona on 4–6 December. Here, these scientists agreed that "Sputnik and the Russian ICBM capability [had] created a national emergency." They also agreed on a course of action that the air force should pursue in response to this crisis. After forming a new ad hoc committee under Stevers, they issued a statement that was presented to General White a few days after the Arizona meeting. It declared that the air force should vigorously pursue the development of ballistic missiles and reconnaissance satellites. With regard to ABM systems, the committee recommended that the air force "pursue an active research program on anti-ICBM problems. The critical elements are decoy discrimination and radar tracking. When these problems are solved, a strong anti-ICBM missile system should be started."[30]

Following these recommendations, General Putt directed SAB to conduct a general review of America's continental defense problem in light of what Sputnik I indicated about Soviet military capabilities. In January 1958, SAB formed another ad hoc committee, this one under Dr. Chalmers W. Sherwin. This committee's report was issued in January 1959 and proved to be something of a disappointment for the air force. It concluded that defense problems had been greatly complicated by the arrival of the ICBM. Moreover, the state of defensive technology was not "sufficiently advanced to enable anyone to conceive reliable systems for intercepting and destroying missiles."[31]

The results of these studies help explain why the air force was so hostile to the army's ABM efforts when Secretary McElroy decided to assign the army principal responsibility for the ballistic missile defense mission. Although McElroy's decision ameliorated the dispute between the army and the air force, it did not end their conflict, which surfaced from time to time in the 1960s as the air force continued to protect its dominant role in the nation's strategy of deterrence. What McElroy's decision had done was to confirm the army in its role as DOD's principal constituency for ballistic missile defense.

Even as McElroy was making his decision on BMD, the army was seeking funds for production of ZEUS in the FY 1959 budget with an eye toward a 1962 operational date for the missile system. Although McElroy had earlier in the month named the army as the principal service for ABM, in hearings later in January he nevertheless argued that there were still too many uncertainties associated with the interception of ICBM warheads. While he favored continued R&D on a BMD system, he considered it too early to begin production. Congress shared the secretary's view and cut the $507 million the army had requested for ZEUS production from its FY 1959 budget. The army's attempts to secure funding for production in FY 1960 and 1961 met with no more success. In addition to the technical problems still associated with stopping an ICBM attack, the nation's political leaders were preparing for a presidential election and did not want to be responsible for the $15 billion commitment associated with a decision to deploy an ABM system. Congress did allocate $137 million in production funds for FY 1960, but the Eisenhower administration refused to spend the money. The decision taken by the government to continue research and development but not to commit to deployment adumbrated the fate of BMD through-out the years when Robert S. McNamara was secretary of defense.[32]

PROJECT DEFENDER

While the army was working to develop the ZEUS system to meet the immediate threat of Soviet ICBMs, other schemes for defending against Russian missiles were being examined by DOD's Advanced Research Projects Agency (ARPA).[33] This agency had been established in the wake of the launching of Sputnik I because DOD officials considered the Soviet satellite a harbinger of new weapons that were so radical they would no longer fit within the traditional bounds of the military services. As Secretary McElroy told the House Armed Services Committee in January 1958: "It seems to us quite obvious that to expect [that] the weapons of the future might fall into a traditional type of service category or service area of responsibility is something which one cannot do." To begin with, the new organization would have responsibility for research and development on advanced systems, specifically ABM missiles and satellites.[34]

One of ARPA's programs was called ARGUS, an experiment suggested by Nicholas C. Christofilos, a scientist at Lawrence Livermore National Laboratory (LLNL) in the 1950s. When the Soviet Union began orbiting its Sputnik satellites in October 1957, there was concern that the Soviets might be able to attack the United States with nuclear weapons delivered from space either by ICBMs or by orbiting nuclear bombs that could be deorbited to strike targets. Christofilos believed that the detonation of several nuclear weapons at the appropriate altitude in space would cause large numbers of electrons to become trapped in the earth's magnetic field, creating a barrier that might damage the nuclear warheads of ballistic missiles and in this way offer a means of defending the United States from nuclear attack. In testing Christofilos's theory, three nuclear devices were exploded in space between 27 August and 6 September 1958. The results showed that large numbers of electrons were in fact trapped in the earth's magnetic field, but their concentration dissipated so rapidly that they offered little prospect of being useful as a shield against a nuclear attack.[35]

Another ARPA undertaking was known as Project Defender. Costing about $200 million a year, Defender was actually a collection of projects that explored "on the broadest front the principles and techniques that might prove useful in the attempt to solve the antimissile problem."

One of these projects was the Guidelines Identification Program for Antimissile Research (GLIPAR). This study examined how exotic technologies such as lasers, particle beams, and "tailored-effects" produced by nuclear devices might contribute to ballistic missile defenses.[36]

Defender also included Project BAMBI (ballistic missile boost intercept). In fact, BAMBI was a category of defensive concepts based on the idea of attacking ICBMs shortly after they were launched. As a result, these concepts generally had to rely on space-based systems for execution of the defense mission. One of BAMBI's concepts was interception by satellite tracking (INSATRAC), which combined a ground-based interceptor with two satellite tracking systems. A scanning satellite in a 2,000-mile orbit would first detect the launch of ICBMs. This information would be used to alert tracking satellites in orbits of 400 to 500 miles. The tracking satellites would relay intercept data to the earth where they would be used to launch and guide MINUTEMAN-like missiles equipped with nuclear warheads and stationed in the Arctic region. These interceptors would meet the attacking missiles over the North Pole where the warheads of the defending missiles would be detonated in the path of these ICBMs.[37]

A second BAMBI concept was known as space patrol active defense (SPAD). The heart of SPAD was a space-based interceptor missile that was expected to be sufficiently accurate to come within 20 to 30 feet of its target. As the interceptor approached a target, it was to deploy a wire mesh 50 feet in radius that increased the probability of kill. These interceptors would have weighed about 300 pounds and been housed in larger vehicles that orbited the earth (one configuration involved six interceptors per satellite "garage"). In the event of an ICBM attack, the interceptors would be launched at the attacking missiles and destroy them primarily by shredding the tanks of boosters, although damage to other parts of the missiles was expected to be effective in stopping them. One advantage of this interceptor was that its "warhead" would have weighed only 3 pounds compared with 50 pounds for the smallest nuclear warhead anticipated at that time.[38] Another form of interceptor was also considered for use under project BAMBI. This device would have weighed about 100 pounds and was to destroy a target by ejecting a cloud of pellets as it approached the target.[39]

Project Defender also made several important contributions to the development of support equipment for ballistic missile defense systems. For one thing, it pioneered the development of large, ground-based phased-array radar systems. Construction of a low-powered radar of this type was finished in the fall of 1960, and this new radar quickly demonstrated the ability to electronically steer a radar beam in two dimensions using computers to control the beam. This success encouraged Bell Laboratories to incorporate phased-array radar into its work on the army's missile defense system.[40] This new radar would play an important role in the transformation of the NIKE-ZEUS program into NIKE-X.

THE BIRTH OF NIKE-X

Soon after the Democrats won the presidential election in November 1960, the army began a vigorous campaign for deployment of ZEUS. The new administration of John F. Kennedy refused to be stampeded but did include ballistic missile defenses in a major review of defense policies undertaken soon after Kennedy took office in January 1961. Two major questions about ZEUS surfaced: Was BMD technically feasible, and if so, Would its capabilities be worth the costs? In April, both questions were answered in the negative when Secretary of Defense McNamara refused to recommend funds for production of ZEUS, citing as his reasons the high cost and technical inadequacies of the missile. With regard to cost, the limited range of a ZEUS missile meant that it would require $15 billion to acquire enough batteries to defend a significant portion of the country. ZEUS's technical problems included its vulnerability to decoys and jamming and the fact that the system could be saturated by a heavy attack. Although McNamara recognized that an ABM system of even limited capabilities would complicate Soviet planning for a first strike, he believed deployment of such a system would also cause the Soviets to expand their ICBM force. In spite of these problems, the secretary did recommend $270 million for a vigorous R&D program that would "develop ZEUS as rapidly as money will permit."[41]

Sixteen months later, another important milestone occurred in the development of America's ABM system. On 19 July 1962, a ZEUS missile fired from Kwajalein test site in the Pacific intercepted an ATLAS D ICBM launched from Vandenberg Air Force Base in California. Although the hydraulic system of the ZEUS failed 10 seconds before the intercept, its dummy nuclear warhead passed within 2 kilometers of the ATLAS's re-entry vehicle (RV). During a test on 22 December 1962, a ZEUS passed within 200 meters of the target RV. All told, thirteen similar tests were run between June 1962 and November 1963. Only the first test on 26 June 1962 was a complete failure. There were three partial successes and nine complete successes.[42]

A NIKE-ZEUS missile successfully intercepts a dummy warhead that had been launched by a TITAN ICBM. The "X" in this time-exposure photograph was formed when the third stage of the NIKE-ZEUS crossed the path of the target, which was moving from the upper right to the lower left. The very large bright streak was produced by the TITAN booster, which had disintegrated and was burning up during reentry into the earth's atmosphere. (Photo SC-603723, National Archives)

In spite of the accomplishments of the test program, McNamara again decided against deployment of the system in 1963, for he believed that ZEUS would not be able to deal with the projected Soviet threat of the late 1960s and early 1970s. His concern focused on several technical matters. For one thing, the ZEUS system still could not discriminate between decoys and warheads. Furthermore, American scientists and engineers had little knowledge of reentry phenomenology, nor did they know how the detonation of a ZEUS warhead would affect other components of the ZEUS system. Because of these problems, McNamara decided that the United States should restructure its ABM efforts by adopting a more advanced program, NIKE-X, which was really a "number of studies and exploratory developments aimed at leading from the . . . outmoded NIKE-ZEUS to the next generation ABM system." The modified program continued the development of the ZEUS missile (which eventually became the SPARTAN), while adding a second interceptor, the short-range, high-acceleration SPRINT. Together, these missiles made up a layered defense. First, ZEUS would attack an approaching swarm of warheads and decoys at an altitude of 70 to 100 miles. Then, SPRINT would intercept the remaining warheads at an altitude of 20 to 30 miles after the atmosphere had stripped away any decoys that might have survived the ZEUS attack.[43]

NIKE-X overcame a major limitation of the ZEUS system by replacing its older radar with the new phased array radar that ARPA had pioneered under Project Defender. The older radar pointed its search beam by physically rotating its antenna. This meant that aiming the beam was a relatively slow process that restricted the number of targets it could handle. As a result, the target tracking and missile tracking sets associated with ZEUS could service only one intercept at a time. Each ZEUS missile had to be supported by two radar sets: one to track the target RV, and the other one to track and guide the missile itself. The new phased-array radar used an antenna with several fixed faces, each of which was covered with an array of radiating elements. One such antenna could generate several beams of radio pulses and rapidly aim them electronically, the direction of a beam being determined by the way electromagnetic energy was fed to the radiating elements. Because of the speed and accuracy with which these beams could be pointed, one radar could perform several functions and service a number of attacking RVs and defending missiles.[44]

Phased-array radar was based on advances in solid-state electronics that also made possible the development of very high capacity computers that were extremely reliable. These computers were needed to process the large amounts of data associated with tracking multiple RV targets and guiding missiles to intercept them.[45]

In addition to the modifications to ZEUS, McNamara also established the requirement for a system of fallout shelters that had to be constructed with the deployment of any ABM system. These shelters were necessary because the Soviets could defeat missile defenses by exploding nuclear weapons upwind, away from defended areas, and allowing the wind to carry radioactive debris into the target area, thus killing the inhabitants with fallout rather than by blast and direct radiation. Additionally, the fallout shelters would provide protection against the detonations of ABM warheads, which could be a threat to the inhabitants of defended areas. The better protected the people were in defended areas, the lower in the atmosphere a SPRINT missile could intercept an attacking warhead; the lower the interception, the better atmospheric discrimination worked to separate warheads and decoys.[46]

In 1964 McNamara expressed cautious optimism about the nation's ABM efforts. Progress was being made in some important technical areas, but unresolved problems still remained. These problems, as well as a projected cost of $16 billion for an ABM system, meant that the United States should proceed carefully. In this assessment, McNamara was supported by General William Dick, the army's chief R&D officer, who believed that a deployment decision could not be taken before 1966.[47]

McNamara's caution with regard to missile defenses was a product of at least two factors: his growing conviction that the most effective way to deter nuclear war was to possess an offensive force that could assure destruction of the Soviet Union as a viable society and increasing opposition to missile defenses in some quarters of the scientific community.

THE RISE OF OPPOSITION IN THE SCIENTIFIC COMMUNITY

By the end of 1964, a number of scientists had concluded that the United States should not begin to deploy a missile defense system. While serving as ARPA's chief scientist, Herbert York had at first favored proceeding with the development and deployment of the NIKE-ZEUS system. Somewhat later, when York had become DOD's director for research and engineering, he learned of the work of DOD's Reentry Body Identification Group (RBIG). In the spring of 1958, RBIG submitted a report stating that the NIKE-ZEUS system could be defeated by the use of multiple warheads on ICBMs. Headed by William E. Bradley,

RBIG detailed several weaknesses of the ZEUS system, including the vulnerability of its radar, the inability of NIKE-ZEUS to deal with decoys, and the fact that nuclear explosions at high altitudes would blind the ZEUS radar. (Even if the Soviets did not detonate a warhead, the explosion of the nuclear warhead of a ZEUS missile would blind its own radar.)[48]

RBIG's report convinced York that the antimissile defense project should be reconsidered. A review directed by Dr. Jack P. Ruina concluded that the NIKE-ZEUS system was vulnerable to countermeasures by attacking forces. This turned York against the deployment of that system.[49] Similar conclusions were reached in early 1959 by a panel of the President's Science Advisory Committee, which included some of the nation's top scientific experts, such as Harold Brown (director of the Lawrence Livermore National Laboratory), Hans Bethe (professor of physics at Cornell University), Jerome Wiesner (professor of engineering at MIT), and Wolfgang Panofsky (director of the High Energy Physics Laboratory at Stanford University).[50]

Given the conclusions of these three reports, it is not surprising that on 16 February 1961, York and Ruina, who was now ARPA's director, advised the House Committee on Science and Astronautics that they were not optimistic about the possibility of developing defenses against ballistic missiles. Specifically, Ruina told the committee "that he felt a 'great deal of pessimism about ever developing a complete and adequate umbrella against ICBM attack.'" In spite of their basic pessimism, both men believed that NIKE-ZEUS might be developed into a system that could defend "selected points" in the United States.[51]

About a year later, the apparent need to test the NIKE-ZEUS warhead by detonating nuclear weapons in the upper regions of the atmosphere threatened to undermine attempts to secure a limited nuclear test ban treaty with the Soviet Union. Bethe, one of the leaders of the effort that eventually led to the establishment of the treaty, publicly expressed his doubts about the feasibility of missile defenses. In an address that focused mainly on arms control and nuclear testing, Bethe "dismissed" the idea that the development of a missile defense system by either the Soviets or the Americans would upset the balance of power. It would be too easy to overcome the defense by means of decoys and increased numbers of offensive missiles. Bethe maintained that developing an effective missile defense was "virtually hopeless."[52]

In October 1964, efforts to overturn the treaty Bethe had been working for (the Partial Test Ban Treaty that had been consummated in 1963) prompted York and Wiesner to lay out the details of their arguments against ballistic missile defenses in an article that appeared in the October 1964 *Scientific American*. Supporters of BMD wished to resume atmospheric testing as part of their effort to develop an effective ABM system. York and Wiesner argued that it made no sense to violate the treaty for this purpose, since such a system would be impossible to develop. Furthermore, the United States should not even attempt to develop a "truly airtight" defense, since it would be extremely destabilizing from the standpoint of the nuclear arms race. Such a defensive system "would effectively nullify the deterrent force of the other [side], exposing the latter to a first attack against which it could not retaliate." This was the "first serious presentation" of the idea that defense could be dangerous in the context of nuclear deterrence.[53]

Wiesner and York criticized Project Defender specifically. Although they agreed that the work being done under the project had to go forward, they considered it counterproductive, for it only kept alive "the forlorn hope of developing an active antimissile defense" while actually undercutting defensive efforts by promoting the development of penetration aids that would nullify defenses. Wiesner and York believed that attempts to develop missile defenses were part of an arms race that confronted the United States and the Soviet Union with the "dilemma of steadily increasing military power and steadily decreasing national security. *It is our considered professional judgment that this dilemma has no technical solution.*"[54]

Within about a year of the appearance of the Wiesner-York article, McNamara had succeeded in integrating BMD into the intellectual framework of the nation's nuclear doctrine. Now any decision to deploy a missile defense required careful consideration of its impact on deterrence.

BMD AND DETERRENCE DOCTRINE

By 1963 McNamara was concerned about how missile defenses would affect the deterrence of nuclear war. That year, he directed the Betts Commission, named after the commission's chairman, army lieutenant general Austin W. Betts, to investigate how an ABM system would affect nuclear war and relations between the Soviet Union and the United States. The commission's key conclusions were favorable from the perspective of missile defenses: (1) offensive technology had not hopelessly outstripped defensive technology—rather, the two technologies were roughly equal; (2) a BMD system would limit damage in case of a nuclear attack, with the amount of limitation dependent on the scenario; and (3) BMD would not disrupt the balance of mutual nuclear deterrence.[55]

Any positive effects that the Betts Report might have had on McNamara with regard to the deployment of a missile defense system were offset by other developments. For one thing, by the time the report reached McNamara at the end of 1964, he was already under the influence of those elements of the scientific community opposed to missile defenses.[56] Furthermore, the conclusions of the Betts Report ran counter to the way McNamara was now thinking.

In the early 1960s McNamara had emphasized counterforce attack as the basis of nuclear strategy on the grounds that this would logically limit the amount of damage a nuclear war would inflict on the warring nations. However, when he sensed that this approach might make nuclear war seem too plausible, too acceptable, he began to emphasize a strategy of "assured destruction." Thus he told the Senate in 1965 that "without question, offensive capability or what I will call the capability for assuring the destruction of the Soviet Union is far and away the most important requirements [sic] we have to meet." This emphasis was reflected in his determination to maintain an offensive force that could absorb a Soviet first strike and still be capable of destroying enough of the Soviet population and industry to ensure that the Soviets could not conclude that it was to their advantage to initiate a nuclear exchange. McNamara's emphasis on assured destruction was also indicated in the R&D priorities he established. First priority was assigned to R&D in support of the Vietnam war, next was R&D on penetration aids for U.S. strategic offensive forces, and third was ABM research.[57]

Not surprisingly, the army's efforts in 1965 to secure a decision for deployment of its BMD system were opposed by McNamara. Once again there had been substantial progress in the ABM program, but McNamara still believed there were too many technical difficulties and problems with the deployment concept. If the nation began fielding a BMD system in FY 1966, changes caused by R&D advances would surely necessitate costly retooling and changes in production. His opposition was bolstered by a comparison of various combinations of offensive and defensive systems to see which one would save the most lives per dollar of cost. He concluded that in 1965 no reasonably priced defense could reduce American casualties in a nuclear war much below eighty million. Therefore, it made no sense to invest in defenses in the mid-1960s because a better return on the dollar could be had by enhancing the ability of offensive forces to penetrate enemy defenses, thereby ensuring deterrence through assured destruction. In his cost-effectiveness analysis, McNamara continued to insist that the cost of fielding an ABM system must include the cost of measures such as beefing up the nation's defenses against bombers to ensure that the Soviets did not simply flow around the missile defense system by expanding its bomber forces. As a result of McNamara's opposition, the deployment of NIKE-X was deferred another year, although the program received $400 million for continued development.[58]

By 1965, however, other developments in the world were beginning to increase the pressure for deploying some kind of ballistic missile defense.

CHAPTER TWO

Fielding an ABM System: Decision and Debate

Defense is moral; offense is immoral!
                    —*Soviet Premier Aleksei N. Kosygin, 23 June 1967[1]*

I discovered that [in case of a nuclear attack against the United States] there are now two grim alternatives—do nothing or push the button that unleashes our devastating nuclear fury . . . . Safeguard provides an additional alternative, an extra button.
                    —*Senator Winston Prouty, 14 July 1969[2]*

THE NTH-COUNTRY THREAT: AN EXPANDED MISSION FOR ABM

Although McNamara refused to field NIKE-X in a configuration that might defend U.S. cities and industrial areas against a heavy Soviet attack in the 1970s, he was led to consider a different deployment option after the Chinese exploded a nuclear device in October 1964. This development caused considerable concern among defense officials (including McNamara) and resulted in the completion of a series of studies examining how NIKE-X might be modified to cope with the kind of light, unsophisticated attack (the "Nth-country threat") that China might be able to deliver in the 1970s.[3]

The possibility that NIKE-X might be required to meet a number of different threats prompted DOD to consider a modular or building block approach to the deployment of a missile defense. This would involve fielding a system that could be expanded or modified to meet other threats. Various forms of the modular system were discussed. One was a full configuration that combined a complete NIKE-X system (ZEUS and SPRINT missiles with appropriate radar systems) with a nationwide fallout shelter program that could protect against a large and sophisticated attack. Another plan envisioned a partial system consisting of ZEUS missiles and a small number of SPRINTs with appropriate radar equipment to deal with a light ICBM attack such as one the Chinese might be able to deliver in the future. A third configuration would have been composed of ZEUS missiles and a phased-array radar system to cope with such things as the accidental firing of an ICBM.[4]

In 1966 several factors militated against a decision to deploy NIKE-X. These included the high cost of the Vietnam war, which limited the availability of funding; opposition from the scientific community; apathy in Congress with regard to the fallout shelters McNamara established as a concomitant to the deployment of a full BMD system; détente with the Soviet Union; and McNamara's own opposition. In defending his decision not to begin deployment, McNamara cited the high cost of a system ($25–30 billion), stated his belief that the Soviets could overcome such a system for much less money, indicated that there was uncertainty as to how deployment would affect the Soviets, and noted that no reasonably priced ABM system could reduce American casualties below fifty million. Although McNamara believed that the Chinese threat was not sufficiently developed to warrant deployment of an Nth-country system, he did note that such a system could be quite effective. An unopposed Chinese ICBM attack in the 1970s might inflict between six and twelve million casualties. A relatively simple defense deployed around some of America's cities and costing around $8 billion could reduce the casualties by about 50 percent. A more extensive system costing around $11 billion could reduce casualties to between zero and two million.[5]

In recommending against the deployment of an ABM system in 1966, McNamara was again overriding the advice of the Joint Chiefs of Staff (JCS). In 1965 the military's top leaders wanted to start work on items in the NIKE-X program that would require long lead times, and in 1966 they supported the army's request for $188 million to begin work on these long lead-time components. The opposition of the JCS to McNamara's position on ABM and a growing feeling that "the Department of Defense did not have a proper sense of urgency in the field of the antiballistic missile defense system" led Congress to allocate funds for pre-production work on NIKE-X with the idea that this money could save as much as a year in the deployment process should the president decide to begin deployment later in FY 1967.[6]

Although this funding was approved by substantial majorities in the House and the Senate, the passage of the measure involved a debate prompted by a small but vocal group opposed to ballistic missile defenses that had developed in Congress by 1966 and continued to grow stronger over the next few years. Among the arguments advanced by opponents of the preproduction funding measure was that NIKE-X could be overwhelmed by a sophisticated ICBM attack. Furthermore, at a time when domestic spending was being restricted, it was inappropriate to begin a costly new defense program. Opponents also argued that deployment of a U.S. missile defense system would disrupt the strategic balance and cause an arms race by provoking the Soviets to expand their forces. Senator Stephen Young (D-Ohio) argued that it was inconsistent for Congress to vote money for preproduction work on NIKE-X at the very time Adrian Fisher, deputy director of the U.S. Arms Control and Disarmament Agency (ACDA), was proposing to the Eighteen Nation Disarmament Committee in Geneva that the United States and USSR agree not to build ABM systems.[7]

Supporters of NIKE-X answered these challenges with arguments of their own. They found little credibility in the opposition's view that the United States should not take measures to defend itself for fear that such actions would antagonize the Soviets. They were more concerned that the United States might be falling behind the Soviets and believed that the nation could not afford to be "second best in defense."[8]

THE ORIGINS OF THE SOVIET ABM PROGRAM

By the end of 1966, four key events had occurred that strengthened the hand of those who favored deployment of an ABM system. Three of these events took place in China and pointed toward a maturing of the Chinese threat. In May the Chinese set off a "nuclear explosion that contained thermonuclear material," and in October they launched a nuclear-tipped test missile that struck its target. On 28 December they conducted another nuclear test. The fourth event occurred six weeks before the second Chinese nuclear explosion—McNamara reported that the Soviets were in the process of fielding an ABM system.[9]

The Soviets had begun basic research on ballistic missile defense right after World War II, in keeping with their practice of beginning work on countermeasures at the same time they start work on a new weapon. By about 1955 they had initiated "specific BMD development programs." In the early 1960s, the Soviets carried out a series of high

The NIKE-X *system featured two types of missiles that formed a layered defense. The longer-ranged* NIKE-ZEUS *missile (shown above during a test firing) was to break up an* ICBM *attack by destroying chaff, decoys, and some warheads at an altitude of about 100 miles. At lower altitudes, the cone-shaped* SPRINT *missile, which had a very high acceleration rate (shown opposite as it emerges from a silo during a test launch), would destroy warheads that survived the attack by* ZEUS *missiles. (U.S. Army Strategic Defense Command, Huntsville, Alabama)*

altitude nuclear detonations that were probably designed to test the effects of electromagnetic pulses on radar systems and determine the lethal radius of warheads for antiballistic missiles.[10]

The Soviet program was markedly different from that of the United States and caused concern that the Soviet Union might be advancing more rapidly toward an operational ABM system than was the United States. Whereas the United States attempted to infer the conditions of nuclear war from basic data, the Soviets actually sought to replicate the conditions of nuclear war and test their systems under these conditions. During one test series, the Soviets exploded nuclear devices at high altitudes on five consecutive days. Another major difference between the two countries was in the philosophy of system development. The Soviets tended to develop and deploy systems rapidly, knowing that there would be operational problems with the systems deployed but expecting to use the knowledge gained from operating an imperfect system to develop a better follow-on system. Americans, on the other hand, insisted on high performance and effective operational capabilities before deploying a system. The result was that the Soviets were more likely to have at least some operational capability before the United States would field a system.[11]

By 1962 the Soviets had deployed about thirty GRIFFON surface-to-air missiles at Leningrad. This system was thought to have a limited ABM capability against tactical ballistic missiles but would have been of questionable value in dealing with an ICBM attack. It was operational for only a short time before it was dismantled around 1964.[12]

The GRIFFON was followed in 1963 by the SA-5, which the Soviets began deploying in the so-called Tallinn Line, named after the capital city of Estonia. Like GRIFFON, the SA-5 had been born at the Soviet ABM development center at Shary Sagan and had at best only a limited capability against ballistic missiles. The Tallinn Line may have been designed to intercept Polaris A-1 missiles, which because of their short range would probably have been launched in the Barents Sea and passed over Estonia enroute to targets in the western Soviet Union.[13]

In 1964 the Soviets displayed for the first time a nuclear-tipped interceptor missile that NATO designated GALOSH. The range of these missiles has been estimated as 200 miles. Original plans seem to have called for 128 launchers to be installed in a ring about 40 miles from the heart of Moscow. Apparently because of radar limitations and other restrictions in the system, these plans were scaled back in 1968 to where only 64 launchers were deployed.[14]

THE POLITICS OF ABM DEPLOYMENT

It was the deployment of GALOSH that McNamara announced to the American people on 10 November 1966. In announcing the Soviet deployment, McNamara sought to head off pressure from Congress to field an American defense system. Had members of Congress discovered the Soviet deployment before McNamara's announcement, they might have gone to the public first with a proposal that the United States field an ABM. However, the defense secretary had the initiative, and he used it to further his position that the appropriate response was to improve America's offensive missiles to ensure they could penetrate the Soviet ABM defenses.[15]

In spite of McNamara's best efforts, the political pressure for deployment of an American missile defense system had reached the point in late 1966 where President Johnson was no longer willing simply to rubber stamp the recommendations of his secretary of defense. Johnson remained more interested in domestic affairs than in defense, but he also recognized that BMD was an important issue. He knew this matter inspired intense feelings in others and was bothered himself by the prospect of a Chinese missile attack on the United States. The president also seems to have been influenced on the ABM issue by several former colleagues in the Senate—Henry Jackson, John Stennis, and Richard Russell. Furthermore, Johnson was impressed by the fact that the JCS favored deployment of a defensive missile system. To all of this should be added President Johnson's realization that in the approaching election the Republicans might well make an issue out of defense and that ABM was becoming a symbol of defense preparedness. Furthermore, at this point McNamara's efforts to influence Johnson on the ABM issue were complicated by the strained relations between the two men that resulted from disagreements over policies in Vietnam, especially those governing the bombing of North Vietnam.[16] For McNamara to continue controlling events in the area of missile defenses would require tremendous powers of persuasion and a shrewd strategy.

Lyndon Johnson was a very capable politician. When it came to controversial matters, he sought compromises to limit any political damage that might arise from his decisions. To keep from having to deploy an ABM system, McNamara would have to offer the president an acceptable compromise. In November 1966 McNamara and the JCS went to Texas to review with Johnson the military budget that he would submit to Congress in January 1967. The JCS unanimously agreed that funds for the development and deployment of a BMD system should be included in the FY 1967 budget. McNamara opposed this, but realized that Johnson would be left in a difficult position unless he showed some commitment to missile defenses. Therefore, McNamara proposed a compromise: Johnson should invite the Soviets to begin arms control talks while calling for money in the FY 1967 budget that could be used for deployment if the effort to start negotiations with the Soviets failed. This appealed to Johnson's sense of history: he might be remembered as the president who started talks that eventually ended the nuclear arms race. It also meant that the deployment of an ABM system might be delayed indefinitely and perhaps never occur. At the same time, this course of action indicated to supporters of ABM that the president would begin deployment if the talks failed to materialize. Here was a position that both friend and foe of missile defenses would have trouble opposing.[17]

The campaign orchestrated by McNamara started in December 1966 when Secretary of State Dean Rusk publicly expressed his hope that the superpowers could agree not to deploy ABM systems and to stop the arms race. The following month, in his State of the Union address, President Johnson indicated that he would pursue an agreement with the Soviets to stop ABM deployments. In his budget message that same month, he called for Congress to appropriate $375 million for the deployment of a missile defense system in case negotiations with the Soviets failed.[18]

To further strengthen his position with the president, McNamara on 23 January convened a meeting at the White House of current and former scientific and technical advisers to the president and current and former directors of defense research and engineering (DDR&E) in DOD. Also present were the chiefs of the armed services. None of the scientists present seemed to disagree with the position put forward by McNamara that a defense against Soviet missiles would not work and should not be built. Although McNamara later claimed unanimous support of his views, the unanimity was achieved through finesse. McNamara "studiously" avoided asking for the opinion of the current DDR&E, Dr. John S. Foster, Jr., who believed in the feasibility of ABM. Foster's silence was taken as concurrence with the other scientific and technical advisers.[19]

In February and March, McNamara made it clear that he still opposed any BMD deployment. With regard to a light system oriented against the Chinese, he pointed out that the technology bases of the two countries should control deployment. An austere BMD system costing about $3.5 billion could be deployed by the United States in less time than the Chinese would require to deploy an ICBM force. By constantly updating this light ABM force, the United States could protect itself from a Chinese attack well beyond 1985. Since the United States could deploy an ABM system faster than the Chinese could field their ICBMs, there was no reason to begin an ABM deployment oriented against the Chinese until they began to deploy their ICBMs.[20]

McNamara's arguments against a Soviet-oriented system were couched in terms of his concept of deterrence. The greatest threat to U.S. security was not a Soviet ABM system but the deployment of an extensive and effective Soviet ABM system coupled with the acquisition of a hard-target kill capability by the Soviet ICBM fleet. This combination could undermine U.S. ability to deter a Soviet nuclear attack, for it would allow the Soviets to threaten the MINUTEMAN force and raise questions about the ability of U.S. residual forces to penetrate Soviet defenses after a Soviet first strike.[21]

In McNamara's view, the answer to this challenge was not an American ABM. Should the United States decide to deploy a system of missile defenses, the Soviets could overcome it with changes in their offensive forces that would cost roughly one-fourth as much as the American defense system. In the end, the superpowers would wind up with a new set of defensive weapons, more-sophisticated offensive weapons, and no improvement in security on either side.[22]

Rather than deploy a costly ABM system that could be cheaply overcome by the Soviets, the United States should improve its offensive strategic forces. Such measures would offset the Soviet ABM system at a fraction of its cost to the Soviets. Indeed, McNamara pointed out that his department had already initiated measures the year before to offset possible threatening developments in the Soviet strategic force structure. These included accelerating the deployment of the new POSEIDON submarine-launched ballistic missile (SLBM), a decision to expand the percentage of the MINUTEMAN force composed of MINUTEMAN III missiles, and improvements in penetration aids. To prepare further for the expected Soviet threat, McNamara asked Congress for funds in FY 1968 to continue those actions started the previous year. In addition, he also asked for funding to develop a new reentry vehicle designed specifically to strike targets defended by ABMs.[23]

THE GLASSBORO SUMMIT

Regardless of how sound these arguments against an ABM deployment might have been, they had little effect on the Soviets whose attitude toward missile defenses was one of the biggest problems McNamara faced in his campaign to keep the United States from fielding a missile defense system. The Soviets were simply not interested in foregoing a BMD deployment. While in London during February 1967, Premier Aleksei N. Kosygin responded to questions at a press conference. He answered one question with these words:

Which weapons should be regarded as a tension factor—offensive or defensive weapons? I think that a defensive system, which prevents attack, is not a cause of the arms race but represents a factor preventing the death of people. Some persons reason thus: Which is cheaper, to have offensive weapons that destroy cities and entire states or to have defensive weapons that can prevent this destruction? At present the theory is current in some places that one should develop whichever system is cheaper. Such "theoreticians" argue also about how much it costs to kill a person—$500,000 or $100,000? An antimissile system may cost more than an offensive one, but it is intended not for killing people but for saving human lives.[24]

On 23 June 1967, Kosygin and Johnson met at Glassboro, New Jersey, for top-level discussions of nuclear arms issues. Johnson's goal was to convince the Soviet premier that the deployment of the GALOSH ABM system would do nothing to improve Soviet security and would merely intensify the nuclear arms race. Johnson was having some difficulty getting this point across, so he asked his erudite secretary of defense, Robert McNamara, to explain what was wrong with the Soviet approach to nuclear strategy. McNamara then laid out the logic of assured destruction for the Soviet premier: "If you proceed with the antiballistic missile deployment our response will not, should not, be to deploy a similar system. . . . [O]ur response will be to expand our offensive weapons." McNamara then told Kosygin that the only way out of this trap was to negotiate restrictions on defensive systems. At this point, McNamara later recalled, Kosygin became red in the face, pounded the table, and declared: "Defense is moral, offense is immoral!" Now it was clear that there would be no superpower talks before Johnson faced the nation with his next budget message.[25]

McNAMARA ANNOUNCES THE SENTINEL DECISION

The Soviets were not the only ones to prove unmanageable. About a week before the Glassboro summit, the Chinese surprised both the United States and the USSR by announcing that they had detonated a hydrogen bomb. This event immediately gave rise to speculation that there would be increased pressure on the Johnson administration to deploy an ABM system against the Chinese.[26] Given the uncooperative nature of the Soviets, the growing concern about Chinese abilities and intentions, and the commitment Johnson had made in January, the time for a deployment decision was obviously at hand.

The Glassboro summit, 1967: With President Johnson on his left, Soviet Premier Kosygin speaks to the press at Glassboro State College. Just visible over Kosygin's left shoulder is Secretary of Defense McNamara; over his right shoulder is Andrei Gromyko, Soviet foreign minister. To the far left is Soviet Ambassador Anatoly Dobrynin. Secretary of State Rusk may be seen over Johnson's right shoulder. (Photo 67-1789, National Archives)

Still, Johnson had grounds for seeking a compromise. For one thing, he wanted to maintain good relations with his powerful defense secretary, who still opposed an ABM deployment. Furthermore, he did not wish to begin fielding a costly, ineffective ABM system with a national election approaching. Thus the president accepted a limited deployment against China and agreed to allow McNamara to announce it as he saw fit, provided the announcement could be taken by ABM supporters as an indication that the deployment was a first step in the fielding of a full-fledged system that ultimately would protect the country against a Soviet attack.[27]

For his part, McNamara had concluded several years earlier that he might be forced to deploy a missile defense and had "begun laying the groundwork for a fall-back position in the form of a small ABM system directed against China." Now he could use his "China card" to head off a deployment against the Soviet Union that he believed would add nothing to U.S. security while touching off an upward spiral in the nuclear arms race.[28]

McNamara's strategy explains the opening of the September 1967 speech in which he announced the Johnson administration's decision to deploy a BMD system against China. He began by lecturing the American people and the Soviet Union on the basics of nuclear strategy, pointing out that neither the Soviet Union nor the United States possessed a first strike capability. Furthermore, such a capability was not within the grasp of either superpower, for there were always things a nation could do to ensure it had a second strike capability that was sufficiently strong to destroy a nuclear aggressor's society. Indeed, based on worst-case analyses, both the United States and the Soviet Union had overbuilt their forces to assure the survival of a second strike capability. Because of this situation, it was pointless for either side to build a missile defense system; rather, both sides should negotiate a treaty that would immediately limit and eventually restrict "offensive and defensive strategic nuclear forces."[29]

McNamara was well over halfway through his speech when he turned to the Soviet deployment of an ABM system and spoke to the American people about the need to "react intelligently" to this Soviet action. The Soviet deployment of an ABM system changed nothing in the deterrence equation, for the United States was already taking actions that would offset any gains the Soviets might achieve with an operational ABM. Furthermore, America's second strike force would remain secure and capable of performing its assured destruction mission. Nor should the United States deploy an ABM system in the hope of defending the nation, for such a defense simply would not work, as a distinguished group of scientists and technical advisers had unanimously agreed. Contrary to what was being said, McNamara continued, it was the ineffectiveness of any ABM system the United States could deploy at this time, not its $40 billion price tag, that made McNamara oppose it.[30]

As he continued discussing the appropriateness of the offensive response to a deployed ABM system, McNamara seemed to be speaking to the Soviets, pointing out the futility of their defensive efforts and assuring them that the U.S. response to their ABM would not be an American ABM. In this way McNamara hoped to convince the Soviets that the ABM deployment he was about to announce was not aimed at them and to persuade them that they need not expand their ICBM fleet to compensate for the American missile defenses. To further assuage the Soviets, McNamara would later insist on a new designation for the nation's antiballistic missile system. On 4 November he announced that the system would be called SENTINEL, with the designation NIKE-X retained for the research portion of the nation's BMD effort.[31]

By the time McNamara began to talk about the Chinese threat and a possible U.S. response, his audience must have been convinced that the United States was not about to deploy an ABM system of any kind. It must have been a considerable surprise when he began to weave the logic for a deployment aimed at a possible Chinese ICBM threat. The situation with regard to China was different from that with the Soviet Union, McNamara said. Clearly, for the foreseeable future the Chinese could develop only a relatively small force of unsophisticated ICBMs. Against such a force, even a thin ABM system would be effective. Furthermore, there were grounds for concern about what the Chinese intended to do with the nuclear force they seemed about to build. In fact, they might be able to launch a nuclear attack on the United States in the mid-1970s. Therefore, as McNamara put it, "there are marginal grounds for concluding that a light deployment of U.S. A.B.M.s against this possibility is prudent."[32]

In addition to protecting against a Chinese attack, this light ABM system would provide some secondary benefits. For one thing, it could be used to protect U.S. MINUTEMAN missile fields and in this way enhance U.S. ability to deter a nuclear attack by the Soviets. It could also be used to provide protection against a possible accidental launch of an ICBM. For those reasons, McNamara announced that the United States would begin deployment of the system at the end of 1967. The announcement of this decision was not, however, McNamara's final comment. That was reserved for a warning against allowing the deployment of a thin ABM system to lead to the thought of expanding it against the Soviets and thus further fueling the nuclear arms race.[33]

Clearly, McNamara's heart was not in the decision to field an ABM system. Twenty years later he stated that he would not change a single word in the first 80 percent of the speech where he had explained why an ABM system aimed at the Soviet threat was unnecessary. He considered this part "one of the best statements of the irrationality of antiballistic missile deployment that has ever been made." On the other hand, he was not pleased with the last part of the speech where he had called for fielding a BMD system against China: "I would like to scrap and remove [it] from the records. . . . The only reason that was in there was . . . to recognize the political pressure and the fact that the Congress had authorized such a system, appropriated funds for it, and was pushing unmercifully to deploy not the thin system but a thick system."[34]

McNamara's announcement of the deployment decision did not mean that he had abandoned his opposition to deployment or that the Johnson administration had given up on arms control. In late November 1967, McNamara's departure from the Pentagon was announced. In his last posture statement, he continued his efforts to see that the Soviets understood that SENTINEL was not aimed at them. He stressed the importance of offensive forces as the key to deterrence and indicated that a SENTINEL system operating against a Soviet attack could not reduce American casualties below one hundred million unless the United States launched a preemptive strike. Furthermore, McNamara, as well as Assistant Secretary of Defense Paul Warnke, indicated that the Chinese ICBM program was a year behind what had been expected, thereby making the deployment of SENTINEL seem less urgent. Warnke's views, at least, were used to bolster a congressional measure to halt deployment. This anti-ABM effort continued throughout the summer and into the fall and was supported by members of the scientific community.[35]

Throughout 1968, members of the administration continued to insist that an agreement to restrict offensive and defensive strategic arms was in the best interest of both the United States and the USSR. On 1 July 1968 Johnson signed the Treaty on the Nonproliferation of Nuclear Weapons and announced that the Soviets and Americans had agreed to begin strategic arms limitation talks (SALT). A summit conference was scheduled for 30 September to begin negotiations, but it was canceled because of the Soviet invasion of Czechoslovakia on 20 August. Nevertheless, the Johnson government continued working on a proposal for the SALT negotiations and in late October announced that the meetings were so important that they would have to take place in spite of the Soviet invasion. Soon after Richard M. Nixon was elected president in November 1968, the Soviets responded positively to the U.S. request to continue talks. When Nixon indicated that he would not be bound by the agreements of the Johnson administration, the Soviets withdrew their acceptance of the invitation to continue the talks.[36]

As the Johnson administration was ending, an important change was occurring with regard to the army's attitude toward ballistic missile defenses. Throughout McNamara's tenure as secretary of defense, the army had been the principal sponsor of ABM development within the defense bureaucracy and on Capitol Hill. However, by the end of the Johnson administration, a significant amount of the army's energy was being absorbed by the war in Vietnam. Furthermore, DOD now adhered to a more diverse strategy in which both limited and conventional warfare were accorded a higher priority. This change in strategy, combined with the army's major role in Vietnam, meant that the army no longer needed a mission associated with strategic deterrence to ensure it received its share of the defense budget. Thus the army was disposed to accept McNamara's decision to deploy only a thin ABM system.[37] This decline in army support came on the eve of a critical national debate on ballistic missile defenses and boded ill for the future of the ABM program.

SENTINEL BECOMES SAFEGUARD

During the last year of the Johnson administration, the army began the process of establishing bases for the SENTINEL missile system. As it became apparent that these bases would in cases be near or within several major U.S. cities, opposition began to develop to the deployment plans. In some instances, this opposition was led by organizations of scientists such as the ABM Committee of the Seattle Association of Scientists and the Chicago branch of the Federation of American Scientists. The principal motivation of these scientists was concern over the implications of the SENTINEL deployment for what the scientists perceived as an arms race. For example, one leader was convinced that the proximity of SENTINEL sites to cities meant that the system would appear to be a "thick," city-defending one rather than a thin one oriented against a putative Chinese missile threat.[38]

There was also apprehension about the possible danger of having nuclear weapons near major residential areas. This concern was apparent as early as September 1968 when, during a congressional debate, Representative Thomas Pelly (R-Wash.) noted that the army, contrary to its promises, was planning to locate an ABM site within 1 mile of Seattle. Pelly pointed out that this was unacceptable to the citizens of that city. Toward the end of 1968, the matter of locating defensive missiles near cities surfaced again. This time Detroit and Chicago were involved. The opposition in Chicago was led by five scientists who formed the West Suburban Concerned Scientists Group. They argued that the deployment near Chicago would make this city a target for Soviet ICBMs. Furthermore, they stated that there was considerable danger that a missile might explode accidentally or that a missile's nuclear warhead might detonate prematurely when the missiles were fired at attacking warheads. Issues of national priorities (defense versus domestic programs) and the technical feasibility of SENTINEL were also raised during this debate.[39]

The SENTINEL controversy continued as Nixon was inaugurated and virtually assured that the new administration would want to review the SENTINEL decision before proceeding with deployment. The likelihood that such a review would occur was increased by a Soviet offer, made on the day of Nixon's inauguration, to begin serious discussions of strategic arms limitations. On 6 February 1969, Secretary of Defense Melvin Laird halted the SENTINEL deployment pending completion of a reexamination of America's strategic programs.[40]

The review was actually initiated on 20 January when Laird directed David R. Packard, deputy secretary of defense, to undertake two very broad studies. One looked at the overall Pentagon budget, and the other examined the status of the U.S. strategic force structure. Naturally, Packard's efforts encompassed a reevaluation of the $1.8 billion SENTINEL program.[41]

On 20 February, after four weeks of intense study, Packard briefed the president on his findings about ballistic missile defenses. He presented four options but made no recommendations. The first called for the United States to deploy a thick system in which a combination of long- and short-range ABMs would be used to protect the twenty-five largest cities in the country. A second option would be to field a thin system to protect only fifteen cities; this was the SENTINEL system chosen by the Johnson administration. The third proposal was known in the Pentagon as I-69; essentially, this would be the SENTINEL system deployed to protect ICBM fields as opposed to cities. The final option was not to build an ABM system at all. Nixon directed Packard to study all four options in greater detail.[42]

Soon after this meeting, Nixon left for an eight-day tour of Europe where he planned to consult with European leaders before beginning negotiations with the Soviets. During this trip, the ABM issue was never far from his mind. He was already leaning toward the I-69 plan primarily because he was concerned about the recent build-up of Soviet offensive strategic forces and the extensive ABM system that the Soviets seemed to be deploying. An American missile defense system could help preserve or restore the strategic balance that was being lost. Furthermore, building a missile defense system around U.S. ICBMs, Nixon thought, was the option least likely to be construed by the Soviets as provocative.[43]

Nixon returned from Europe on 2 March. Three days later, Packard presented his findings to him. Strongly favoring the I-69 deployment option, Packard supported his recommendation with arguments similar to views already entertained by the president. These arguments were summarized in a forty-page briefing book prepared for Nixon by his national security adviser, Henry Kissinger, who also played an important role in the final missile defense decision. Also included in the book were the arguments against the I-69 deployment, which had been drawn up at Kissinger's direction by Laurence Lynn of the National Security Council (NSC) staff. On the weekend of 8–9 March, Nixon took this briefing book with him to Key Biscayne, Florida, where he read it and decided to deploy an ABM system to protect U.S. ICBM fields (the I-69 plan).[44]

Having taken this basic decision, Nixon faced the next issues: the timing and method of deployment. These matters were decided after the president returned to Washington on Monday evening. One option supported by members of the academic community and some in Congress was to delay deployment in favor of more research. Nixon rejected this possibility, for he believed that the nation's missile defense effort had progressed as far as it could in the research and development mode; only through a deployment and the actual operation of ABM facilities could the program be advanced. Under the I-69 plan, missile defenses could be constructed at twelve sites depending upon how the strategic situation evolved. The sites would be selected to tailor the system to meet several goals, and the sites would be established through a phased deployment program that would cost only $800–900 million the first year. This funding level would support continuing R&D and permit construction to begin at two phase-one sites—air force bases at Malmstrom, Montana, and Grand Forks, North Dakota—where the ABM systems would defend MINUTEMAN fields. The need to construct the ten remaining sites would be reviewed each year by the President's Foreign Intelligence Advisory Board. These additional sites, if and when constructed, were to expand protection for the MINUTEMAN force and provide a thin defense against a Chinese missile attack or a small, accidental missile launch from any source. Furthermore, this expanded system could become the basis for further expansion of the system to one that could provide broader protection against Soviet ICBMs. Nixon announced his decision on 14 March 1969. The new system was to be called SAFEGUARD.[45]

Nixon's ABM decision was consistent with his concept of nuclear sufficiency, which held that the United States should possess a strategic force structure that was sufficient "to deny other countries the ability to impose their will on the United States and its allies under the weight of strategic military superiority." This concept represented a compromise between those who favored nuclear superiority and those who supported what had come to be known as mutual assured destruction. Like those who favored strategic superiority, Nixon was unwilling to grant the Soviets a clear, unopposed advantage in any one area of strategic weaponry. Thus the Soviet deployment of an ABM system was a challenge to be answered by the fielding of an American system. On the other hand, like the advocates of offensive nuclear deterrence, Nixon recognized the need to establish a stable balance between the American and Soviet strategic force structures. An ABM system deployed to defend missiles and not cities should not alarm the Soviets, for it would be seen by the Soviets as an effort to protect America's second strike retaliatory force from a Soviet first strike and not as an effort to protect U.S. cities from a weak second strike attack by Soviet rockets that might survive an American first strike.[46]

Additionally, Nixon's SAFEGUARD had two strong political advantages over SENTINEL. First, by moving the defensive missiles and their nuclear warheads away from populated areas, it eliminated one of the major objections to Johnson's missile system. Second, by rejecting a program designed to defend a limited number of U.S. cities, it avoided the impossible political decision of which cities to defend.[47]

THE ABM DEBATE OF 1969

In spite of its advantages, Nixon's SAFEGUARD decision did not silence the opposition, which had been working feverishly to turn Laird's temporary halt of deployment into a permanent one. Not only had there been hostile hearings in Congress, but the academic-scientific community had been mobilizing its resources against deployment. For these opponents, SAFEGUARD had become the symbol of all that they disliked about U.S. defense policies from Vietnam and cost overruns to what they perceived as a nuclear arms race. This meant that the administration's fight for deployment would be difficult.[48]

By 1969, opposition to the Vietnam war was common on the nation's university campuses. One facet of this opposition was a "strike" organized in early 1969 by graduate students in the physics department at MIT. The purpose of the strike of 4 March was to call attention to abuses of scientific and technical knowledge. The efforts of these student protesters was supported by some of the leading members of their department. On the actual day of the strike, Hans Bethe described why in his view the SAFEGUARD system was not technically feasible. The strike movement itself eventually spread to over thirty campuses.[49]

Somewhat later, over 2,000 people were drawn to a session on missile defenses during a meeting of the American Physical Society in Washington, D.C. After the meeting, 250 physicists marched from their hotel to the White House, where they met with the president's science adviser. Other groups of physicists visited Capitol Hill, where they spoke against SAFEGUARD to over 60 senators.[50] Their petitions fell upon sympathetic ears in the Senate, for there was strong opposition to SAFEGUARD among liberal senators and members of the Senate Foreign Relations Committee. Other senators supported the program, as did most members of the House of Representatives.[51]

The division in the Senate in 1969 was a mirror of a nation confused and divided about the ABM issue. Four years earlier, a survey had revealed that two out of three Americans believed the United States already had a missile defense. In April 1969, another poll showed that only 47 percent favored deployment of an ABM system, while 26 percent opposed it and 27 percent were undecided. Another poll released somewhat later showed that 84 percent of all Americans thought the United States should have a missile defense system. A Gallup poll in July showed that 58 percent of the people were uninformed or undecided about deployment of a BMD system and only 23 percent favored it. Other manifestations of this division were the stances for and against deployment taken by established organizations and the substantial number of ad hoc groups formed to oppose or support SAFEGUARD. Those who opposed the system tended to believe that SAFEGUARD would not work and was not needed, whereas those who supported it believed that the United States had to keep up with the Soviets, that the protection was needed, and that the nation should trust the president's judgment.[52]

One of the leading opponents of SAFEGUARD was New York publisher Cass Canfield, who raised money for a lobbying effort in Congress. The list of those he recruited "read like a Who's Who of the liberal intelligentsia." Among the leading lights of this group were Jerome Wiesner, president of MIT and erstwhile science adviser to John Kennedy, and Hans Bethe, a Nobel laureate in physics.[53]

One of the most important groups supporting SAFEGUARD was the Committee to Maintain a Prudent Defense Policy, established through the initiative of Paul Nitze and Dean Acheson. To Nitze, the scientists who opposed SAFEGUARD were not thinking clearly about the issues involved and were caught up in fashionable, erroneous attitudes toward nuclear weapons. They were making their judgments based upon what they believed should happen rather than what could happen. The spade work of the committee was done by four young analysts: Peter Wilson, Paul Wolfowitz, Richard Perle, and Edward Luttwak. Nitze would later brag that "with these fellows and only fifteen thousand dollars, half of which came out of my own pocket, we ran circles around Cass Canfield, his millions, and all his big-name experts."[54]

Multiple warhead

In this political cartoon, a "multiple warhead" of senators erupts through the dome of the Capitol during the ABM *debate in the summer of 1969. (Copyright by Paul Conrad, 1969,* Los Angeles Times; *reprinted with permission)*

Throughout the spring and into the summer, national discussion of SAFEGUARD intensified. DOD was accused of altering data, keeping information from Congress, and basing its analysis of BMD on worst-case scenarios. In early May a congressional report hostile to SAFEGUARD was published by Senator Edward Kennedy (D-Mass.), who in February had hired a private committee headed by Wiesner and Abram Chayes to review the issue of an ABM deployment. The report argued that missile defense was neither feasible nor desirable; it was answered promptly by a DOD rebuttal that attacked the report for inadequate methodology, numerous factual errors, and faulty conclusions. There was also a major dispute between Secretary of Defense Laird and the director of the CIA, Richard Helms. Laird held that the Soviets were attempting to achieve a first strike capability, and Helms disagreed. Secret Senate hearings, it was later revealed, showed that both men were concerned about the Soviet threat. The difference between DOD and the CIA concerned whether the Soviets would continue their strategic build-up into the 1970s and whether they could do the things Laird suggested they would do in modifying their strategic force structure.[55]

On 27 June the Senate Armed Services Committee approved an appropriation bill for the armed services that contained funds for SAFE-GUARD. However, the vote of 10 to 7 reflected disagreement over the bill's $345.5 million for the deployment of SAFEGUARD and was an ominous sign for ABM proponents, for the committee normally sent such bills to the floor with unanimous approval. As Senator John Stennis (D-Miss.) prepared to take the bill into the debate of the full Senate, one of his aides took a quick head count of senators: 50 favored and 50 opposed SAFEGUARD. No wonder Stennis declared at this moment: "I feel like I'm going off to war."[56]

Stennis's committee had been conducting hearings for months, and as the bill emerged, the committee's report presented the arguments that had been advanced by both sides in the ABM battle. Among the reasons presented in favor of SAFEGUARD was an apparent drive by the Soviets to achieve a first strike capability. Unless the United States acted expeditiously, developments in the Soviet strategic force structure would threaten all three legs of the American strategic TRIAD by the mid-1970s. Moreover, actions other than SAFEGUARD that the nation might take to offset enhancements of Soviet nuclear forces could be more destabilizing and lead to an escalation in the arms race. Finally, since President Nixon was about to begin strategic arms talks with the Soviets, a decision to begin deployment of an ABM could strengthen his hand.[57]

The minority view argued in the main that SAFEGUARD could not be effective. In addition to its extreme complexity, which raised questions about whether or not it would work, the radar element of the system was extremely vulnerable to nuclear attack. Furthermore, the Soviets could easily overwhelm SAFEGUARD with relatively simple changes in their nuclear force structure, such as increasing the number of SS-9 missiles. And finally, opponents observed that there were just too many demands on U.S. resources to waste money on a system that would not improve U.S. security.[58]

The critical debate on SAFEGUARD got under way on 9 July when the defense authorization bill was laid before the Senate. Margaret Chase Smith (R-Me.) began these deliberations by delivering an introductory statement upon which other senators based their own remarks. The first to speak specifically about ABM during this session was Senator Albert Gore (D-Tenn.). Alluding to Smith's earlier comments, Gore stated that the basis of deterrence is offensive power, and ABM did not fit that paradigm. The Soviets, he maintained, would no more fear the American ABM than the United States would theirs.[59]

Somewhat later, Senator Henry M. Jackson (D-Wash.) delivered a longer speech in favor of SAFEGUARD. After reviewing the make-up of the Soviet leadership and declaring it part of the Soviet threat, Jackson discussed the Soviet progress in deploying its GALOSH ABM and described new developments in Soviet missile defenses. He then explained SAFEGUARD's mission and answered the opposition's criticisms. Against those who proposed offensive answers to the emerging Soviet threat, Jackson argued that a defensive response would be less destabilizing. To opponents who favored a delay in deployment until the United States had had time to negotiate with the Soviet Union, he replied that America should both deploy and negotiate, as the deployment would improve its negotiating position. "In my judgment," Jackson told his colleagues, "anyone who wants a successful negotiation with the Soviets to halt the further evolution of dangerous strategic armaments should be a strong proponent of the SAFEGUARD ABM." Then, almost prophetically in view of the 1972 ABM treaty, Jackson said: "I believe the chance is promising that we could come to an agreement with the Soviet Union for a limited ABM defense on both sides—an agreed ceiling on the number of ABMs, for example—provided that we do not foolishly throw that chance away by now scuttling our own program."[60]

Jackson was answered by two of the staunchest opponents of SAFE-GUARD—Senators John Stewart Cooper (R-Ky.) and Philip Hart (D-Mich.). Cooper argued that "arms control is the best means of security," and even if the Soviet threat increased as Jackson predicted (which Cooper doubted), the appropriate American response was an increase in offensive forces, not SAFEGUARD. Hart followed Cooper with information gleaned from a report by scientists at the University of Michigan. Problems with SAFEGUARD's radar and computers, along with inadequate testing, meant that the system was not likely to provide a reliable defense. Furthermore, this report put the cost of SAFE-GUARD at $28 billion, with the expanded system costing $40 billion. For only $5 billion, the United States could harden its MINUTEMAN silos to the point that the Soviets would require six thousand missiles to destroy them, and Secretary of Defense Laird projected a Soviet threat of only five hundred missiles by the mid-1970s.[61]

Later in the proceedings, Cooper introduced for himself and Hart an amendment (S. 2546) that would bar the use of any money provided in the authorization bill for the deployment of SAFEGUARD or any component thereof. Also precluded was the acquisition of any site for a SAFE-GUARD facility. DOD would be permitted to spend money for "research, development, testing, evaluation and normal procurement thereto."[62]

Later still, a sharp exchange took place between Gore and Jackson and Stennis. The senator from Tennessee accused proponents of SAFE-GUARD of shifting their arguments. When President Nixon announced his decision on television to the American people, he justified it by saying that a BMD system was necessary to "preserve the integrity of our deterrence." Later, Secretary Laird confirmed this position. The day before, Gore said, Senator Stennis had said SAFEGUARD was necessary to improve our bargaining position vis-à-vis the Soviets. "We are back to the canard," Gore continued, "of arming in order to parley." According to Gore, Laird had also retreated from his earlier position.[63]

Jackson and Stennis immediately challenged Gore's allegations. Stennis said that improving Nixon's negotiating position and enhancing the U.S. deterrent were both valid reasons for supporting SAFE-GUARD. Certainly, the Congress should not pull the rug from under the president as he was preparing for the negotiations. Jackson seconded Stennis's remarks.[64]

As the debate continued through July, things were not going well for the pro-ABM forces. One shock came early in that month when Senator George D. Aiken (R-Vt.) cast his lot with those opposing SAFEGUARD. This was an especially serious loss. Aiken was "a white-maned Yankee whose flinty wisdom on foreign affairs command[ed] respect on both sides of the aisle." At seventy-six, he was the dean of Republican senators and was sure to bring with him to the opposition the junior Republican senator from Vermont, Winston Lewis Prouty. Some began saying that the loss of these two senators would force the president into a compromise if he was to save SAFEGUARD.[65]

About a week later, on 14 July, Prouty provided one of the most dramatic moments of the debate when he surprised his colleagues by

Winston Lewis Prouty was born into a prosperous New England family in 1906 and began his political career in 1938 when he was elected mayor of Newport, Vermont. In 1950 he was elected to the House of Representatives where he served four terms before being elected to the Senate. During the ABM debate of 1969, Prouty surprised political pundits by breaking with the senior senator from Vermont, George D. Aiken, and announcing his support for the SAFE-GUARD program. (Special Collections, Bailey/Howe Library, University of Vermont)

breaking with Aiken. In a seventy-minute speech, Prouty first considered the plight of a president confronted with an oncoming Soviet missile attack and then declared that he wanted to give the president an "extra button":

> I envisioned a president faced with the knowledge that enemy missiles were heading toward the United States. I inquired as to what options are now available to him in response to such attack. I discovered that there are now two grim alternatives—do nothing or push the button that unleashes our devastating nuclear fury. . . .
>
> But if there was another button available, a button to trigger our missiles designed to intercept and destroy these incoming weap-

ons, the president could push it and halt the attack without immense loss of lives at home or the catastrophic consequences of full retaliation. . . . Safeguard provides an additional alternative, an extra button.[66]

Within a week of Prouty's announcement, the anti-SAFEGUARD forces received another shock. The Democratic leadership, particularly Senators Mike Mansfield (D-Mont.) and Edward Kennedy, had been working hard to align the Democrats in opposition to ABM when on 18 July Kennedy was involved in an accident. Mary Jo Kopechne, a passenger in the senator's car, was drowned when Kennedy drove his car off a bridge from Martha's Vineyard to Chappaquiddick Island. This was a major national news event and seriously impaired the senator's effectiveness for the moment.[67]

By the time the ABM amendments came to a vote, the Senate was evenly split on the issue of SAFEGUARD deployment; one vote could literally carry the issue. Critics of deployment had thrown their support behind the leading opposition amendment, the Cooper-Hart bill, which would stop deployment of SAFEGUARD but provide $759 million for continued research and development. Senator Smith, who had opened the debate on the Senate floor on 9 July, was known as a staunch foe of SAFEGUARD. She had been one of the seven senators on the Armed Services Committee to vote against the system.[68] Naturally, the opponents of an ABM deployment counted her in their fold. They should have known better, for Smith was one of the most colorful members of the Senate with a reputation for doing the unexpected. In her thirtieth year in Congress, the last twenty in the Senate, she held the record for consecutive roll calls—2,946—a string that had been broken a year earlier because of a hip operation and late plane. The most predictable thing about her was that each day she would be wearing a rose when she answered the Senate roll call. On the day President Kennedy was assassinated, she had removed her rose and laid it on his old desk in the Senate chamber.[69]

On 6 August the Senate was scheduled to vote on the authorization bill containing the provision for SAFEGUARD deployment. True to her character, Smith would help make it a memorable vote for all senators. Early in the day she surprised her colleagues by sending them a note suggesting that if they were really against SAFEGUARD they should join her in voting down all funds for it, including R&D money. Later, as the Senate was gaveled into order, a woman dressed in black stood up in the gallery and shouted: "I prophesy against ABM in the name of Jesus

Christ!" After she was removed, the senators began their deliberations on amendments that would restrict authorized funding for SAFEGUARD; Smith's amendment was the first of the anti-ABM measures considered. In midafternoon, it was defeated by a vote of 89 to 11.[70]

During a brief recess following this vote, Gore and Smith worked out another anti-ABM amendment. Cooper and Hart agreed to support this proposal in the hope that Smith would support their amendment if hers failed. Known as the Smith-Cooper-Hart amendment, this measure would cut off all funds for SAFEGUARD but would allow the $759 million in the bill to be used for R&D on other antiballistic missile systems, including components of SAFEGUARD. The vote of 50 for and 50 against the new measure marked the high-water point of opposition to the SAFEGUARD deployment. Although a tie vote defeats an amendment under Senate rules, Vice President Spiro Agnew voted against the amendment so that the final tally was 50 for and 51 against.[71]

The opponents of SAFEGUARD next brought up the original Cooper-Hart amendment, but it was defeated by a vote of 49 for and 51 against. The change in the vote line-up reflected Smith's vote against an amendment that would have stopped deployment while still providing money for SAFEGUARD R&D.[72]

Why was the opposition to SAFEGUARD so strong? For some, at least, the ABM system had come to stand for all they detested in American defense policies. It represented costly and unnecessary weapons that were draining the national treasury. But above all, it symbolized the unpopular Vietnam war. For these senators, their vote against SAFEGUARD was an effort to "reassert Congressional control over defense spending" and redirect America's national energies.[73]

Although Nixon's victory had been by the narrowest of margins, he believed that the vote for SAFEGUARD showed that America was "still prepared to maintain its military strength." The president was now in the position of strength he considered essential to negotiate meaningful arms reductions with the Soviets.[74]

Part Two
The SALT Decade

If we have not reached an agreement well before 1977, then I believe you will see an explosion of technology and an explosion of numbers at the end of which we will be lucky if we have the present stability, in which it will be impossible to describe what strategic superiority means. And one of the questions which we have to ask ourselves as a country is: What in the name of God is strategic superiority? What is the significance of it, politically, militarily, operationally, at these levels of numbers? What do you do with it?
—*Henry Kissinger, 1974*[1]

The decade of the 1970s was the age of SALT. As the 1970s dawned, the Soviet Union and the United States were negotiating the agreements that led to the demise of America's SAFEGUARD missile defense system in 1976. The decade ended with the Soviet invasion of Afghanistan and President Jimmy Carter's withdrawal of the SALT II treaty from Senate consideration.

Although the SALT I ABM Treaty placed severe restrictions on BMD systems and effectively killed the American ABM program, it did little where offensive systems were concerned beyond recognizing the offensive force structures the superpowers had established by 1972. Furthermore, the treaty on offensive systems that emerged from the SALT II negotiations would have done nothing to reduce what Americans considered the most dangerous element in the Soviet strategic force structure: the heavy ICBMs that many feared would give the Soviets a first strike capability against American MINUTEMAN missiles by the early to mid-1980s.

As the 1970s wore on and the Soviets began equipping their large missiles with multiple independently targeted reentry vehicles (MIRVs) and improving their accuracy, several national leaders and strategic analysts in the United States began to worry about the Soviet strategic build-up. What motives were behind it? How should the United States respond? The debates spawned by increasing Soviet strategic power and by the SALT agreements constitute the background that is essential for understanding the termination of the SAFEGUARD program, which was followed by a resurgence of interest in missile defenses as the SALT decade ended.

CHAPTER THREE

SALT I and the Institutionalization of MAD

I agreed with the conclusion that we should go forward with ABM. The decisive arguments in my view were both military and diplomatic. Soviet leaders and military theorists had never espoused the Western academic notions that vulnerability was desirable or that ABM was threatening and destabilizing. As Premier Kosygin declared at a London news conference in February 1967, an antiballistic missile system "is intended not for killing people but for saving human lives."
—*Henry Kissinger,* White House Years[1]

In July 1970 we watched with some concern the debate in the Senate on the Safeguard ABM program, judging that a congressional setback to Safeguard would take steam out of the ABM negotiation, by reducing any Soviet disposition to make concessions.
—*Gerard Smith,* Doubletalk[2]

THE SALT TALKS BEGIN

In his inaugural address of 20 January 1969, President Nixon noted that the "greatest honor history can bestow is the title of peacemaker" and indicated an interest in negotiations to reduce "the burden of arms" and "to strengthen the structure of peace." Nevertheless, his new administration proceeded cautiously in devising and implementing its strategic arms policy, for Nixon wanted first to gauge Soviet attitudes and goals in the area of strategic arms and then to develop a coherent policy to guide American efforts in the negotiations. Furthermore, as previously noted, he hoped to improve the strategic force structure of the United States so that he could negotiate with the Soviets from a position of strength. Hopefully, a part of this improved force structure would be a defensive missile system. Such a system would match the one the Soviets were already deploying and at the same time serve as a bargaining chip that might persuade the Soviets to accept limitations on strategic arms. Without an ABM system, American negotiators might well have to give up some other element of the U.S. force structure to secure meaningful limitations on Soviet systems.[3]

Nor were the Soviets likely to begin negotiations on strategic arms as long as there was a prospect that Washington politics might kill the SAFEGUARD system. To start strategic arms talks before Congress finished its deliberations on SAFEGUARD would spoil the argument of ABM critics that a decision to deploy a missile defense system would be "incompatible with arms control negotiations." Such an attitude on the part of the Soviets would help explain why Nixon's 11 June invitation to begin negotiations was "met by four months of Soviet stonewalling." In the wake of the 6 August vote in the Senate, it was anticipated that the Soviets would soon propose a date for beginning the talks, since the vote in the House was not expected to be close. However, the Soviets did not make a concrete proposal for talks until 20 October. By then, SAFEGUARD had cleared the House with a comfortable 3-to-1 majority. Now, with an end to Soviet hopes that Congress might rule against SAFEGUARD and with Nixon in a stronger bargaining position, the conditions were right for negotiations to begin. On 25 October the Nixon administration announced its acceptance of a Soviet invitation to begin exploratory strategic arms talks at Helsinki on 17 November.[4]

From the start of negotiations, two major problems relative to SAFEGUARD would continue to plague American negotiators. One of these was the lack of a strong political consensus, especially in the Senate, favoring deployment of an ABM system. For SAFEGUARD to be an effective bargaining chip, the Soviets had to be convinced that the United States was committed to deployment. The obvious difficulty the Nixon administration would have in sustaining political support for the SAFEGUARD program would constantly undermine the program's credibility as a bargaining chip. For example, throughout the SALT I negotiations Nixon would have to keep a steady eye on the Senate to ensure that SAFEGUARD survived until an arms agreement was reached. As Nixon put it to a group of Republican senators in April 1971: "If SALT is to have a chance, we cannot give away in the Senate things we might want to negotiate with the Soviets. They will say, 'Why should we continue to negotiate SALT when the United States is going to take these actions unilaterally?'"[5]

A second problem that would vex U.S. negotiators was a gap that had opened between the bargaining position of the United States in the arms talks and the ABM program Congress had approved and was most likely to continue supporting. The first phase of the SAFEGUARD program, it will be recalled, involved the deployment of ABM systems to protect two MINUTEMAN missile fields. Only later would the United States deploy a system to protect the national command authorities (NCA) at Washington, D.C. Nevertheless, the Nixon administration maneuvered itself into proposing an agreement under which the United States and USSR would be allowed to deploy a single ABM system to protect each nation's NCA. This proposal would require a major, costly reorientation of the SAFEGUARD program and might cause a less than enthusiastic Congress to kill the program. Although the Soviets were confused by the contradiction between this proposal and the congressionally approved ABM system, they quickly accepted a position that obviously would pose difficulties for the Americans. In addition to confusing the Soviets, this proposal sowed seeds of disunity among U.S. negotiators.[6]

These two problems haunted the Americans throughout the SALT I negotiations. In all, there would be seven rounds of talks, leading two and a half years later to the Nixon-Brezhnev summit in Moscow and the SALT I agreements signed in Moscow on 26 May 1972. Discussions of ABM systems were of major significance throughout these talks, and the resulting ABM accord was the principal fruit of the negotiations.

THE FIRST U.S. POSITION ON ABM

The first round of SALT I got under way at Helsinki on 17 November 1969. In these talks, the negotiating teams worked out the ground rules and definitions that would guide the talks; each team also laid out its broad negotiating position. The United States indicated its desire to negotiate restrictions on defensive as well as offensive weapons and insisted on linking the two. The United States was interested especially in establishing limits on Soviet ICBMs, including a sublimit of 250 on the largest Soviet missile, the SS-9.[7]

American negotiators were somewhat surprised, given Soviet attitudes expressed at Glassboro, to find that the Soviets were "most eager" to talk about ABM systems, but failed even to mention the issue of MIRVs, a recent development that prompted considerable concern for many in the United States who feared that MIRVing, along with ABMs, would heat up the arms race. With regard to missile defenses, Soviet negotiators presented three options (a heavy deployment, a limited deployment, and a complete ban) and indicated a clear preference for something in between a complete ban and a limited deployment. U.S. negotiators interpreted the Soviet preference to mean that the Soviets preferred to keep the GALOSH system they were building around Moscow.[8]

Because of the asymmetry in the initial positions of the negotiating teams, the American delegation sought to be conciliatory on the ABM issue in the hope that the Soviets would reciprocate on offensive systems. When round two of the talks started in Vienna on 16 April 1970, the American delegation was prepared to make two proposals. The first contained three elements: limits on the number of offensive launch vehicles, a ban on the testing and deployment of MIRVs to be verified by on-site inspections, and either a complete ban on ABMs or a deployment restricted to one location near each nation's capital to defend the national command authorities. If the Soviets rejected this offer, the second U.S. proposal would be advanced. It also called for limits on offensive systems but contained no restrictions on MIRVing. Where ABMs were concerned, it advanced the same two options that were contained in the first proposal. When presenting their position, U.S. negotiators were directed to begin with the option that allowed each side to have one NCA-oriented site.[9]

This position on ABM was a "first-class blunder" according to Henry Kissinger. It arose from a bureaucratic compromise and placed the United States in an impossible negotiating position. That the Nixon administration did not make the original twelve-site SAFEGUARD program the basis of its negotiating position was not all that unwise, since few senators who voted for SAFEGUARD in August 1969 continued to support the original concept. However, the lack of wisdom in the NCA-oriented option should have been apparent, for though an ABM facility to defend Washington was one of the twelve in the overall plan for SAFE-GUARD, protecting the U.S. capital was bound to raise prickly political questions about why Congress might choose to defend only Washington. It should have been equally apparent that the DOD would not support a complete ABM ban because having at least one operational site would help sustain development efforts and give the military valuable experience in operating a missile defense system. These considerations notwithstanding, the State Department and the Arms Control and Disarmament Agency favored a complete ban on ABM. But since DOD would not support this option and the Soviets were already building the GALOSH system to protect their national command authorities, the State Department was willing to support the option allowing one NCA-oriented site as the ABM proposal most likely to be accepted. Thus the Nixon administration found itself in the difficult position of making an offer to the Soviets that Congress was not likely to approve. Not only that, but the NCA proposal would also give considerable advantage to the Soviets, since about three hundred of their ICBMs were close enough to Moscow to be protected by the GALOSH system being installed near the Soviet capital. There were no ICBMs near Washington to be protected even in the unlikely event that Congress would approve construction of an ABM facility there.[10]

The Soviets quickly rejected the first U.S. proposal, perhaps because it required on-site inspections to confirm compliance with its restrictions on MIRVing. They also refused to accept the second proposal's limitations on offensive systems because they believed the Americans were trying to restrict their land-based ICBMs, which the Soviets considered their greatest strategic asset. Yet, "with amazing and totally unprecedented speed," Soviet negotiators accepted the American proposal on ABM restricting both sides to one site for defense of their respective national command authorities. In this way, the Soviets closed the box that the Nixon administration had built for itself with its ABM proposals. To add insult to injury, the American offer on ABM systems that had been designed to be conciliatory failed to win any concessions from the Soviets in the area of offensive systems.[11]

By late May it was apparent that no progress was being made in the second round of discussions. The talks had become bogged down principally over the issues of forward-based systems (FBS)[12] and MIRVing. At this point the U.S. delegation informed the president of the stalemate and proposed on 15 June that the United States adopt a new negotiating position that might get the talks rolling again. This Vienna Option called for an initial ABM treaty and an agreement on three central offensive strategic systems (heavy bombers, ICBMs, and SLBMs). The sticky issues of medium- and intermediate-range ballistic missiles and cruise missiles would be deferred in return for a Soviet agreement to postpone the matter of FBS. After these first agreements, a more comprehensive treaty would be negotiated to include limits on other offensive weapons.[13]

On 23 June, while this proposal was being considered, Henry Kissinger, Nixon's national security adviser, and Anatoly Dobrynin, Soviet ambassador to the United States, began special "back channel" talks in an effort to break the log jam in Vienna.[14] These talks would continue throughout the critical period of the official negotiations and involved considerable diplomatic maneuvering in which the Soviets sought to separate negotiations on ABM limitations from those dealing with restrictions on offensive systems while the United States continued to insist on linking the two. Since decoupling the talks on offensive and defensive systems would have destroyed SAFEGUARD's value as a bargaining chip, from the U.S. perspective, linkage was arguably the dominant issue until the SALT I accords were signed almost two years later. Furthermore, the negotiations that were most important in resolving this issue took place in the back channel.[15]

On 4 August the United States tabled a new position on missile defenses at the Geneva talks. It insisted on the continued linkage of negotiations on offensive and defensive weapons, offered a new proposal on offensive systems, and proposed a total ban on ABM systems. With this new position, the United States was attempting to recover from the difficulties created by its earlier proposal to allow each side a single ABM system to defend its national command authorities. When the Soviets failed to respond effectively to these proposals, the talks were adjourned on 14 August.[16]

PRESERVING THE BARGAINING CHIP:
THE HOME FRONT

In early 1970 the Nixon administration announced plans to begin the expansion phase of SAFEGUARD by adding six sites to the two authorized by Congress in the fall of 1969. Construction was to begin on one site at Whiteman Air Force Base, Missouri, where its missiles would defend a MINUTEMAN field. Preliminary work was to start on five other sites. One of these, Francis E. Warren Air Force Base, Wyoming, would protect an ICBM field. The four remaining sites, including one at Washington, D.C., would become the basis for a thin system to protect against an attack from China or an accidental launch of a Soviet missile.[17] The Washington, D.C., site would also protect the national command authorities.

In announcing these plans, officials of the Nixon administration stressed the flexibility offered by the proposed expansion of SAFE-GUARD. Not only was it a reasonable response to evolving Chinese and Soviet threats, but it would sustain a strong bargaining position for the United States in the SALT negotiations. This latter point had to be handled delicately, and in an apparent effort to see that America's new ABM efforts did not alarm the Soviets and therefore have the wrong effect on SALT proceedings, government spokesmen soft-pedaled the expansion as being less ambitious than Nixon's original SAFEGUARD plan.[18]

The expansion program soon ran into congressional opposition. In mid-June, while the second round of talks was still in progress, as if to underline its differences with the administration, the Senate Armed Services Committee rejected the House-approved plan for expanding SAFEGUARD. The Senate committee announced it would restrict America's ABM to the protection of missile fields. This meant that Congress would support the two sites already under construction near Grand Forks and Malmstrom Air Force Bases, as well as the sites planned for Whiteman and Francis E. Warren Air Force Bases. At the same time, the Senate committee voted to cut the funds for preliminary work on the four sites that were to form the basis of an area defense to protect the United States from a Chinese ICBM attack. These included, of course, the Washington location, which would have covered the national command authorities. The death of this part of the SAFEGUARD program sent a clear message to Soviet and American SALT negotiators: an agreement to restrict BMD to one NCA-oriented site was tantamount to killing the American ABM program. Moreover, it relieved members of Congress of the sticky political questions they would have faced from constituents wondering why Congress would vote funds for an ABM site near Washington but not for the nation's other major cities.[19]

As the authorization bill moved from the Senate Armed Services Committee toward another crucial vote on the floor of the Senate, there appeared to be some sentiment for cutting funds for the sites at Whiteman and Francis E. Warren. Nixon and his staff now faced a rather delicate political situation. A number of key administration officials believed that a strong ABM program was America's most powerful bargaining tool in the SALT negotiations and knew that the value of ABM as a bargaining chip was one of the best arguments for strong congressional support for SAFEGUARD. At the same time, the use of this argument required great subtlety. Too much emphasis on ABM as a bargaining chip could convince the Soviets that they need only stall the talks long enough and support for SAFEGUARD would evaporate. Moreover, building an ABM system as simply a ploy to strengthen the U.S. negotiating position could lead to embarrassing political questions on the home front about why the government was spending so much money on a system it was likely to abandon. Furthermore, there was the difficulty one would face with members of Congress who had been convinced in the debate of 1969 that SAFEGUARD was crucial to the defense of the country: how could Nixon consider bargaining away a system that was vital to U.S. security? All of this was further complicated by the American negotiating position on ABM. The delicacy of this situation explains why the Nixon administration moved cautiously to sustain support for SAFEGUARD in the summer of 1970.[20]

To keep the SAFEGUARD program as strong as possible and protect its status as a bargaining chip, Kissinger met with a select group of Senate and House leaders on 23 July. Since Nixon recognized that his administration could not talk publicly about a bargaining chip and have it retain its power, the meeting was held behind closed doors. It did not go well. To begin with, the session was not as well attended as Kissinger and Nixon had hoped and was interrupted frequently by members of Congress coming in and then leaving to participate in roll-call votes. Furthermore, Kissinger's comments generated some hostile reaction. He stressed the value of SAFEGUARD in persuading the Soviets to limit the size of their SS-9 force. Some members of Congress considered this an effort to pressure them into voting for the system. Senator J. William Fulbright (D-Ark.) criticized the Nixon administration for briefing NATO allies on the SALT proceedings before he briefed Congress. As if the outcome of the meeting were not bad enough, the next day the *New York Times* and the *Washington Post* carried articles disclosing information on what had been discussed.[21]

Three weeks after this meeting, SAFEGUARD faced its second do-or-die vote in the Senate. The test came over an amendment put forward by Cooper and Hart, the same senators who had combined their efforts a year earlier in an attempt to prevent deployment of the system. This measure would cut from the defense procurement bill the $322 million earmarked for the two new ABM sites at Whiteman and Francis E. Warren Air Force Bases, leaving $1.027 billion for the two sites being constructed at Malmstrom and Grand Forks. The arguments of those supporting the Cooper-Hart amendment were essentially the same as a year earlier: ballistic missile defense was not technically feasible, deployment would escalate the arms race, and a missile defense system would take money from social programs. Senator Jackson, leader of the pro-SAFEGUARD forces, argued that the Senate had to send a message to the Soviets that the United States was prepared to meet any expansion in Soviet strategic programs. The Soviets would then be convinced that the only sensible course of action for them was to agree to strategic arms limitations.[22]

As the time of the vote approached, the White House circulated among uncommitted senators a communiqué from Gerard Smith indicating the importance of SAFEGUARD to the talks under way in Vienna. Apparently, Smith's message influenced at least two senators who were sitting on the fence, Thomas J. McIntyre (D-N.J.) and James B. Pearson (R-Kans.). On 12 August they voted with the majority, defeating the Cooper-Hart bill 52 to 47. The anti-SAFEGUARD forces concluded that the key to Nixon's victory had been effective use of the bargaining chip argument.[23] With the bargaining chip now relatively secure on the home front, the question became whether or not the Nixon administration could use it to obtain meaningful limitations on Soviet offensive systems.

PRESERVING THE BARGAINING CHIP:
THE SALT TALKS

The third round of SALT negotiations took place in Helsinki in November and December 1970. It was a short and stormy session that marked the "nadir of SALT I." Again the center of contention was forward-based systems, an issue used skillfully by the Soviets in their continuing effort to separate negotiations on defensive systems from those on offensive systems. The U.S. delegation began by standing pat on its proposal of 4 August, insisting that the Soviets must respond to this proposal before the talks could proceed. For their part, the Soviets continued to demand that U.S. FBS be included in the count of U.S. strategic systems. When on 1 December the Soviet chief negotiator, Vladimir Semenov, formally proposed separating talks on offensive and defensive systems, he used U.S. intransigence on the forward-based systems issue as the reason for his proposal. Since discussions of offensive weapons were deadlocked over the FBS issue, the two sides should put off an offensive agreement while pursuing a treaty on ABM systems.[24]

In discussing the ABM issue, the Soviets said they were confused by the American position (one NCA-oriented site or a complete ABM ban), which ran counter to the program Congress seemed willing to support (a broad system principally to defend American ICBMs). Nevertheless, the Soviets agreed to the NCA-oriented ABM option. One site would be permitted within a given radius of the center of each country's national capital. Also, limits on the numbers of launchers, missiles, and radar systems should be specified in the treaty.[25]

Unofficially, the Soviets encouraged the United States not to reject their new proposal outright, hinting that details on the proposal would follow. Although the White House reply left the door open for the Soviets to elaborate on their offer, there was little that was concrete in what the Soviet delegation had to say during the remainder of round three. The Soviets seemed to be at pains to show that their new proposal did not completely separate negotiations on offensive and defensive systems, but they offered no firm timetable for negotiations on offensive weapons and specified no limitations on offensive systems that might then be negotiable.[26]

The third round of talks highlighted the different approaches to negotiation taken by the Soviet and U.S. teams. The Soviets tended to table general proposals devoid of details and to insist on acceptance of the principles in the proposal as the price for getting more details. On the other hand, the U.S. team would offer detailed proposals and expect the Soviets to negotiate on the details. By the time the third round of talks ended on 18 December, the Americans had tabled a number of detailed proposals to which the Soviets had continued to respond with their usual general ones. The American delegation had come to feel that it was negotiating with itself.[27]

With the Soviets now pushing for the NCA-oriented ABM agreement offered by the Americans and attempting to separate talks on defensive and offensive systems, it was apparent that the United States had painted itself into a corner in the SALT negotiations.

ANOTHER THREAT TO THE BARGAINING CHIP: A SIGNAL NEVER SENT

In the three months between rounds three and four of the SALT negotiations, SAFEGUARD and Nixon's negotiating position became the center of a maelstrom of domestic pressures as scientists and newspaper editors, among others, took positions supporting the Soviet effort to separate negotiations on offensive and defensive systems. Nevertheless, Nixon seemed to be holding his ground when his State of the World report was delivered to Congress on 25 February 1971, for he argued against splitting the SALT talks on the grounds that this approach would do nothing more than channel the arms race in an offensive or defensive direction.[28]

One development that supplied support to opponents of the Nixon administration was a "signal" from the Soviet Union that it would bargain in good faith. About the time round three of the talks was ending, Secretary Laird announced that there was evidence the Soviets had stopped constructing silos for their large SS-9 ICBMs. These missiles were of special concern, because American strategists believed they eventually would give the Soviets a first strike capability against the U.S. MINUTEMAN force. This "signal" seemed to promise that the Soviets would continue to bargain in earnest even if a separate ABM treaty stripped the United States of its SAFEGUARD bargaining chip.[29]

President Nixon's foes called for reciprocal action on the part of the United States. Senator Hubert Humphrey (D-Minn.) saw this as an ideal opportunity for the United States to halt its part of the arms race, something it could do with impunity by freezing the U.S. MIRV and ABM programs. Even Gerard Smith, the U.S. chief negotiator, seems to have taken this position, for he suggested to President Nixon that the U.S. halt further ABM deployments as an indication of America's commitment to arms control.[30]

Those who supported the president's hard-line position felt vindicated when the Soviet signal turned out to be nothing more than wishful thinking on the part of ABM foes and other administration opponents. On 7 March Senator Jackson revealed new intelligence data showing that the Soviets had ended their SS-9 moratorium. The stoppage really had not been a signal after all. Rather, it had been a pause in their construction program as the Soviets shifted from building silos for the SS-9 to constructing bigger silos for a new and larger missile, the SS-18. By the end of 1971, there had been "more Soviet missile starts . . . than in all but one year of the previous decade."[31]

THE BACK CHANNEL AGAIN

While these events were unfolding, Nixon and Kissinger were working through the back channel to establish the framework for a SALT treaty. Throughout these discussions, the Soviets proved to be tough and wily negotiators, seeking every advantage and giving ground only grudgingly as they sought to separate talks on defensive and offensive systems while Nixon and Kissinger worked to establish linkage as the basic principle of any SALT accord.[32]

By early February 1971, the Soviets had agreed to linkage in principle. If an agreement on defensive systems were reached before an accord on offensive weapons was arranged, the Soviets "would consider a freeze on offensive deployments pending the completion of negotiations." Then, just as the superpowers seemed on the verge of an agreement, a crisis developed when the Soviets sent a submarine tender to the port of Cienfuegos, Cuba, indicating that they might again be trying to establish a submarine base there.[33] Although this issue was resolved rather quickly, it was followed by a period in which Soviet leaders stalled negotiations so that a firm agreement still had not been reached in the back channel as the first week of March ended.[34]

The SALT talks were scheduled to resume on 15 March in Vienna, and the Nixon administration had hoped to complete the back channel discussions in time to draw up new instructions to guide the American delegation in the next round of negotiations. When it became apparent that this would not be possible, President Nixon was faced with having to issue interim instructions to Gerard Smith. In doing so, he had to ensure that the instructions would not conflict with agreements likely to be arranged in the back channel. Not surprisingly, then, Nixon chose to stick largely to the position the United States had tabled in Vienna the previous August. The only significant change pertained to the U.S. position on ABM.[35]

The domestic debate swirling around SAFEGUARD in the winter of 1971 convinced Nixon that an ABM agreement based on the NCA option would be the death knell of SAFEGUARD. Something had to be done to bring the U.S. negotiating position into line with the reality of domestic politics. The interim instructions offered an opportunity to start this realignment. Accordingly, on 11 March the Nixon administration issued National Security Decision Memorandum (NSDM) 102, which directed Smith to add a third option to the U.S. negotiating position on ABM. This new option would allow the United States to continue its SAFEGUARD program as approved by Congress and permit the Soviets to keep the NCA-oriented system they were building.[36]

On 12 March, about a month after the Soviets had accepted linkage in principle, Dobrynin gave Kissinger a note in which the Soviets reneged on their earlier agreement. The new Soviet position was that the superpowers should first conclude an ABM agreement that would allow the deployment of one site near each nation's capital. After this, the Soviets would agree to discuss limits on offensive systems. As soon as Kissinger advised Dobrynin that this position was unacceptable, the Soviet ambassador offered to work with him to blend the arrangements being advocated by the U.S. and Soviet governments. The two met again on 15 March and exchanged draft agreements. Dobrynin's draft still called for an accord on ABM before offensive limitations were agreed to, but it did drop the Soviet insistence that the only ABM site would be at each nation's capital. Kissinger's draft still insisted on linkage. On 25 March Kissinger again informed Dobrynin of the U.S. insistence on linkage: the ABM treaty and the conditions of the freeze on offensive weapons would have to be negotiated simultaneously and concluded at the same time. The next day, according to Kissinger:

> Dobrynin brought the Soviet reply to our March 16 [sic] draft, which it neither accepted nor rejected. The principle of a freeze on strategic offensive weapons was accepted, but the details were to be discussed *after* an agreement on defensive weapons had been reached. . . . [T]his implied a compromise: that the agreements be discussed successively but signed simultaneously. This we could not accept. Once an ABM treaty was known to exist, we would be under irresistible pressure to sign; the minute we had signed, the offensive freeze would evaporate. (Even if we did not sign it, the Congress would never vote funds for the ABM program, so that the ideal outcome from the Soviet point of view would be an unconsummated ABM agreement in which the United States abandoned its program unilaterally.)
> We were making progress, but at an excruciatingly slow pace.[37]

The pace of progress in the Kissinger-Dobrynin talks was further slowed for some time by what seemed to be a Soviet effort to use the secrecy of the back channel against the Nixon administration. This was done on 4 and 9 May by Semenov, who advanced to Smith a proposal that Kissinger had rejected in the back channel six weeks earlier. In this way, the Soviets apparently hoped to improve their position by playing Smith against Kissinger. On 11 May, Kissinger ended this ploy by telling Dobrynin bluntly that if the Soviets did not halt this practice promptly, the United States would close the back channel and thenceforth conduct all negotiations with the Soviets in public, including the delicate negotiations on Soviet interests in Berlin,[38] which were being conducted in a separate set of talks that the Soviets wished to conclude quickly. At the same time, Kissinger demanded from the Soviets within forty-eight hours an answer to a U.S. proposal of 26 April that made it clear that the United States would not accept an NCA-only restriction on its ABM system.[39]

Dobrynin brought the reply on 12 May. The Soviets agreed to drop their requirement that each country be limited to a NCA-oriented site at its capital, thereby letting the Nixon administration off the hook of its own fashioning. Furthermore, the Soviets agreed to negotiate offensive and defensive agreements simultaneously. These arrangements brought the superpowers "onto negotiable grounds" and a joint announcement was made by the national leaders on 20 May.[40]

The back channel agreement was far from perfect. It had not re-solved sticking points like the Soviet position on FBS and the U.S. insis-tence on equality in strategic nuclear systems; it simply removed them from the negotiating agenda at this first stage of the talks. The agree-ment also tolerated a good deal of ambiguity about what each side meant by such terms as "freeze" and "simultaneity." Furthermore, dif-ficult issues relating to offensive systems remained unresolved. On top of all this, there remained a good deal of bargaining to be done right in Washington, where the "truly nasty problem was to find a position on defense—on limiting ABMs—that the various parts of the town could live with and that might be negotiable."[41]

NARROWING THE DIFFERENCES

Although the Soviets had dropped their insistence on the NCA-oriented system in the back channel discussions, in the formal talks of round four they rejected the new U.S. proposal contained in the president's in-terim instructions to the U.S. delegation. This proposal would have al-lowed each country to keep the system it was currently deploying. The United States would be permitted to field its four-site SAFEGUARD sys-tem protecting missile fields, while the Soviets would be allowed to keep their one NCA-oriented site. The Soviets considered this arrange-ment "manifestly inequitable."[42] They would not find the first U.S. po-sition in the next round of the talks much more to their liking.

The fifth round of talks started at Helsinki on 8 July with the two delegations sparring over the meaning of "simultaneity." The U.S. po-sition was that the discussions could focus on ABM matters for two to three weeks, but after that negotiations on offensive and defensive sys-tems had to be carried out in parallel. On the other hand, Semenov, speaking for the Soviets, claimed not to understand the concept of par-allel talks and argued that after an agreement was reached on ABM, "some measures would be agreed on in the sphere of limiting strategic offensive arms."[43]

To emphasize its requirement for simultaneous negotiations, the American delegation on 27 July tabled proposals for an ABM accord and an interim agreement on offensive systems. The U.S. position on ABM was the so-called three-to-one proposal, an attempt to blend the SAFE-GUARD system with the NCA-only proposal. Each side was to have the option of defending its NCA with one hundred ABMs or defending three missile fields with three hundred ABMs. If the United States chose to defend missile fields, its ABM sites would have to be west of the Mississippi River; if the Soviets chose this option, their sites would have to be east of the Ural Mountains. The last U.S. proposal on ABM was tabled on 20 August and offered each side the option of building either two sites to protect missile fields or one site to defend its national command authorities.[44]

There were at least two reasons behind the three-to-one proposal advanced by the United States. First, the Soviets were likely to emerge from the SALT negotiations with a superior number of ICBMs. And second, the Soviet GALOSH system at Moscow could defend three hundred Soviet ICBMs. Nevertheless, the Soviets were not likely to accept a three-to-one disparity in ABM facilities. Further undermining this proposal was the fact that the American SALT delegation and part of the Washington bureaucracy opposed it.[45]

Those who opposed the president's position raised again the possibility of achieving a complete ban on ABM systems. Their opposition set off an extensive and rancorous debate that threatened to turn U.S. policy making into the "greatest seminar on arms control in history" without producing a decision. The debate was finally resolved with the issuance of NSDM 127, which reaffirmed the three-to-one proposal while acknowledging a ban on ABM as the ultimate goal of U.S. arms control policy. The document specified that this ultimate goal could be pursued only after limits were negotiated on ABM systems and after an interim agreement limiting offensive weapons was arranged.[46]

For their part, the Soviets advanced four ABM proposals during the fifth round, the last of which was made in early September. Its provisions resembled those finally incorporated in the ABM treaty. Each side was to be allowed one NCA-oriented site. Additionally, the United States could keep one of the sites it was already constructing, and the Soviets were to be allowed to build an additional ABM facility to protect the same number of missile silos as the American site would defend. While this Soviet proposal was similar to the agreement eventually signed at the summit, the U.S. delegation was not prepared to accept it at this stage of the negotiations, partly because of its vagueness about the second ABM system the USSR would gain. The Nixon administration rejected this proposal and reiterated its position of 20 August. On 24 September round five ended.[47]

Three weeks later, President Nixon announced that a summit meeting had been scheduled for the following May. This added a new sense of urgency to the talks when they resumed at Vienna on 14 November. The focus remained on ABM, with each side still maneuvering for an advantage. The American delegation suggested that the Soviets keep the system they were deploying and allow the United States to keep both of the SAFEGUARD sites it was currently building.[48]

The credibility of this position may have been undermined by American officials involved in the SALT process who placed little value on the expected capabilities of SAFEGUARD. In the eyes of one U.S. official: "The Russians have something of value to them—their Galosh, which at least has some anti-China capability—we have two Safeguard sites that protect nothing." This attitude was not shared by Soviet officials, who, according to Gerard Smith, "took [SAFEGUARD] seriously, especially its potential for a nationwide defense which could eventually neutralize the danger to the United States from Soviet retaliatory missile forces." Given such views, the Soviets naturally continued their efforts to restrict the deployment of the American ABM. They proposed to keep their NCA-oriented site and construct another facility to protect an ICBM field while holding the United States to one facility at Grand Forks.[49]

Several other important developments took place during the sixth round of the talks. For one thing, the Soviets agreed in principle to a sub-limit on their large SS-9 missiles, thus allowing the United States to achieve one of its most important strategic goals. Additionally, an agreement was reached regarding a ban on futuristic ABM systems. Still unresolved were the issues of what limits, if any, were to be placed on Soviet SLBMs and what was to be the exact configuration of each side's ABM force structure. Nevertheless, a number of issues were still unresolved when the talks were recessed on 4 February 1972, with the Moscow summit only three months away.[50]

During this break, the American arms control bureaucracy was busy grinding out a position for the negotiations that were to resume at the end of March. On 23 March the White House issued NSDM 158, which directed the U.S. delegation to offer the Soviets an agreement allowing two ABM sites for each side. The U.S. sites would be at Grand Forks and Malmstrom Air Force bases; the Soviets would have their GALOSH system at Moscow, and one site to defend ICBMs. This offer was contingent upon the Soviets agreeing to limits on SLBMs.[51]

The talks were now entering a crucial stage with only two months remaining before the summit. Nixon and Kissinger were determined to keep a firm grip on the negotiations. Thus no fallback position from NSDM 158 was authorized in spite of a request from the American delegation for some negotiating room. If the talks did not show progress within three weeks, Smith was to return to Washington for consultations. One reason for this rigid position was to avoid a repetition of the "Beecher leak" in which a *New York Times* article revealed a secret fallback position of the U.S. delegation during round five. Additionally, the Nixon administration wanted to convince the Soviets that the United States would not back down on its requirement for restrictions on SLBMs as a prerequisite for a SALT agreement.[52]

EXECUTIVE DIPLOMACY: KISSINGER'S MOSCOW MISSION AND THE SUMMIT

The final round of talks got under way on 28 March and had reached an impasse by 14 April. As a result, the focus of negotiations shifted once more to the back channel where Kissinger and Dobrynin had been talking since early March. This time Kissinger's efforts culminated in a special secret meeting in Moscow between 20 and 24 April 1972. Here Kissinger and General Secretary Leonid Brezhnev worked out the final framework of the SALT I agreements. A major step in establishing this framework was the Soviet acceptance of limitations on SLBMs. Where missile defenses were concerned, the Soviets suggested that each side be allowed one ABM site to defend ICBMs and one site to defend its national command authorities.[53]

After Kissinger's return to Washington, the Nixon administration quickly worked out instructions to guide America's SALT delegation in the last-minute negotiations that were to be completed in Helsinki. These were spelled out in NSDM 164, which was issued on 1 May. In this document, the United States agreed to Soviet numbers for a freeze on SLBMs and accepted the Soviet ABM proposal presented to Kissinger in Moscow. Kissinger's work in the back channel now merged with that of Smith in the front channel. The U.S. delegation at Helsinki began working out the details of the SALT I agreements.[54]

Several key issues pertaining to ABM systems were not settled until the eleventh hour. On 22 May, the day Nixon arrived in Moscow, two such matters were resolved, although one of these was to resurface during the Moscow summit. The first related to the language determining where the ABM sites could be located. The Soviets objected to terminology that would have called for their second site to be east of the Ural Mountains. For the treaty to specify such details was considered to be injurious to Soviet prestige. Compromise wording stated that the second site installed by a nation had to be 1,300 to 1,500 kilometers from its NCA facility. This was the distance between Moscow and the back side of the Urals. The Soviet delegation said that it would recommend that its leaders accept the lower number, but the distance was to be finalized at the summit. The second issue concerned restrictions on phased-array radar systems that might be capable of supporting a missile defense system. A compromise was reached on the main sticking point—a technical parameter would be used to determine if a phased-array radar was ABM-capable.[55]

By the time Brezhnev welcomed Nixon to Moscow on 22 May, the ABM Treaty, the interim agreement on offensive weapons, and a series of "agreed interpretations" were almost complete. Nevertheless, there were some tense moments as a few remaining issues were resolved in top-level negotiations that were handled principally by Kissinger. The last details were worked out during the late evening and early morning of 25-26 May, and the SALT I agreements were signed at 11:00 P.M. on 26 May.[56]

SALT I AND THE INSTITUTIONALIZATION
OF MUTUAL ASSURED DESTRUCTION

In its final form, the ABM accord allowed each superpower to have one ABM facility within a 150 kilometer radius of its capital and one site within a 150 kilometer radius of a missile field. The agreed interpretations further specified that there must be at least 1,300 kilometers between the center of the site at the national capital and the center of the site protecting an ICBM field. The radar facilities that could be installed at each of the ABM sites were specified in the treaty. Each ABM site could have one hundred missiles and one hundred launchers with each side authorized up to fifteen additional launchers at test ranges. Each side was allowed to update its ABM system, but the treaty forbade either side "to develop, test, or deploy ABM systems or components which are sea-based, air-based, space-based, or mobile land-based." Although the treaty was of indefinite duration, it was to be reviewed every five years and could be abrogated by either side with six months' notice.[57]

The other major agreement signed in Moscow was an interim accord on offensive systems that was to remain in effect for five years. It froze land-based ICBM deployments at the point they would reach as of 1 July 1972. The United States was allowed 1,054 ICBMs, a force level that had remained fixed since it was achieved in the mid-1960s. On the other hand, the Soviets, who had been adding steadily to their ICBM force during the thirty months of the SALT talks, were allowed 1,618 ICBMs. With regard to SLBMs and ballistic missile submarines, the Soviets were allowed 62 boats and 950 missiles to America's 44 boats and up to 710 missiles. No limitations were prescribed for MIRVing, bombers, forward-based systems, or mobile ICBMs.[58]

From the U.S. perspective, the SALT I agreements effectively institutionalized the doctrine of mutual assured destruction (MAD), for while placing severe and strict limitations on ABM systems, they set no comparable restrictions for offensive systems. John Newhouse put it this way: "The ABM Treaty had at last been signed, with each side renouncing the defense of its society and territory against the other's nuclear weapons. That is the treaty's historic essence." In confirming deterrence through assured destruction as U.S. nuclear doctrine, the SALT I accords effectively killed the American SAFEGUARD system.[59]

CHAPTER FOUR

The End of the SALT Era: Strategic Crisis

All SALT issues arise from instabilities, real or potential. Some instabilities are no less real for being rooted in suspicion and fear instead of hard fact. What is stabilizing for one side—something it is doing—may seem wildly destabilizing to the other. Although each side seeks stability, neither is willing to accept a heavier weight of relative insecurity—a sense of strategic inferiority—than the other.

Stability's handmaiden is MAD.

—*John Newhouse, 1973*[1]

A CAUTIOUS CONFIRMATION FOR THE SALT I ACCORDS

The SALT I agreements left liberals as well as conservatives dissatisfied. Liberals disliked the fact that improvements in weapons systems were permitted under the agreements and were especially upset that no restrictions were placed on MIRVing. On the other hand, conservatives were not pleased that the interim agreement gave the Soviets a significant edge in the numbers of missiles (both ICBMs and SLBMs) as well as in the area of missile throw-weight. "In effect, conservatives believed that the SALT agreements reduced America to a second-rate status in the nuclear equation and thereby made her vulnerable to Soviet nuclear blackmail."[2] Thus the SALT era began under a dark cloud of suspicion rather than a bright sun of hope.

Problems surfaced as soon as the SALT accords were submitted to Congress for approval. Since the interim agreement was not a formal treaty, it required approval only by a simple majority in both the House and the Senate. The ABM Treaty, on the other hand, required approval by two-thirds of the Senate.[3] On 3 August 1972, the latter breezed through the Senate with the support of eighty-eight senators. Only Senators James L. Buckley, a conservative Republican from New York, and James Allen, a Democrat from Alabama, opposed the treaty. Buckley stated that he had "strong misgivings as to both the prudence and the ultimate morality of denying ourselves for all time—or denying the Russians for that matter—the right to protect our civilian populations from nuclear disaster."[4]

The situation was altogether different where the interim accord on offensive systems was concerned. It immediately ran into stiff opposition led by Senator Henry Jackson, a conservative Democrat. Jackson understood that the interim agreement allowed the Soviets a substantially larger number of missiles to compensate them for the fact that the United States held a three-to-one advantage in bombers and was about to begin MIRVing some of its missiles. The senator from Washington said that the United States advantage was illusory and temporary. Within five years, the Soviets would be able to overtake and surpass the United States in nuclear power by MIRVing their missiles. Particularly troublesome was the idea that the Soviets would MIRV their huge SS-9 missiles. If that happened, Jackson warned, the Soviets would have a first strike capability. To preclude this eventuality, Jackson offered an amendment that would allow the United States to abrogate the agreement if the Soviets put multiple warheads on their heavy ICBMs. Furthermore, in future agreements, the United States should be allowed the same number of launchers as the Soviets. This amendment would apply only to the wording of the congressional resolution of approval and would not be binding on the president or change the wording of the interim agreement itself. Since the Nixon administration believed the Jackson amendment was in consonance with the interim agreement, it supported Jackson's change.[5]

The Jackson amendment prompted a rancorous debate in the Senate that lasted into the middle of September. Led by Senator J. William Fulbright (D-Ark.), opponents of the Jackson amendment argued that his bill would seem to require the Soviets to freeze their forces in an inferior position and would therefore poison the atmosphere of future negotiations. In spite of strong opposition and a good deal of parliamentary maneuvering, Jackson's measure was approved on 14 September with the Senate passing the amended resolution by a vote of 88 to 2.

House approval of the Senate resolution came on 25 September with a vote of 306 to 4.[6]

The Soviets approved the SALT I agreements on 29 September. In the discussions that preceded the approval by the Presidium of the Supreme Soviet, Defense Minister A. A. Grechko assured the Soviet people that the SALT accords "did not put any limits on the carrying out of research and experimental work that is directed toward solving the problems of the defense of the country from nuclear rocket attack." Other Presidium members noted that the United States had recognized the existence of nuclear parity between the two superpowers. President Nixon signed the agreements on 30 September.[7]

SALT II

The opposition of Jackson and other conservatives to SALT I signaled possible difficulties for future strategic arms agreements as the Nixon administration started the SALT II talks in November 1972. A goal of the American negotiators was an agreement in which the total throw-weights of the United States and Soviet Union would be roughly equivalent and the throw-weight of the MIRVed missiles of each country would be the same. The Soviets rejected this negotiating position and insisted that the advantages in throw-weight and launchers they had negotiated in SALT I must become a part of any SALT II agreement. They also refused to accept limits on the MIRVing of their missiles.[8]

The issue of MIRVing was still unresolved when President Nixon and General Secretary Brezhnev held their second Moscow summit at the end of June 1974. Although they could not reach an agreement on MIRVs, they did sign a protocol to the ABM Treaty that reduced to one the number of ABM sites allowed each nation. As the meeting ended, the two leaders issued a joint communiqué indicating their intention to push for a new eight-year agreement to take effect in 1977 when the 1972 interim agreement was due to expire.[9]

As the summit ended, Kissinger met with the press to discuss its outcome. He explained that the ABM Treaty was designed to keep either side from maintaining an effective ballistic missile defense. By allowing each side only one site instead of the two provided in the basic treaty, the 1974 protocol reenforced that intention and made it more difficult for either superpower to break out of the 1972 treaty. Under the terms of the protocol each country could reverse its decision on the location of its site one time. That is, the United States could decide to shift its SAFEGUARD system to defend Washington, but having done so, it could not reverse that decision and return to the defense of an ICBM field. Kissinger emphasized that the absence of a strong ABM system removed a major incentive for deploying MIRVed ICBMs. The absence of defenses, Kissinger said, meant that the term "superiority" was "devoid of any operational meaning."[10]

Later in the news conference, a reporter asked about the prospect for an arms race if a follow-on agreement were not reached by 1977. Kissinger's response contained a hint of frustration as he returned to his earlier point about the meaning of nuclear superiority.

> If we have not reached an agreement well before 1977, then I believe you will see an explosion of technology and an explosion of numbers at the end of which we will be lucky if we have the present stability, in which it will be impossible to describe what strategic superiority means. And one of the questions which we have to ask ourselves as a country is: What in the name of God is strategic superiority? What is the significance of it, politically, militarily, operationally, at these levels of numbers? What do you do with it?[11]

At the time of the Moscow summit, the Watergate scandal was on the verge of overtaking President Nixon, and on 9 August he resigned his office and was succeeded by Gerald Ford. Although Ford was eager to keep the SALT process going, only limited progress was made in negotiations during his presidency. At Vladivostok in November 1974, Ford and Brezhnev agreed to a ceiling of 2,400 strategic delivery systems of which 1,320 could be MIRVed. In January 1975 the formal SALT II negotiations began at Geneva and immediately produced disagreements on the counting of MIRVed missiles, how to consider cruise missiles, and whether or not to include the Backfire bomber in the Soviet count of strategic systems. Furthermore, these talks occurred against a background of deteriorating relations between the superpowers as the Soviets deployed their first MIRVed missile, "bitterly renounced" their trade agreement with the United States, and supported North Vietnam's successful invasion of South Vietnam. It was also about this time that several people, including former Secretary of Defense Melvin Laird, began to charge the Soviets with violations of the SALT I agreements.[12]

Some progress was made in resolving these disagreements during the remainder of the Ford administration. Real progress, however, was undermined by continuing tensions in broader superpower relations,

Soviet intransigence on the issues of the Backfire bomber and cruise missiles, and Ford's growing preoccupation with the election campaign against Jimmy Carter.[13]

Having won the election, Carter came to office promising to work for the elimination of "all nuclear weapons from this earth." Displeased with the approach of previous Republican administrations, Carter set a new course based on the idea that a nuclear arms agreement was too important to be hostage to the routine clashes of interests that punctuated relations between the two great powers. In February, Carter announced that he would push ahead with a treaty to establish the general limits that Ford and Brezhnev had agreed to at the end of 1974, postponing until SALT III the touchy issues associated with cruise missiles and Backfire bombers.[14]

The effort of the Carter administration to negotiate a second SALT treaty began in March 1977 and lasted twenty-seven months. The main objective of American negotiators was an agreement to restrain what appeared to be a Soviet drive to achieve clear strategic superiority that would carry with it the ability to execute a successful first strike against American ICBMs. Thus an early American proposal would roll back the number of modern heavy ICBMs allowed the Soviets under SALT I from 308 to 150. Furthermore, it would fix at 550 the number of MIRVed ICBMs permitted each side. For their part, the Soviets insisted on keeping the gains they had achieved in SALT I and at Vladivostok and would not agree to curbs on their heavy ICBMs.[15]

Despite more than two years of negotiating, the Soviets refused to accept any reduction in their force of 308 heavy missiles. The superpowers agreed that each side could have a total of 2,250 launchers, 1,200 of which could be MIRVed. These limits were to be achieved on 31 December 1981. Carter and Brezhnev signed the SALT II treaty in Vienna on 18 June 1979.[16]

Nevertheless, the same tensions that had plagued relations between the United States and the Soviet Union while the treaty was being negotiated persisted after the signing ceremonies in Vienna and played a major role in undermining the treaty in the minds of U.S. senators. As the treaty was being considered by the Senate, reports of a Soviet combat brigade in Cuba caused a political furor in the United States. This incident, combined with the Soviet invasion of Afghanistan, raised questions about the long-term goals of the Soviets and "shattered the crumbling structure of American-Soviet détente."[17] In early January 1980, Carter asked the Senate to delay its consideration of the SALT II agreement, since he did not "consider this 'a propitious time' to take up the treaty." The agreement had still not been approved when Carter left office a year later. Although the new Reagan administration refused to push for ratification, the provisions of the SALT I and II agreements would be observed by the United States until President Ronald Reagan renounced the restrictions in May 1986.[18]

AMERICAN CONCERN
OVER SOVIET MISSILES GROWS

Arguably, the SALT agreements did little to restrict Soviet plans to expand their offensive strategic forces. The SALT I negotiations lasted two and a half years, with the Soviets refusing to link restrictions on ABM systems and limits on offensive systems until they reached the desired point in their offensive build-up. In 1970, shortly after the SALT I talks began, Soviet ICBM strength stood at 1,300 missiles. By the time the treaty was ratified, this number had risen to 1,530. A RAND study of the "SALT experience" made the following statement about SALT I: "With the signing of the SALT Interim Agreement of May 1972, the Soviet Union could be said to have brought the quantitative buildup of its land-based ICBM forces to a successful close. It then held a numerical lead of around 50 percent over the United States in ICBM launchers, and this margin was assured for at least the five-year life of the agreement." SALT II did not improve this situation. It came too late and its provisions were too generous to eliminate the growing Soviet threat to America's ICBM fleet. It did virtually nothing to constrain the primary hard-target kill system in the Soviet nuclear arsenal, as the Soviets refused to accept a reduction in their heavy ICBM force of 308 missiles. Moreover, by the time the provisions of the treaty were established, the Soviets had already tested the SS-18 (the replacement for the SS-9) with 10 warheads.[19]

The steady increase of Soviet strategic power became a matter for concern soon after Congress accepted the SALT I interim accord on offensive systems. In the spring of 1974, Secretary of Defense James R. Schlesinger warned about the growing Soviet missile threat, stating that the USSR appeared determined to "exploit" asymmetries in the Soviet and American force structures. The secretary noted that the United States was "troubled by Soviet weapons momentum, and we simply cannot ignore the prospect of a growing disparity between the two major nuclear powers."[20]

The United States had hoped to control the total throw-weight of the

Soviet missile force by restricting the largest Soviet missile (the SS-9) and its replacement (the SS-18), the latter having a throw-weight that was 30 percent greater than the 12,000 to 15,000 pounds of its predecessor. However, the United States was caught off guard by the unexpected development of the SS-17 and SS-19 as replacements for the SS-11. The throw-weights of these new missiles were three to five times that of the SS-11, which had a payload of 1,500 pounds. Moreover, by late 1974 the SS-17 had been tested with four MIRVed warheads and the SS-19 with six. One variant of the SS-17 was tested with a single warhead and in this configuration possessed hard-target kill capability. Overall, Schlesinger projected that the Soviets could have a combined throw-weight in their ICBM fleet "in the out years" of 10 to 12 million pounds compared to only 2 million pounds for the United States. With such a throw-weight, the Soviets had the potential to field up to 33,000 reentry vehicles equivalent to those carried by the U.S. POSEIDON missile.[21]

Less than a year after Schlesinger's warning, the Soviets started to deploy the SS-18 and tested this giant missile with multiple warheads. These tests and other developments prompted Secretary Schlesinger to state publicly his disappointment in an apparent Soviet drive to achieve "major counterforce capabilities." As large Soviet missiles with multiple warheads became operational, the United States would push its own MIRV program, which was already well along.[22]

Schlesinger's outspokenness on strategic defense issues and his feud with Kissinger were major causes of a break between him and President Ford. Particularly troublesome was Schlesinger's hard-line stand on arms negotiations with the Soviets. While Ford and Kissinger seemed eager for an additional strategic arms agreement, Schlesinger insisted that such an agreement must include limits on the throw-weight of Soviet missiles and restrictions on the number of MIRVed missiles on both sides. These difficulties culminated in the so-called Halloween massacre of 1975 in which Ford replaced his troublesome secretary of defense with Donald Rumsfeld. Although Rumsfeld was also a hard-liner on defense issues, he was more of a team player than the man he replaced.[23]

Ford's firing of Schlesinger led Lieutenant General Daniel O. Graham to resign his position as director of the Defense Intelligence Agency and retire from the army. Schlesinger had allowed Graham to circulate in the Pentagon a "cold warish study of 'Détente in Soviet Strategy'" that charged that the Soviets were clearly determined to break up NATO and considered détente advantageous to their cause.[24]

Soon after he retired, Graham became a national security adviser on the campaign staff of Ronald Reagan, who was running against Ford for the Republican nomination.[25]

Graham's views were indicative of growing suspicion among some about Soviet intentions toward the West. Graham and those of his persuasion were apprehensive that the Soviets might use their advantage in offensive forces, combined with their operational ABM system and their civil defense program, to coerce the United States in a political crisis. In the mid-1970s, concerns such as these "generated an intense and spreading debate about what Soviet military development means, and how the United States should respond."[26]

THE DEFENSE DEBATE OF THE 1970s:
THE UTILITY OF MILITARY POWER

Although not infallible, the resources and methods of modern intelligence make it possible to estimate the number and characteristics of enemy systems with reasonable accuracy. However, when one moves into the realm of strategy and intentions, one leaves the relative certainty and comfort offered by the domain of numbers for the uncertain realm of qualities where intuitive judgments based on history and theory prevail. It was in this latter region of uncertainty that the most important issues of the "intense and spreading debate" of the mid-1970s were argued.

One part of the debate centered on the utility of military power, especially nuclear arms. The post–World War II portion of this debate stretches back to Bernard Brodie's statement in 1946 that in the nuclear age military power is virtually useless except as a deterrent to the use of other military power.[27] In the 1970s this fundamental issue was raised again by Kissinger's frustrated questions: "What in the name of God is strategic superiority? What is the significance of it, politically, militarily, operationally, at these levels of numbers? What do you do with it?"[28]

Similar views were expressed by Paul Warnke, who believed that nuclear superiority was meaningless, since both the Soviets and the Americans had enough weapons to annihilate each other. With regard to the superior number of strategic launchers the Soviets possessed in 1977, Warnke said that this kind of superiority is "clearly without any kind of significance, *unless by our own rhetoric we give it political sig-*

nificance that it does not deserve."[29] He had little more regard for conventional military forces and weapons. In his view, they had not furthered American interests, but rather had undermined them. Matters such as assuring an adequate supply of raw materials for the United States were "not military problems; they're problems of diplomacy and foreign policy."[30]

Jan Lodal expressed views similar to Warnke's. According to Lodal, the only possible benefit of nuclear superiority

> might be to create adverse political perceptions in the rest of the world concerning the relative strengths of the United States and the Soviet Union.
>
> But we must not forget that our own rhetoric largely determines these political perceptions. To the extent that we emphasize measures in which the Soviets have an advantage, such as missile throw-weight, we ensure that others will perceive us to be at a disadvantage. On the other hand, if we pursue sensible programs designed to protect our deterrent capability, and explain carefully why we have decided to forego a "throw-weight race" or a "megatonnage race," I see no reason why we should be the subject of adverse political perceptions.[31]

Conservatives like Paul Nitze viewed things differently. He was specifically concerned by Kissinger's questioning of the utility of strategic superiority. Nitze believed the United States was in a long-term struggle with the Soviet Union in which the Soviets would do everything possible to achieve an advantage that could be used to gain their ideological goals. Faced with such an intransigent opponent, America must respond to Soviet actions such as the deployment of a new generation of missiles even if it meant acquiring new strategic systems beyond the TRIDENT program and B-1 bomber. Otherwise, as the correlation of forces changed more in favor of the USSR, American leaders could expect the Soviets to attempt to take advantage of their superior forces. Among the things the Soviets might achieve was an increased accommodation toward the Soviet view in the Third World. Nitze summed up his point as follows: "If one does not want to see either an increase in the prospects for general Soviet hegemony or an increase in the risk of nuclear war, it is necessary to maintain the quality of deterrence, crisis stability, and rough strategic parity." In short, nuclear superiority has real world consequences.[32]

THE DEBATE:
WHAT ARE THE SOVIETS' INTENTIONS?

What, if anything, the Soviets might do with military superiority was a function of Soviet intentions, and perhaps the most influential statement on this subject was a study produced during the second half of 1976 by CIA Team B, a group of defense analysts invited by the agency's director, George Bush, to complete an independent evaluation of Soviet forces and strategic intentions that would offer an alternative view to the CIA's own analysis. One reason for the appointment of this team was the steady criticism of CIA estimates of Soviet strength that came from Generals George Keegan and Daniel Graham (both of whom had held high-level positions in the intelligence community) and Paul Nitze and Richard Pipes (both of whom were outside the intelligence community). Furthermore, the Republican primary elections were being held during the spring of 1976, and Ronald Reagan was making an issue of national security. As a result, Gerald Ford was sensitive to this criticism of the CIA and thus was willing to allow Bush to appoint the independent review group.[33]

The committee was designated Team B to distinguish it from Team A, the CIA analysts who normally performed this function.[34] Pipes, a Harvard professor of Russian history who had been recommended by the President's Foreign Intelligence Advisory Board, was the leader of Team B.[35] All told, there were eleven members of Team B, seven from outside the government and four from within. The outsiders were Pipes, Paul Nitze, Foy Kohler, William Van Cleave, Daniel Graham, Thomas Wolfe of RAND, and retired air force general John Vogt, Jr. Members from inside the government included air force major general George Keegan (a strong critic of the CIA), air force brigadier general Jaspar A. Welch, Paul D. Wolfowitz of the Arms Control and Disarmament Agency, and Seymour Weiss of the State Department.[36]

Team B began its work in June 1976. The focus of its efforts was the official intelligence estimates of Soviet military capabilities generated by the CIA. These estimates are an important factor in determining the U.S. military budget and in planning the American force structure. Shortly after Team B finished working, its findings appeared in unclassified form in an article published by Pipes in the July 1977 edition of *Commentary* magazine.[37]

According to this article, U.S. and Soviet leaders held divergent views of strategic nuclear war. Because the Soviet experience in the twentieth century included sixty million deaths as a result of wars (twenty million in World War II alone), famine, and political upheaval, Soviet leaders considered "conflict and violence as natural regulators of all human affairs." Therefore, the Soviets naturally followed the teachings of Clausewitz, who considered war an extension of politics by other means. Even after the advent of nuclear weapons, Soviet leaders continued to believe that "thermonuclear war is not suicidal, it can be fought and won, and thus resort to it must not be ruled out." Far from being useless, nuclear weapons served as "compellants" in peacetime and in war would be used in the decisive, early phases to disrupt the enemy's home front and prepare the way for later successful operations carried out by other arms of the Soviet military establishment.[38]

On the other hand, the United States had experienced only 650,000 casualties in all of its wars since 1775 and had never had a famine or a political purge. In the American view, war is "the result of an inability or an unwillingness to apply rational analysis and patient negotiation to disagreements: the use of force is *prima facie* evidence of failure." After World War II ended with the use of atomic weapons against Japan, Pipes wrote, an important segment of the American strategic community followed the lead of Bernard Brodie and other civilian strategists who concluded that nuclear armed military forces could have no other useful purpose than to deter war, which would be an unmitigated disaster for humanity. Thus, for these Americans, Clausewitz's view that war is policy extended had lost its validity.[39]

The views of Team B were in wide circulation as the Carter administration took office. Team B's conclusions were reflected in the new National Intelligence Estimate of Soviet Strategic Capabilities and Objectives that was completed on 21 December 1976.[40] Furthermore, Secretary of Defense Donald Rumsfeld supported the Team B analysis. As he was ending his term as secretary of defense, Rumsfeld noted that though U.S. leaders cannot know Soviet intentions with certainty, Americans can evaluate Russian military capabilities, which "indicate a tendency toward war fighting . . . rather than for the more modish Western models of deterrence through mutual vulnerability."[41] George Bush also used his influence to push the Team B report. As a result, it became the generally accepted national estimate of what the United States faced when Jimmy Carter became president.[42]

There are still other indications of the importance of Team B's findings. Drew Middleton summarized the Pipes article for the *New York Times* before the publication date of the July *Commentary*.[43] Moreover, Pipes's article was reprinted in the July 1977 edition of *Air Force Magazine*, an influential journal with a wide circulation in the national security affairs community, which includes active duty military and defense industry leaders. Also, it was referenced in several later articles on strategic military thought.[44] The manner in which this piece was published marked it as the flagship article for a movement among conservative strategic analysts who aimed to bring about a fundamental reassessment and revision of American strategic thought.

To say that the Team B report was highly influential is not to say that its views were universally shared. Paul Warnke believed that even if the Soviets believed that nuclear war is winnable, the United States should not respond "to this kind of thinking [which] is on a level of abstraction which is unrealistic." To debate with the Soviets as if nuclear war might be winnable would be to "indulge what I [Warnke] regard as the primitive aspects of Soviet nuclear doctrine." Instead, Americans "ought to be trying to educate them into the real world of strategic nuclear weapons, which is that nobody could possibly win. Nor could anybody calculate what the consequences would be in the event of a strategic nuclear exchange."[45]

Warnke's comment about educating Soviet strategists elicited a scathing response from Richard Pipes in his later *Commentary* article: "On what grounds does he, a Washington lawyer, presume to 'educate' the Soviet general staff composed of professional soldiers who thirty years ago defeated the Wehrmacht—and, of all things, about the 'real world of strategic nuclear weapons' of which they happen to possess a considerably larger arsenal than we?"[46] From Pipes's perspective, people such as Warnke were dangerous. They were like the scientists he described in his *Commentary* article who were not well versed in Soviet strategic literature and did not understand the Soviet culture. These Americans reached their own conclusion that nuclear war was unthinkable, and when they did not find these views mirrored in Soviet strategic literature, they simply dismissed the Soviet writings as unsophisticated and wrong. The resultant asymmetrical views of nuclear war were destabilizing, in Pipes's opinion, for "as long as the Soviets persist in adhering to the Clausewitzian maxim on the function of war, mutual deterrence does not really exist." Only by meeting the Soviets on their own ground and denying them the possibility of succeeding in a nuclear war could Americans continue to maintain deterrence.[47]

THE DEBATE: IS THE ARMS
RACE REALITY OR MYTH?

Another strategic issue debated in the 1970s was the concept of a strategic arms race that was much in vogue among those who believed the

United States should use restraint in developing and deploying strategic systems. They argued that America was constantly overestimating Soviet strategic forces and using these overestimations to justify its own arms build-up. By building to meet the exaggerated Soviet threat, the United States stimulated Soviet military developments.[48]

In the mid-1970s, this arms race syllogism came under attack from Albert Wohlstetter. One of the early RAND fellows, Wohlstetter was a mathematical logician and master of its spin-off discipline, systems analysis. One of the main points for his attack was what he considered the empty rhetoric of those who made use of the arms race concept to fight for restrictions on U.S. strategic systems.[49]

Wohlstetter closely examined several tenets of the arms race thesis. For example, with regard to the idea that American analysts constantly overestimated the deployment of Soviet strategic forces, Wohlstetter presented information indicating that after the most famous episode of overestimation, the so-called missile gap of the Kennedy-Nixon campaign of 1960, the United States had consistently underestimated the development rate of the Soviet strategic force structure. Based on extensive research,[50] Wohlstetter argued that "in 49 out of 51 cases the eventual Soviet deployment exceeded the mid-range of the secretary's estimates. In 42 of the 51, it exceeded the secretary's high." Not only that, but U.S. analysts underestimated the speed with which missile technology would advance. ICBMs and fusion bombs were available to the Soviets sooner than expected. Furthermore, the accuracy of Soviet missiles was virtually always better than predicted.[51]

Based on his analysis, Wohlstetter concluded that the arms race thesis "is clearly mistaken in all of its principal tenets." The United States had clearly not been racing in the sense that the arms race doctrine maintained.

The gross shape of the U.S. curve of strategic spending, if extended back to 1945, would show a sharp drop after World War II, a surprisingly low level during the late 1940s when "atomic diplomacy" was supposed to have been in full sway, a rapid rise after Korea to a high plateau in the mid- and late-1950s, then another sharp decline beginning at the start of the 1960s. These gross changes in American, and the simultaneous quite different changes in Soviet strategic spending, cannot be understood in terms of a closed cycle of tightly coupled interaction between U.S. and Soviet processes of decision to acquire weapons—as is assumed in the usual action-reaction theory.[52]

Wohlstetter's articles in *Foreign Policy* were the opening round of a rather lengthy debate over the myths and realities of the arms race conducted in the pages of that journal.[53] In the spring 1975 edition, Paul Warnke answered Wohlstetter in an article that essentially granted Wohlstetter's point that the United States had most consistently underestimated the Soviet deployment of strategic systems. Nevertheless, Warnke dismissed Wohlstetter's argument as an idle "contest in semantics," for even if "race" was not the appropriate metaphor, there was indeed something akin to an arms race in progress. Perhaps the proper analogy was to see the superpowers as apes jogging in tandem on a treadmill. Thus the real dynamic of this process was that the Soviets were "aping" the Americans, a case of "monkey see, monkey do." Therefore, ideas like negotiating from strength and developing strategic bargaining chips were invalid, because they only encouraged the Soviets to behave in the same fashion. The proper thing for the United States to do was exercise restraint, for the "Soviets are far more apt to emulate than to capitulate." The "only victory in the arms race" was to "be the first off the treadmill."[54]

THE VULNERABILITY OF THE TRIAD

Although reasonable people could disagree over issues like metaphors, hard numbers such as the 12 million pounds of throw-weight ascribed to the Soviet strategic missile fleet by Schlesinger left far less room for divergent opinion. By the mid-1970s, these numbers pointed increasingly toward a Soviet first strike capability that threatened the ICBM leg of America's strategic TRIAD.

In early 1975 Paul Nitze had described how the Soviets might use the massive throw-weight advantage they were accumulating to overwhelm the TRIAD. After estimating that the Soviets would eventually have 10 to 15 million pounds of throw-weight, Nitze described how the Soviets might use this to attack the TRIAD. His attack scenario was based on the following assumptions: 2,000 pounds of throw-weight would be required to achieve a 95 percent probability of killing a fixed, hardened target; 3,500 pounds could be used to blanket an area of 400 square miles so as to destroy an aircraft flying anywhere in this area; 15,000 pounds of throw-weight would produce a nuclear barrage that would disable a submarine known to be somewhere in a 300-square-mile area of ocean. Based on these estimates, Nitze concluded that the Soviets could destroy twelve hundred hard targets, blanket 400,000 square miles of bomber escape routes, and strike one hundred aim points at sea using a total of 6.9 million pounds of throw-weight, about half of the total within the Soviet arsenal.[55]

Other disquieting news appeared in statements of defense secretaries during the second half of the 1970s. Both Donald Rumsfeld and Harold Brown regularly warned about the growing threat to the American MINUTEMAN force. For example, in 1977, Brown was reasonably certain the strategic posture of the United States was adequate to deter Soviet leaders. However, as he looked ahead to the 1980s he was worried that some future Soviet leader might be tempted to try a "cosmic roll of the dice." A chart in Brown's statement for FY 1980 showed that by 1988 only about 10 percent of America's ICBMs would survive a Soviet first strike.[56]

Others considered the situation worse than Brown's assessment. By early 1979 some were saying that the United States had drastically underestimated the growing Soviet threat to its ICBMs. Before 1978 U.S. analyses had projected that it would be the mid-1980s before the Soviets could place America's ICBM fleet at risk. In early 1978 the Soviets unexpectedly demonstrated a .1 nautical mile circular error probable (CEP) for the warheads on their SS-18 missiles, prompting American analysts to advance the time of vulnerability to the early 1980s when the Soviets might be able to destroy America's ICBMs using only about one-third of their own ICBM warheads.[57]

In the winter of 1978 Jacquelyn K. Davis, foreign affairs editor for *Strategic Review*, sounded a warning. Without SALT II restrictions or action on the part of the United States, by 1985 a preemptive strike by the Soviet Union might destroy 90 percent of the MINUTEMAN III force. In addition to the threat against MINUTEMAN missiles, Soviet work with depressed trajectory SLBMs indicated that in the future a substantial portion of America's bomber force could be eliminated by a surprise attack from Soviet ballistic missile submarines. Moreover, Soviet efforts in antisubmarine warfare, some of which were quite sophisticated, warned of technical breakthroughs that might jeopardize the sea leg of the TRIAD.[58]

Not surprisingly, by the time Carter signed the SALT II agreements in Vienna, there was a growing feeling that the SALT process had failed. An editorial in the *Wall Street Journal* noted that the decade of SALT had witnessed "one of history's great arms build-ups." In 1969 the United States had 1,054 ICBMs and 656 SLBMs. In 1978 it had the same number of missiles, although it had MIRVed part of this force. Over the same period, the Soviets had expanded their ICBM force from 1,028 to

1,400 and increased their submarine-launched missiles from 196 to 1,015. In the next few years, the Soviets could be expected to have 6,000 warheads deployed on their ICBMs. Half of these would be on their heaviest missiles and would have CEPs of 600 feet. This meant that the Soviets would soon have confidence that they could cripple the MINUTE-MAN force using only a small number of their own ICBMs. As a result of the Soviet strategic arms build-up, the vulnerability of American ICBMs to a Soviet first strike was arguably "the largest strategic problem" facing the United States. Yet in 1976 the United States had deactivated its only operational ABM facility (as we shall see in the next chapter) and as of 1979 still had not taken decisive action to deploy the MX missile in a secure basing mode.[59]

Still, in November 1979 Bernard T. Feld and Kosta Tsipis argued that the vulnerability then being imputed to the MINUTEMAN was greatly exaggerated because of unrealistic assumptions about such things as the ability of silos to withstand attack and the CEP of missile warheads. Moreover, they were skeptical about the prospect of conditions arising that would tempt Soviet leaders to launch a first strike against U.S. ICBMs. However, since the perception that MINUTEMAN was vulnerable might "well generate political problems for the U.S. Government, both domestically and internationally," and since "there is little doubt that in the long run fixed land-based missiles will appear to become increasingly vulnerable to a MIRV attack," it was reasonable "to explore alternatives that could offer some relief of the perceived MINUTEMAN vulnerability."[60]

Thus, in the second half of the 1970s, the warnings sounded earlier by Jackson and Kissinger began to have the ring of prophecy about them. The growth of Soviet offensive forces that threatened the survivability of American ICBMs and raised questions about the ability of the TRIAD to deter nuclear war created pressures for the United States to shore up its strategic deterrent. One measure advocated was the deployment of ABM systems to protect the MINUTEMAN and its follow-on system, the MX missile.

Part Three
An American Phoenix

FENIX: the Bird of Arabia is called this because of its reddish purple colour (*phoeniceus*). It is unique: it is unparalleled in the whole world. It lives beyond five hundred years.

When it notices that it is growing old, it builds itself a funeral pyre, after collecting some spice branches, and on this, turning its body toward the rays of the sun and flapping its wings, it sets fire to itself of its own accord until it burns itself up. Then verily, on the ninth day afterward, it rises from its own ashes!

—*The Book of Beasts,*
Twelfth-century bestiary[1]

The SALT I agreements sounded the death knell of the SAFE-GUARD missile defense system. In 1969 SAFEGUARD had survived congressional scrutiny only by the narrowest of margins and then principally on the basis of its being used as a bargaining chip to be traded for restrictions on offensive systems. With the completion of the SALT I negotiations, SAFEGUARD was no longer a bargaining chip. Furthermore, because of the limitations imposed on defenses by the ABM Treaty and the July 1974 protocol, SAFEGUARD had no chance of coping with a massive attack of the kind made possible by MIRVing and the large throw-weights of Soviet missiles, neither of which was adequately constrained by the SALT I agreements. Congress was unwilling to fund what it considered a largely useless system.

With the closing of the SAFEGUARD site in North Dakota, the focus of America's ABM program changed from developing an improved system as a replacement for SAFEGUARD to conducting research as a hedge against a possible technological breakthrough by the Soviet Union. Then, toward the end of the decade when the strategic balance seemed to be tilting toward the Soviets, U.S. leaders began to search for a means of offsetting the growing Soviet advantage. Under these circumstances, the idea of defending missile fields again became a viable policy alternative. Once the idea of missile defense was resurrected, advances in missile defense technology that had come from DOD's continuing R&D efforts, especially developments in the area of directed energy weapons, excited interest in the possibility of a more general defense against ballistic missiles.

CHAPTER FIVE

The Death of SAFEGUARD and the Reorientation of America's ABM Program

ABM would have a difficult time outliving SALT negotiations no matter what their outcome.

—*Gerard Smith,* Doubletalk[1]

THE DEMISE OF SAFEGUARD

The build-up of Soviet strategic forces had not been prompted by developments in strategic defenses, for the severe limitations imposed on defensive systems by the SALT agreements ensured that neither side could deploy a strategically significant ABM system. In spite of the restrictions on defenses, the United States continued with the deployment of a treaty-compliant ABM system at the Mickelsen SAFEGUARD complex. Located 100 miles northwest of Grand Forks, North Dakota, this complex was to defend 150 MINUTEMAN missiles.

In a number of ways, the Mickelson facility was a technological marvel. The 80-foot-tall truncated pyramid that housed the antennas for the missile site radar (MSR) dominated the flat landscape around the town of Nekoma. The structure's four-foot-thick concrete walls were sloped at a 35-degree angle to provide hardening against the effects of nuclear blast. Each sloping surface of the pyramid held a radar antenna that was 13 feet in diameter and contained five thousand phased-array elements. These elements and the circular shape of the antenna gave the appearance of a gigantic, multi-lensed insect eye. The shape of the building and the antennas marking each face of the struc-

ture reminded some people of a religious shrine and invited compari-
sons with the ancient Pyramid of Cheops and the Stonehenge ruins.[2]

The four faces of the MSR allowed it to search for targets coming from
all directions, and it could acquire these targets at a range of 300 miles.
The MSR worked in conjunction with a perimeter acquisition radar
(PAR) near Cavalier, North Dakota, 25 miles northeast of the missile
site. This was also a phased-array radar, but it was designed to search
in only one direction—toward the north. In the event of a Soviet attack,
the PAR would detect incoming missiles at a range of 1,800 miles, about
the time the warheads were passing over the North Pole. Detection at
this range would allow only six minutes to plan the battle against the
approaching reentry vehicles. Computers associated with the PAR
would determine the trajectory of incoming missiles and pass the information to the MSR for control of the defensive missiles that would attack the warheads.[3]

Two types of missiles were employed in the SAFEGUARD system. The
high-altitude SPARTAN missile was built by McDonnell Douglas. It was
a three-stage, solid-propellant rocket armed with a nuclear warhead
that killed warheads by blast and by X-rays that were lethal to warheads several miles away. SPARTAN was 55 feet long. The second missile, SPRINT, was a marvel of aeronautics and space technology. Built by
Martin Marietta, it was designed to operate at hypersonic speeds in the
earth's atmosphere; at its top speed, the missile's skin became hotter
than the interior of its rocket motor and glowed incandescently. If one
somehow could have trained an acetylene torch on the nose of the missile at this speed, the hot gases of the torch would have cooled the nose.
The electronic components of SPRINT were designed to withstand accel-
erations of 100 times gravity. The missile was 27 feet long, consisted of
two stages, and used solid fuel. Like SPARTAN, SPRINT carried a nuclear
warhead.[4]

Together these missiles provided a "layered" defense. SPARTAN was
designed to attack the incoming "threat cloud" of warheads, boosters,
and decoys while it was still above the atmosphere. SPRINT would then
attack surviving warheads after they had penetrated the atmosphere
where the resistance and friction of the air would separate the warheads from decoys and booster debris.

In the end, however, SAFEGUARD's "technical sweetness" was over-
shadowed by its limitations. With only one hundred missiles, the system could provide only limited protection to the ICBMs near Grand
Forks and supply some measure of protection to the central United
States against an accidental missile launch or a light ICBM attack.[5]

The landscape around the SAFEGUARD complex in North Dakota was dominated by the system's two large radar antenna structures. Above is the single-faced antenna for the long-range perimeter acquisition radar (PAR). This massive structure was over 100 feet high and contained 17 million pounds of steel reinforcing rods and 58,000 cubic yards of concrete. Below is the four-faced antenna for the missile site radar (MSR), which rose 80 feet above the ground. (U.S. Army Strategic Defense Command, Huntsville, Alabama)

A mock-up of the SPARTAN missile (top). Like the earlier NIKE- ZEUS, the SPARTAN missile was designed to intercept the "swarm" of decoys and warheads at an altitude of about 100 miles. A high-speed SPRINT missile is shown during a test flight in 1965 (bottom). The second stage of the SPRINT missile reached such a high velocity that air friction heated the missile to the point where parts of its surface were hotter than the inside of its rocket motor and the missile's skin glowed incandescently. (Photos SC-644735 and SC-617812, National Archives)

Moreover, SAFEGUARD was not the optimum system for the point defense of hard targets. It started out as the SENTINEL project, which was supposed to provide nationwide protection against a light ICBM attack. When President Nixon shifted the emphasis of the program to defending ICBM fields, the United States wound up using an area defense system for a point defense mission. The area defense concept involved the use of the large, powerful long-range radar systems that were hallmarks of the Mickelsen complex. In addition to being subject to blackout caused by the detonation of nuclear warheads, these radar systems could be attacked directly. Once they were destroyed, the SPARTAN and SPRINT missiles were electronically blind and therefore useless. One nuclear war scenario envisioned the SAFEGUARD complex being attacked by relatively light SS-11 warheads that could easily destroy the large radar antennas. These attacks would be followed by a wave of SS-9 warheads that would destroy the MINUTEMAN missiles. Had the army started off with the mission of defending only missiles, it would probably have deployed only SPRINT-type missiles to take full advantage of atmospheric discrimination.[6]

The known weaknesses of SAFEGUARD help explain why the army was developing a follow-on missile defense system even before SAFEGUARD became operational. Called the Site Defense system and developed by McDonnell Douglas, it was to include only one kind of missile, a modified SPRINT interceptor (SPRINT II) that featured such things as greater accuracy, a much expanded capacity for maneuvering, greater hardening of its silo through the addition of a concrete door that could be opened in a single second, and better maintainability. Site Defense was also to include an improved radar system composed of smaller, less vulnerable radars and a powerful, commercially proven computer. Only in the case of the system's software did the army believe it was working with an unproven system component. This new system was considered a hedge against improvements in the Soviet ICBM force and was to be ready for deployment in four to eight years, being designed specifically to protect missile fields against advanced Soviet ICBMs such as the SS-18 and SS-19.[7]

To facilitate deployment and provide greater flexibility in protecting missile fields, the Site Defense system was developed around a modular concept. A module was to consist of three radars, each of which controlled a SPRINT battery. Together, the three batteries of a module would contain about one hundred missiles. The number of modules deployed in defense of MINUTEMAN silos would be a function of the severity of the threat to American ICBMs.[8]

The prototype of Site Defense was to be built at the army's Kwajalein Missile Test Range. To support this program, Secretary of Defense James Schlesinger asked for $160 million in FY 1975. Site Defense, he said, would give the United States the option of defending its MINUTEMAN missiles and expanding the nation's ABM system to include the national command authorities should that become desirable. Construction of the Site Defense facility was to begin in the fall of 1974 with a completion date in early FY 1977. When finished, the facility would be used in tests to resolve the target discrimination and designation problems that would be associated with an attack by Soviet SS-17, SS-18, and SS-19 missiles.[9]

In the fall of 1975, the same limitations that hampered SAFEGUARD and caused the army to initiate the Site Defense program inspired Congress to begin the proceedings that led to the deactivation of the Mickelsen SAFEGUARD complex. On 2 October 1975, one day after SAFEGUARD became operational, the House voted to deactivate the system. DOD Studies made available to the House Committee on Appropriations in September had shown that Soviet missiles with multiple warheads would be able to overwhelm the system. The vulnerability of SAFEGUARD's radar systems was also a factor in the committee's decision. DOD itself drove the final nail in SAFEGUARD's coffin. During proceedings of the House, it was discovered that DOD had been planning for two years to deactivate the North Dakota site on 1 July 1976.[10]

The House vote against SAFEGUARD prompted Defense Secretary Schlesinger to ask Senator John McClellan (D-Ark.), chairman of the Senate Appropriations Committee, to keep SAFEGUARD operational. In his 3 October letter making the request, Schlesinger emphasized the valuable experience that would come from actually operating the complex missile defense system and pointed out that SAFEGUARD's perimeter acquisition radar could spot incoming missiles over the Arctic region and thus supplement America's early warning system. Moreover, Schlesinger did not think the United States should abandon its BMD system without seeking some concession from the Soviets. McClellan and the Appropriations Committee agreed with Schlesinger. Since almost $6 billion had been spent on the ballistic missile defense program, the committee concluded that it made good sense to pay the small cost of operating SAFEGUARD for a time before placing it in caretaker status.[11]

The full Senate did not agree with McClellan's committee and in November 1975 voted against continued operation of SAFEGUARD in a series of "relatively close votes."[12] Senator Edward Kennedy had led the anti-SAFEGUARD forces in the 1969 ABM debate, and he again played a pivotal role in opposing the system. On Friday, 14 November, he proposed amending the Senate defense appropriations bill to require closing the ABM site as the House had already voted to do. This measure was narrowly defeated. The following Tuesday he offered a compromise bill that would allow operation and testing of the site's perimeter acquisition radar but would close down the remainder of SAFEGUARD. Kennedy's second bill passed by a vote of 52 to 47.[13] Efforts to reverse this decision were undermined by awareness of DOD's own plans to deactivate SAFEGUARD, and House and Senate conferees agreed to the provisions of Kennedy's amendment. The appropriating law of 9 February 1976 specified that operation and maintenance funds for the Mickelsen facility could be used to operate and maintain only the perimeter acquisition radar and to deactivate all other functions of the facility.[14]

In February 1976 the army began carrying out the directions of Congress. Specifically, site technicians stopped the radiation of power from the missile site radar and began removing warheads and missiles from their launching cells. Furthermore, the army started transferring personnel to other locations and began to dispose of excess property according to government regulations. The Office of Economic Adjustment began working with the local communities to ameliorate the impact of the site closing. The large structures of the site were to remain intact until the proper dismantling procedures were issued by the Standing Consultative Commission, a joint U.S.-Soviet agency established to oversee the implementation of the ABM treaty.[15]

The *New York Times* marked the passing of SAFEGUARD with an "I told you so" report of the congressional decision. According to this story, the House Appropriations Committee stated that the Soviet deployment of MIRVed ICBMs "essentially nullified" the capabilities of SAFEGUARD; this was the same basic argument used six years earlier by those who tried to stop the development of SAFEGUARD.[16]

REORIENTATION OF THE ARMY'S BMD PROGRAM

In the wake of the ABM treaty, the emphasis in the army's BMD program began to shift from developing deployable systems to research and development aimed at maintaining America's technological edge in the area of missile defenses and to hedge against a possible Soviet breakthrough. Total funding for the program reflected this change. In FY 1972, the total for all aspects of the program came to $1.4 billion; DOD requested only $440 million for FY 1975. The R&D program that resulted from this shift was designed to push BMD technology in six areas: radar, optics, data processing and software development, interceptors, discrimination, and new concepts arising from basic research.[17]

The shift toward research and development was accentuated when Congress instructed the army to redirect its Site Defense program from prototype development to R&D. These directions were given when Congress ordered the dismantling of the SAFEGUARD site. The result was a fundamental reorientation of the army's BMD program described in these words by Major General Robert C. Marshall, the army's ballistic missile defense program manager:

> For the past 20 years the major activities of the BMD community have, for the most part, been directed toward the achievement of one primary goal—the development and deployment of a BMD system. Finally designated SAFEGUARD, the system had as its primary purpose the defense of MINUTEMAN. Today our situation is quite different. We do not have a specific system deployment objective as a follow-on to SAFEGUARD. Instead our emphasis now is on R&D as a hedge against the uncertainties of the future. In response to your guidance, we are terminating and deactivating SAFEGUARD, keeping only the Perimeter Acquisition Radar (PAR) operational for missile attack characterization. Last year, also in response to . . . [congressional] guidance, we abandoned our plans for a prototype demonstration of the Site Defense system. This year we have further reoriented our R&D program to emphasize technology relevant to a broader range of R&D possibilities than in the past; we have formulated this program based on a relatively constant, sustaining level of effort for the foreseeable future.[18]

There were two basic parts to the army's restructured BMD program. The first part was an advanced technology program (ATP) that aimed to produce major innovations in missile defense components and functions. The second part was the reoriented Site Defense project, which became a broad systems technology program (STP). Marshall explained succinctly how these two programs were to work together: "From the ATP we want a futuristic, imaginative search for better ways to do the BMD job—while from STP we require an objective evaluation of systems applications of emerging components and concepts." Marshall stressed the importance of the systems technology program. Advances in technology by themselves were of questionable value until they were tested in a systems environment. "To capitalize on technological improvements in components, it is necessary to integrate the components and validate, through field tests against realistic targets, their capability as an ensemble to accomplish the basic BMD system functions." Within this framework, research and development would concentrate mainly on terminal defense for missile silos as opposed to an area defense concept that could protect cities. As part of these efforts, in FY 1977 the army planned to start investigating new BMD system concepts that would be applicable in the exoatmospheric, high endoatmospheric, and low-altitude regions.[19]

In spite of the army's careful efforts to comply with congressional directions regarding the reorientation of its BMD program, in the spring of 1976 the Senate reduced funding for the systems technology portion of the BMD program from $118 million to $100 million. This move was vigorously opposed by Secretary of Defense Rumsfeld, who believed that the army had followed the Senate's instructions and was now being penalized for doing so. These sentiments were shared by Senator James B. Allen (D-Ala.), who scored his Senate colleagues for their inconsistency in dealing with the army ABM program. Allen told the Senate that "our inconsistency and our tendency to micro-manage research and development programs is demonstrably inefficient and detrimental to the cost effectiveness of the programs and products."[20]

Allen's colleagues on the Senate Appropriations Committee were unchastened by his remarks and reduced the funding still further to $75 million. After an appeal from Deputy Secretary of Defense William P. Clements, Jr., a conference committee restored the funding level to $100 million. In his letter to Representative George M. Mahon (D-Tex.), chairman of the House Appropriations Committee, Clements stated that the Senate reduction would "probably create a major asymmetry between the United States and the USSR in BMD system capability." The major funding reduction passed by the Senate, combined with the closing of the SAFEGUARD site, could indicate a serious lack of resolve on the part of the United States and might lead the Soviets to lose interest in maintaining the ABM Treaty, which was to be reviewed by both powers in 1977.[21]

BMD AFTER SAFEGUARD: R&D CONTINUES

In the years following the deactivation of SAFEGUARD, the army was forced to conduct what was essentially a research-only program under strict guidelines imposed by Congress and the ABM agreements. Not only that, but Congress continued to reduce BMD funding. In addition to these obstacles, the army had to contend with the considerable difficulty that a research-only program poses within the context of the American defense acquisition process. Such a program generates no requirements for the production of hardware. Without the prospect of orders for equipment, it is difficult to keep contractors interested in defense work, for only production requirements are likely to result in appreciable profits. These difficulties contrasted sharply with a Soviet program that was funded at a level estimated to be three times that of the United States effort. This meant that the goal of the army's program, maintaining a technological lead over the Soviets, might prove impossible to achieve.[22]

In spite of these problems, the army pursued a vigorous program driven by three possible ABM missions: protecting American ICBM fields; securing the national command authorities as well as the command, control, and communications (C[3]) system that controls United States nuclear forces; and providing a limited defense for urban industrial areas.[23] The army had gained a thorough understanding of the nature and magnitude of the problems associated with ballistic missile defense from its work with SAFEGUARD, and this experience determined to some extent the direction of the R&D effort.[24]

R&D CONTINUES: COMPUTERS

One major requirement of an effective BMD system is a powerful computer possessing the ability to store and process huge quantities of data with great speed. The data processing requirement associated with controlling an ABM system is illustrated nicely in the example of a battle in which two hundred enemy warheads are scanned by a radar system at the rate of twenty pulses per second. This requires a computer to handle twelve million instructions per second (MIPS).[25]

When the SENTINEL-SAFEGUARD system was being developed there were no commercial computers available with sufficient capacity. Therefore, in 1967 a data processing package was designed and developed specifically for the ABM system through a cooperative effort involving Bell Laboratories, Western Electric, and Lockheed Electronics. The SAFEGUARD computer was capable of performing ten MIPS.[26]

By the time the army was working on the Site Defense system, the quality of commercial computers had advanced to the point where a commercial machine could be used. The computer selected was a Control Data Corporation (CDC) 7700, which had twice the capacity of the SAFEGUARD data processing system and was one of the largest and fastest commercial computers in 1976.[27]

The army was also working with computers more powerful than the CDC 7700. These machines were in the army's Advanced Research Center, which included a computer complex containing four major computers. The most impressive of these, PEPE (parallel element processing ensemble), was built by Burroughs Corporation to meet the specific demands of ballistic missile defenses—keeping a huge, complex data base up-to-date; controlling search radar; tracking objects and distinguishing warheads from decoys; and so on. Although the other computers might operate as fast as twenty-five MIPS, PEPE could handle as many as eight hundred MIPS.[28]

By mid-1978 the army's R&D program included an examination of techniques and equipment that would permit the distribution of some of the command and control functions from a centralized control center to individual interceptors in a missile defense system. A special computer for installation on interceptor missiles was being developed to handle these functions. The goal of this effort was to provide an onboard computer that could handle 100 million operations per second. One machine being developed was to be about 1 foot in height and 14 inches in diameter and weigh about 80 pounds.[29]

Two years later, the army's Advanced Research Center was evaluating a minicomputer designed by Lockheed. Using "residue-number arithmetic" this device could perform the equivalent of 500 million additions per second or 120 million multiplications per second. The speed of this machine was achieved by processing its computations in parallel.[30]

R&D CONTINUES: OPTICAL SENSORS
AND INTERCEPTOR CONCEPTS

By the end of the 1970s, the army was beginning to combine the advances being made in computer technology with developments in the area of sensors to set the stage for the development of a new generation of interceptor missiles. It was apparent to the army that one way to overcome the single-site limitations imposed by the ABM Treaty and offset the advantages MIRVed ICBMs had enjoyed to this point was to extend the range at which an ABM system could attack incoming warheads.

One reason for pursuing research on optical sensors was the operating limitations of radar. For example, radar could not distinguish between decoys, boosters, and warheads during the midcourse phase of flight. Moreover, great power and large antennas are required to pick up the elements of this threat cloud. The antennas, however, make the radar vulnerable to direct attack, as in the case of the SAFEGUARD system. Still another problem with radar is encountered when it is used to direct attacks against warheads in the terminal phase of their flight. As the threat cloud reenters the atmosphere, two phenomena occur. First, the large booster breaks up and fills the air with debris. Second, the lighter decoys and some booster debris are slowed more rapidly by the atmosphere and fall behind the warheads and dense chunks of debris. The latter phenomenon helps the defender to distinguish warheads from decoys. However, some of the booster debris is large enough to present radar returns similar to warheads and therefore tends to confuse the defender.

To overcome these problems, the army began to develop optical sensors in the infrared radiation range. In a test conducted in 1979 at Kwajalein, a ground-based infrared sensor had been able to find and follow a warhead in the middle of booster debris forty percent of the time. During this same period, radar sensors were totally incapable of finding the warhead.[31]

Work also was being done with optical sensors that could be launched into space. Boeing Corporation, working with Hughes Aircraft Company, was developing a designating optical tracker (DOT) for the army. This recoverable sensor package would be sent aloft and used to study the infrared signatures of warheads and booster debris from space. In September 1980 the army successfully tested the DOT system. In spite of the deployment of penetration aids by the "attacker," the infrared sensor was able to track the test warhead.[32]

One scheme for taking advantage of the new sensors was called the forward acquisition sensor system (FASS). The idea here was to launch the sensor into a ballistic trajectory so that it could pick up the approaching threat cloud and relay trajectory data to ground facilities. These data would be used in launching a fleet of mother vehicles equipped with their own sensors and carrying several nonnuclear kill vehicles equipped with homing sensors. The mother ships would cooperate in designating targets for the fleet's kill vehicles and launch them at approaching warheads. The kill vehicles would then home in on their assigned targets.[33]

By combining the improved capabilities of infrared sensors with small, high-capacity computers, the army produced hit-to-kill, or kinetic kill, interceptors. These vehicles represented the first major revolution in ballistic missile defenses since the United States began BMD research in the 1940s. To this point, the accuracy of guidance systems was such that an ABM missile required a nuclear warhead to assure a reasonable kill probability. Yet nuclear warheads brought with them a number of problems, such as the fact that nuclear explosions interfere with the operation of the radar systems that were supposed to control the battle between defending missiles and incoming warheads. Now it was reasonable to think of destroying a reentry vehicle with a missile that literally collides with the vehicle and destroys it with the kinetic energy of the colliding bodies.[34]

By 1980 the army was planning to demonstrate this new interceptor concept in the homing overlay experiment (HOE)[35] scheduled for the 1982–1983 time frame. In this demonstration, an experimental vehicle would be launched from Kwajalein Missile Range using a modified MINUTEMAN rocket. In addition to a computer and an infrared sensor package for guidance, the vehicle would be equipped with a kill device that resembled the folded skeleton of an umbrella with weights attached to its ribs. Once above the atmosphere, a sensor and computer on board the MINUTEMAN would locate and track a test reentry vehicle launched from Vandenberg Air Force Base by a second MINUTEMAN missile. Then the onboard computer of the launch rocket would pass tracking data to the computer on the intercept vehicle. At the appropriate time, the interceptor would be launched and home in on the target using its own infrared sensor and onboard computer. Once free of the mother ship, the kill vehicle would deploy its umbrella structure, thereby increasing the probability that it would hit and destroy the target.[36]

THE ORIGINS AND DEVELOPMENT
OF DIRECTED ENERGY WEAPONS

The army's nonnuclear kill vehicle was not the only revolutionary concept being pursued by the DOD in the 1970s. Throughout this decade, defense organizations supported an impressive array of R&D programs focused on the development of directed energy weapons (DEWs) and the

This artist's conception shows the Homing Overlay Experiment vehicle with its "umbrella-ribbed" structure extended. This apparatus was deployed to increase the probability of collision as the vehicle approached its target. (U.S. Department of Defense)

application to these devices to the ABM mission. By 1980 significant advances in these programs were inspiring confidence that DEWs would soon offer the means of defeating attacks by ICBMs. The roots of these exotic weapons are found in science fiction and the realization before World War II that nature produces radiations that can kill human beings.

Ancient history provides what is probably the first description of a weapon that achieved its destructive effects by directing energy onto a target. In the third century B.C., the Greek scientist Archimedes reportedly used sunlight to destroy the ships of a Roman fleet that had laid siege to the port of Syracuse. Using concave mirrors he had constructed, Archimedes supposedly set the Roman vessels ablaze by focusing the sun's rays on their sails.[37]

More recently, a description of a directed energy weapon was presented in H. G. Wells's famous science fiction novel, *The War of the Worlds*. In one passage he described how the Martians used a heat ray to kill people:

> It is still a matter of wonder how the Martians are able to slay men so swiftly and so silently. Many think that in some way they are able to generate an intense heat in a chamber of practically absolute non-conductivity. This intense heat they project in a parallel beam against any object they choose, by means of a polished parabolic mirror of unknown composition, much as the parabolic mirror of a lighthouse projects a beam of light.[38]

Perhaps more relevant to the actual development of directed energy weapons are the stories that abound in the *New York Times* of the 1920s and 1930s concerning doctors and scientists who contracted cancer and often died as a result of their work with radiation. So many people perished in this manner that a monument to the "heroes of science" was established at the Roentgen Institute of St. George's Hospital in Hamburg, Germany. In 1935 the names of forty Americans were added to this monument. It was common to refer to the radiation that killed these scientists as a death ray.[39]

There are also stories about various inventors who claimed to have developed death rays that could kill animals and people. One of the most famous was Nikola Tesla. Following his tradition of announcing a major invention on each of his birthdays, he stated in 1935 that he had invented a death ray that could kill an army of one million men instantly and bring down a fleet of aircraft at a range of 250 miles.[40]

Several episodes related to radiation weapons occurred during World War II. When Sir Robert Watson-Watt developed the concept for British radar, he was responding to a query as to whether or not it was possible to produce a radiation weapon that could bring down an airplane. Sir Robert calculated the amount of energy that would have to be concentrated on an aircraft to make the blood of its crew boil and concluded that this scheme was impractical. However, he reported to his superiors that it would be possible to direct enough radio energy onto an aircraft to produce a reflection that could be used to detect the presence of the plane.[41]

As World War II was beginning in Europe, there is evidence that the United States Army was at least aware of the idea of radiation weapons, even if its R&D officers did not have much faith in their potential. Shortly after the German invasion of Poland, the U.S. government established the Uranium Committee to serve as a liaison with physicists who were involved in research that might lead to the development of an atomic bomb. During an October 1939 meeting of this committee, Lieutenant Colonel Keith F. Adamson noted that the army was offering $10,000 to anyone who could produce a ray that would kill a goat tethered on a 10-foot rope at the Aberdeen Proving Ground. The colonel added sarcastically that no one had yet claimed the money.[42]

In a 1940 movie, "Murder in the Air," an American agent thwarted an attempt by Communist spies to steal an "inertia projector" that had been invented by American scientists and could transmit "electrical waves capable of paralyzing alternating and direct currents at the source." The hero of the movie was Brass Bancroft, who was played by Ronald Reagan. He used the inertia projector to stop the spies' escape by turning the device on their airplane and making it crash.[43]

American bomber commanders directing the Combined Bomber Offensive against the Nazis in 1943 and 1944 were worried that the Germans had developed a device like the inertia projector that could stop an internal combustion engine and bring down American bombers. A research project carried out under the Office of Scientific Research and Development concluded that such a device was not feasible because of power limitations.[44]

As the war was ending, Professor Theodore von Kármán reported to Henry H. Arnold, commanding general of the Army Air Forces, on potential applications of science in air wars of the future. One possibility he evaluated was using a beam weapon to defend against attacking missiles by exploding the bombs they carried or by otherwise disabling them. Von Kármán concluded that "even if twice the total electric power of the United States were placed in a single beam from a reflector 50 feet in diameter, the intensity at one mile would just reach the sparking voltage in air. . . . Thus, present scientific knowledge offers no hope for, but on the contrary distinct evidence against, the possibility of detonating bombs at a distance."[45]

The actual origins of modern directed energy devices are considerably more mundane than the science fiction of H.G. Wells and "Murder in the Air." One source of these revolutionary devices was the work of Charles H. Townes, who in 1951 conceived of using the phenomenon of stimulated emission to produce an improved source of microwave energy. According to the theory of stimulated response first advanced by Albert Einstein in 1916, it should be possible to cause an atom to produce light of a given wavelength by directing light of that same wavelength on the atom. In 1953 this principle was used to build the world's first maser (microwave amplification through stimulated emission of radiation). Within a few years, the application of the principle was expanded to a light amplification device called a laser (light amplification through stimulated emission of radiation), which was first demonstrated in July 1960.[46]

Soon after the first laser demonstration, DOD began to consider several different weapons applications. Among these was the use of powerful lasers to defend against ballistic missiles. In fact, before the end of 1961 DOD's Advanced Research Projects Agency (ARPA)[47] began to fund research on lasers for missile defense under Project SEASIDE, which was managed by the navy's Office of Naval Research (ONR). The major challenge of this project was to increase the power of lasers to the point where they could destroy a missile's warhead.[48]

In the first half of the 1960s, efforts to produce high energy lasers were hampered by a commitment to solid-state lasers that earlier had shown considerable promise with regard to scalability. In this early activity, researchers had used glass and ruby crystals as the lasing material and believed that increasing the laser's power to the point where it would be effective as a weapon was largely a function of improving these crystals. As a result, a major program was launched in 1963 to find the best lasing substances. The project eventually became so extensive that the Naval Research Laboratory established a center to evaluate the materials developed. By the mid-1960s, difficulties in the scaling of solid-state lasers had resulted in a shift of focus in the ARPA-ONR program from ABM applications to radar applications. Additionally, more emphasis was placed on efforts to understand fundamental lasing phenomena.[49]

Until about 1965 the concentration on solid-state lasing in the ARPA-ONR program had blinded researchers to the potential of the gas laser. This device had been invented in 1960 and at first gave little indication that its power could be increased to the level required of a weapon. However, in 1964 C. N. K. Patel of Bell Laboratories invented the carbon dioxide laser, which did lend itself to up-scaling. Soon after this, both the army and the air force built large carbon dioxide lasers, as did Raytheon Corporation. These devices were referred to as "sewer pipe" lasers because of their long, slender appearance. One device constructed by the army was 178 feet in length and 2 inches in diameter and produced 2,300 watts of power.[50]

The next major advance came in 1967, when a carbon dioxide laser was combined with aerodynamic techniques to produce the carbon dioxide gas dynamic laser (GDL), which showed great promise for scaling to high energy levels. In this type of laser, the electrons of a gas are excited to the higher energy state required to produce lasing by burning a fuel in oxygen or nitrous oxide and then expanding the resulting hot gas through nozzles into a vacuum. By the time news of this device reached the public it had achieved powers of 60,000 watts.[51]

In the early 1970s, progress in increasing laser output power led DOD to almost double its budget for laser technology. A decade earlier, the output power of a continuous wave (CW) laser had been measured in tens of watts. By 1972 laser power had been increased more than a thousand times and was approaching a level that would allow it to destroy an aircraft. Although the exact power of the strongest laser (a GDL laser) was classified, *Aviation Week* reported that it was in the realm of 200 kilowatts and noted that power levels might reach the megawatt range by the end of the 1970s. At the same time, the Defense Advanced Research Projects Agency (DARPA) and the military services were hard at work on tracking systems with the high precision required to point a laser weapon. These developments indicated that lasers could be a threat to missiles by 1980. Further cause for optimism came in 1973 when the air force used a laser to shoot down a drone aircraft on the Sandia Optical Range near Kirtland Air Force Base, New Mexico. Three years later, the army accomplished similar feats at its Redstone Arsenal in Alabama. And about two years later, the navy used a laser to destroy a tube-launched, optically tracked, wire-guided (TOW) missile fired by army technicians at San Juan Capistrano in California.[52]

Thus, as the 1970s came to a close, lasers had demonstrated that they could be integrated with pointing and tracking devices to form effective weapons systems and had given indications that they might be effective against missiles in just a few years. By this time, the army was also at work on a second form of the directed energy weapon—the particle beam, which would destroy its target by transferring energy to it in the form of a concentrated beam of atomic or subatomic particles.

At the end of the 1970s, the army's particle beam program included both ground-based and space-based concepts. The major ground-based system was a proton particle beam that could be operational by 1990. The major space-based program was a neutral particle beam being developed in the army's Project SIPAPU, an American Indian word meaning sacred fire. The SIPAPU particle beam would be produced by accelerating a stream of negative hydrogen ions and then neutralizing the beam by passing it through a "charge exchange cell." Once neutralized the beam would be suited for use in space, since it would be unaffected by the earth's magnetic field. An antisatellite version of SIPAPU could be orbited in as little as three to five years.[53]

The potential power of the neutral particle beam made it one of the more promising technologies around 1980. Its powerful stream of particles traveled at nearly the speed of light, and when this beam struck a target, it tended to "produce near-instantaneous destruction of the target surface" and also penetrated deeply into the object, where it did further damage. Not only could such a beam destroy a satellite at a range of several thousand kilometers, but the beam's power made it difficult to counter.[54]

While the army was pursuing a DEW program with obvious potential for BMD, the air force was involved in a more generic laser program with several weapons applications in mind. Part of the air force effort was an adaptive optics program centered around the development of deformable mirrors to compensate for distortions in laser beams caused by such things as atmospheric heating produced by laser beams passing through the air and by deficiencies in other optical components in the system.[55]

The year 1980 witnessed several significant changes in the Department of Defense's DEW program. Around the middle of the year, Secretary of Defense Harold Brown ordered a shift in DOD priorities. Noting that lasers had the potential to revolutionize warfare, he directed the military services to explore all possible uses of these devices but to focus on the development of space-based, high energy lasers. Part of the reason for this emphasis was the difficulty of operating lasers in the atmosphere where thermal blooming and scattering weaken the beam. With this shift in priorities, the Pentagon's DEW efforts began to focus on a technology program that might permit the deployment of "laser battle stations" in space in seven to ten years. These could be used to defend U.S. satellites or to defeat an attack by ICBMs. Furthermore, as the shift was occurring, DARPA began to play a more important role in the DOD's directed energy weapons program. It became the manager of a consolidated particle beam technology program with responsibility for demonstrating particle beam feasibility in two major areas: neutral particle beam propagation and the propagation and target interaction of a charged particle beam.[56]

As a part of the consolidation, the army's SIPAPU program was transferred to DARPA control beginning in FY 1981 and was redesignated WHITE HORSE to avoid antagonizing American Indians, who consider *sipapu* a religious word. Under DARPA, WHITE HORSE shifted from the army's five-year schedule to a seven-year program designed to demonstrate the feasibility of using particle beam devices in a space-based defense against ICBMs. Also transferred to DARPA control was the army's autoresonant accelerator program. Although authority over these programs was passed to DARPA, the army continued to manage them and was allowed to keep a very modest high energy laser program.[57]

DARPA was also managing a project at Lawrence Livermore National Laboratory that sought to develop the ability to fire an electron beam through the atmosphere. One immediate application of such a capability might be a device to protect major naval vessels from attacks by aircraft and cruise missiles. In the more distant future, there was the prospect of developing ground-based particle beams that could be used as ABM weapons.[58]

In addition to its particle beam work, DARPA was supporting R&D in the field of high energy lasers where the focus was the DARPA TRIAD, a space-based laser project. The first part of the TRIAD was the ALPHA program, which aimed to develop a hydrogen fluoride laser with a wavelength of 2.7 microns and a power output of 5 megawatts. The second element was the large optics demonstration experiment (LODE), which involved the "fabrication" of a large mirror 4 meters in diameter. The third component was TALON GOLD, an undertaking to develop precise pointing capabilities. A TALON GOLD experiment was to be conducted in mid-1985 on a space shuttle flight to demonstrate a pointing accuracy of "at least 0.2 microradians." Boeing was responsible for combining these three elements for a system demonstration.[59]

The fabrication of large mirrors was the pacing technology for lasers as the 1970s came to a close. A 3-meter mirror had already been built and work was under way on the LODE project. There was no scientific or technical reason that a mirror as large as 10 meters could not be built.

The problem was that mirror fabrication was still a "cottage industry," and there was no production facility available to construct the larger mirror.[60]

One proposal to overcome the fabrication problem was advanced by the United Technologies Research Center in early 1981. It involved using lightweight composite materials to construct segments that could be combined to form a 10-meter mirror. This device, a "graphite fiber-reinforced glass matrix composite optical system," would be the result of a three-part program. The three parts would run in parallel and would include research to resolve the remaining basic technology issues, production of a smaller, 2.4-meter mirror, and finally construction of the 10-meter mirror. This last element would require about four and a half years to complete because of the ticklish nature of the fabrication procedures. It was the delicacy of these procedures that made mirror construction the pacing technology of laser weapons. The total cost of this program was estimated at $87.2 million.[61]

The pointing and tracking problem was also a difficult challenge. NASA's space telescope was designed to meet a higher level of accuracy—25 nanoradians, which equates to 1-foot error at 7,575 miles. However, NASA had the advantage of having much more time to focus its telescope. A laser weapon must be swiftly pointed and changed from one target to another, all with great precision. Still, according to Senator Malcolm Wallop, a Republican from Wyoming and a member of the Senate Intelligence Committee, by May 1981, the United States had the technology to achieve the necessary accuracy in pointing and tracking. Wallop stated that an accuracy of .2 microdegrees was required to destroy an ICBM at 3,000 to 5,000 miles. He further reported that he had seen equipment that routinely achieved a higher accuracy than that.[62]

THE PROMISE OF DIRECTED ENERGY WEAPONS

As the 1980s began, several people believed that prospects were bright for the development of an effective defense against ballistic missiles. As the discussion of DEW research indicates, directed energy devices seemed especially promising. Pessimistic estimates indicated that not until the 1990s would DEWs mature to the point where they could serve in an ABM capacity. More optimistic projections fixed this date at sometime in the late 1980s. The development of such weapons and the possibility of deploying them in space not only promised a solution to the problem of ICBM vulnerability, but again raised the possibility of protecting the U.S. population, as had been the intention with NIKE-X and SENTINEL in the 1960s. "The implications become awesome," as one official put it.[63]

This comment and others like it suggest that there was considerable optimism among those concerned with the nation's DEW and BMD programs. A February 1981 article reported that a soon-to-be-released DARPA study concluded that an effective space-based laser weapon was near at hand. This chemical laser would develop 2.5 megawatts of power. Using a mirror 4 meters in diameter to focus its energy, it could deliver 1.5 kilojoules per square centimeter at distances up to 2,200 miles. This was sufficient to destroy an ICBM in the boost phase since an energy level of only 1.0 kilojoules per square centimeter was considered lethal for such missiles. A network of one hundred such lasers with their power increased to 25 megawatts and equipped with 15-meter mirrors would have the ability to blunt a Soviet missile attack on the United States. Although the 5-megawatt laser could be tested in nine years, it would take twenty to twenty-five years to deploy the one-hundred-laser constellation that would constitute "a full or robust BMD capability." These deployment projections were based upon an aggressively pursued, not a crash, program. Also assumed were necessary advances in surveillance and C[3] systems and in the development of the requisite heavy-lift space vehicles.[64]

Later the same month, *Aviation Week* reported that X-ray lasing had been demonstrated by the Livermore Laboratory during a test at an underground site in Nevada. The test was part of a series known as the DAUPHIN project. An X-ray laser would consist of a central nuclear explosive device surrounded by a ring of approximately fifty lasing rods between 3 and 8 feet long, each of which could be independently aimed. When "pumped" by a small nuclear explosion, each rod would produce an extremely powerful series of energy pulses lasting for only 10 microseconds. So powerful would these pulses be that they could destroy a target in a single microsecond by evaporating the surface where the beam strikes. Countermeasures that would protect a warhead or missile from conventional lasers would be ineffective against the X-ray laser. Yet, in spite of their great power, these devices were reportedly so small that a single shuttle flight could orbit enough of them to stop a Soviet missile attack against the United States. One operational concept called for placing a constellation of these devices into polar orbits.[65]

A few months later, *Aviation Week* reported that Boeing proposed to construct a space-based laser that would be effective against airborne and spaceborne targets. This device would use a 2.5-meter mirror and develop 2.2 megawatts of power. It would be placed in orbit by the space shuttle and could be demonstrated as early as 1985.[66]

A sense that DEWs had reached a critical point in their development was also reflected in congressional (especially senatorial) efforts to increase funding for DEW work. In FY 1980, DARPA spent $48.8 million for high energy lasers. The following fiscal year this figure increased to $69.1 million. Moreover, some members of Congress wanted to increase the FY 1981 figure by $20 million more. Floor amendments in the Senate that would have increased this total to $180 million were only narrowly defeated. About $30 million was provided for particle beam research in FY 1981.[67]

Furthermore, in May 1981 Wallop and six colleagues sponsored an amendment that would have added $250 million to the military authorization bill for FY 1982. Of this money, $152.5 million was to be earmarked for DARPA's space-based, high energy laser program with the remainder going to support air force work on lasers. This was reduced to $50 million by the House-Senate conference.[68]

Thus, from the closing of SAFEGUARD to the beginning of the 1980s, several important technical advances had occurred. Of these, the promise of directed energy weapons more than any other development excited renewed interest in deploying an ABM system. To visionaries, the revolutionary characteristics of these devices, especially their "muzzle" velocity, which in the case of the laser was the speed of light, promised capabilities that would allow defensive systems to overcome the advantages that the nuclear-tipped ICBM had enjoyed for two decades and end the stranglehold that the mutual assured destruction doctrine had on the thinking of American strategists. One of these visionaries was Maxwell W. Hunter II, who in the late 1970s was a senior aerospace engineer working for Lockheed Corporation. His story is part of the next chapter.

CHAPTER SIX

The Reemergence
of Ballistic Missile Defense
as a National Issue: 1977–1981

This is like looking at the Wright brothers and not realizing you
have to learn about bomb shelters.
—*Maxwell W. Hunter II, 1987*[1]

The 1970s was marked by a steady increase and improve-
ment in Soviet strategic offensive forces and a concomitant rise in concern among American strategists that the Soviets would soon have the
ability to launch a disarming first strike against the U.S. ICBM fleet
and retain sufficient reserves to destroy the United States if it chose to
retaliate. In spite of this concern, America terminated SAFEGUARD and
abandoned plans to develop the Site Defense follow-on system. Yet even
as SAFEGUARD was being deactivated, there were discussions about using terminal defensive systems to improve the survivability of the MIN-
UTEMAN and MX missiles.

Later in the 1970s as the army was developing new ABM technologies
and concepts, the vision of strategic analysts began to expand as they
contemplated the advantages offered by attacking ICBMs in midcourse
and perhaps earlier. Their horizons were further broadened as work on
DEWs progressed, giving analysts a glimpse of the revolutionary potential of these devices, especially space-based directed energy weapons.

The possibility that technical advances would bring the strategic defense abreast of the strategic offense and the need to respond to the
growth of Soviet strategic forces combined to trigger an intragovernmental debate over the appropriate response to the changing strategic
environment. Moreover, the prospect that defenses might be broadened

to include population centers raised serious questions about the dominant U.S. strategic doctrine of assured destruction. By the beginning of
President Reagan's first term in office, the debate within Congress, the
Department of Defense, and the State Department and between these
major segments of the government had reached the point where it was
necessary to establish some policy guidelines to give direction to government activities that were becoming increasingly chaotic.

RENEWED PRESSURE TO DEFEND ICBMS

Long before SAFEGUARD was deployed, several cheap, quick-fix approaches to ICBM defense had been advanced as alternatives to developing a system such as SAFEGUARD. Among the first to suggest schemes
for defending MINUTEMAN fields was Richard Garwin, a research scientist with IBM Corporation. One of his ideas was the "bed of nails" concept in which steel spikes erected in missile fields would destroy warheads just before they detonated on the ground. Another of Garwin's
proposals was to electronically jam the radar fuses of warheads. He also
suggested the destruction of warheads by means of a "curtain of steel
pellets" that would be thrown into the air over a missile field by the
detonation of conventional explosives. Another concept Garwin offered
was to plant nuclear charges in the missile fields and detonate them as
Soviet warheads approached. This would lift a large amount of debris
into the air and destroy approaching warheads. Since the debris would
stay in the air for some time, the MINUTEMAN missiles would be protected for up to an hour.[2]

As the threat to American ICBMs increased following the deactivation of SAFEGUARD, schemes similar to those advanced by Garwin were
again discussed. For example, Bernard Feld and Kosta Tsipis suggested
a variant of a Garwin defensive concept. Two small radar systems
would be placed north of each silo and used to control launchers that
would fire swarms of small rockets at approaching warheads when they
were about a kilometer above the MINUTEMAN silos. Although an attacking force could eventually overwhelm such a defensive system, this
method of defending U.S. missiles would force an attacker to expend a
much larger number of missiles for an effective first strike and would
introduce great uncertainty into the work of Soviet planners. Since
these "minirockets" would be unguided, they would probably not constitute a violation of the SALT I ABM Treaty. However, it might be neces-

sary, Feld and Tsipis thought, to negotiate with the Soviets to be sure this system did not even appear to be a treaty violation.[3]

Similar schemes found their way into army plans for emergency defense of U.S. missile fields. Project Quick-Shot involved the development of a small, inexpensive rocket with high velocity for use in terminal defense. Groups of such rockets would be fired in salvos at enemy warheads once they had penetrated to very low altitudes. To improve effectiveness, each of the small missiles might be equipped with a simple guidance system.[4] The same shot-gun principle underpinned another plan the army devised. Here optical sensing probes would be launched into space to meet an attack. These probes would guide swarms of nonnuclear homing intercept vehicles that would then be rocketed into a volume of space through which the attacking warheads would pass. From this position they would use their own guidance systems to attack the warheads.[5]

While considering these short-term solutions to the problem of terminal defense, the army continued to explore more permanent ways of defending ICBM fields. In the fall of 1976 an army contract with McDonnell Douglas called for exploring the feasibility of a low-altitude ABM system (ST-2) to defend the new MX missile that was entering the engineering development stage. This system would intercept incoming missiles below 50,000 feet where the warheads would be distinguishable from most booster debris and decoys. Consideration of this new system included the recognition that ST-2 would have to be mobile if a mobile basing mode was selected for MX. The prospect of a mobile ABM system raised the specter of treaty violation, for such systems were banned by the 1972 ABM Treaty.[6]

As the 1970s advanced, the idea of defending the MX missile became more appealing as the survivability of U.S. ICBMs became increasingly problematic. Although the number of warheads in the Soviet ICBM fleet tripled in this ten-year period, it might still be possible to offset this increase in Soviet forces by means of an appropriate basing mode combined with an ABM system incorporating the latest advances in defensive technologies. Such a combination could confer considerable leverage to even a small ABM force of one hundred missiles. For example, take the case of a basing mode in which a small number of ICBMs is shuttled among a relatively large number of protective shelters. Since the defender knows the location of his ICBMs, he needs to defend only occupied shelters, whereas the attacker must strike all shelters and cannot concentrate to overwhelm the defense. There was also an important advantage in defending missiles as opposed to defending cities—

when defending protectively based ICBMs, limited leakage is acceptable.[7]

In 1979 as an "endless procession of Defense Department officials"
were telling Congress that by the early 1980s the Soviets would be able
to destroy American ICBMs using only one-third of their own warheads,
the army was planning to defend the MX missile in the two basing
modes considered most advantageous by the air force—the multiple
protective shelter (MPS) mode and the air mobile mode. For defense of
the MPS mode, the army planned a system that would intercept attacking warheads below 50,000 feet. As a result, the system was called low-
altitude defense system (LoADS). The interceptor was to be a SPRINT-like
missile 15 feet in length. Early versions were to be nuclear armed, but
as the army's work with kinetic kill technology advanced, the nuclear-
tipped missiles would be replaced by kinetic kill vehicles (KKV). In one
variant of LoADS, a battery of three missiles and a radar system were to
be carried on a launch vehicle that would move about in an underground launch tube. One of these batteries could be installed in each of
the shelter complexes of the MPS basing mode for MX. Under attack,
the radar system and missiles would be pushed up through the surface
of the underground launch tube. The missiles would be capable of accelerating to 8,500 feet per second in only 1.5 seconds and would reach
an altitude of 4,000 to 5,000 feet in about one second. If the air mobile
basing mode were to be selected over MPS, the army planned to defend
it with an ABM system using exoatmospheric interceptors with nonnuclear warheads.[8]

The army, profiting from its experience with SAFEGUARD, had
planned considerable flexibility into its LoADS. First, it would be able to
protect the vulnerable MINUTEMAN missiles. If a land-based mode was
selected for the MX missile, LoADS would be adaptable to defending the
new missile. Moreover, the army even envisioned LoADS becoming the
lower tier of a broader two-tiered BMD system that was part of long-
range army plans.[9]

EXPANDING HORIZONS: SPACE-BASED BATTLE STATIONS

LoADS and the army's long-range plans for a multitiered missile defense system are indicative of how the pressure of dealing with the issue of ICBM vulnerability under the restrictions imposed by the ABM
Treaty had combined with advances in technology to expand the conceptual horizons of American missile defense experts. In September

1976 Clarence Robinson summed up the situation neatly for readers of *Aviation Week*: "Since the U.S. and U.S.S.R. have both agreed to a single ABM site, the U.S. is convinced that exoatmospheric interception of ICBMs is critical to successful defense. The eventual use of space platforms with energy directed ABM weapons and interceptors using nonnuclear warheads is considered vital by ABM planners." With defensive systems in space, the next logical step would be to use these systems to multiply the power of the defense by attacking the ICBM while it was still in its boost phase when its warheads and decoys still represented a single target. By mid-1978, army personnel were confident they would "be capable of reaching out into space to attack intercontinental ballistic missiles . . . in midcourse trajectory, or just after launch from enemy silos, to halt nuclear weapons attacks on the U.S."[10]

Where boost-phase interception was concerned, the most promising technological concept at this time was space-based directed energy weapons. By the late 1970s this concept was rather well developed as Clarence Robinson showed in the 16 October 1978 *Aviation Week*. Robinson had been covering ABM and DEW developments for several years; the major source for his report was an anonymous official of Lockheed Corporation.[11]

The article focused on space-based "battle stations" and may be the first appearance of this concept in U.S. defense literature. These stations were to be armed with directed energy weapons such as the army's SIPAPU particle beam. The "muzzle" velocity of such weapons was 50,000 times greater than that of rockets and made them revolutionary in nature. Furthermore, the laser possessed an extraordinary ability to focus energy into a narrow beam. The concentration of energy exceeded that of a nuclear weapon, yet its narrowness precluded it from being used as a weapon of mass destruction. In short, it was a weapon of surgical precision that offered "the distinct possibility that the rapid delivery of nuclear explosives can be prevented by a weapon system that is itself not capable of mass destruction. Such a system clearly would give the nation that possesses it options in strategic posture and activity that are now denied everyone, including returning to those in charge the time to permit adequate decision making, which was taken away by the unholy synergism of nuclear weaponry and ballistic missiles." The potential of the laser for killing an ICBM during its boost phase meant that as soon as a sufficient number were deployed in space the era of mutual assured destruction would be at an end.[12]

The feasibility of this revolutionary space-based missile defense system would be founded upon another revolution that appeared to be at hand—a drastic reduction in transportation costs associated with the debut of the space shuttle. The dramatic economies made possible by the shuttle justified a reevaluation of earlier, more pessimistic studies of space-based systems that relied on conventional rocket capabilities.

> When space transportation attains sizable economies, then space weaponry must be evaluated on the basis of military utility rather than being summarily dismissed because of huge logistics costs. Such weaponry need not be placed in primitive, flimsy satellites. Rather, heavy weights of shielding and hardening materials become feasible in space. The term battle station is more descriptive of these weapons than the images conjured up by the terms satellite or space station.

These battle stations would be assembled in space using multiple trips by the space shuttle to transport the required materials into orbit.[13]

In considering the costs of transportation, Robinson's anonymous source assumed that the cost of orbiting 1 pound of material during the era of the shuttle would be $150, which meant that it would cost $750 million to $1.5 billion for the space transportation system to field the requisite system of battle stations. The required size of the battle station constellation varied depending on the range of the lasers carried by the stations. With a 1,000 kilometer laser, 406 stations would be required. A laser of 5,000 kilometer range would reduce the required number of stations to 21; and if the range of the lasers could be extended to 10,000 kilometers, the number of battle stations was reduced to 9.[14]

Robinson carefully avoided naming the source of his information on space-based missile defenses, noting only that he was quoting extensively the words of an "industry official connected with laser weapons work" and "a Lockheed study of lasers." The anonymous official was Maxwell W. Hunter II, and the industry study was Hunter's "Strategic Dynamics and Space-Laser Weaponry," which Hunter completed on 31 October 1977 and referred to as the Halloween paper.[15]

MAXWELL HUNTER AND THE ORIGINS OF THE CONCEPT OF SPACE-BASED DEFENSE

In 1978 Hunter was a senior aerospace engineer with Lockheed Corporation. He had received a bachelor's degree in physics and mathemat-

In the late 1970s when he advanced the idea of space-based, laser-armed battle stations, Maxwell W. Hunter II was a senior aerospace engineer with Lockheed Corporation. He had been involved with work on ballistic missile defenses since the mid-1950s. In 1978 Hunter was introduced to missile-defense advocate Senator Malcolm Wallop (R-Wyo.) through Angelo Codevilla, an aide to Wallop. (Courtesy Maxwell W. Hunter II)

ics from Washington and Jefferson College and a master's degree in aeronautical engineering from MIT. By the late 1970s, when he became involved in an effort to apply lasers to ballistic missile defense, he had been working for over thirty years as an aeronautical and space systems design engineer. While employed by Douglas Aircraft Corporation between 1944 and 1961, he had been responsible for the aerodynamic design of several missiles, including the NIKE-AJAX, NIKE-ZEUS, and HERCULES. He had been a member of the Douglas team that worked with Bell Laboratories on the NIKE II ABM study that the army had started in March 1955. He had served on the professional staff of the National Aeronautics and Space Council between 1961 when he left Douglas and 1965 when he started working for Lockheed Missiles and Space Company, where he was employed until retiring in 1987.[16]

In late 1966 Hunter led a study of missile defenses that was completed by Lockheed in anticipation of possible government interest in the development of an ABM capability. After concluding that an upgraded BAMBI system would require too much weight in orbit, the group examined a proposal by Ben Dunn that consideration be given to using carbon dioxide lasers in orbit as the basis of a ballistic missile defense system.[17]

Calculations soon showed that such a system could be placed in orbit at a reasonable cost. However, the idea seemed too advanced at the time, and the Lockheed study team decided merely to watch this field for later developments. Hunter was now aware that lasers might play a useful role in missile defenses. About two years later, when he knew more about lasers, specifically gas dynamic and chemical lasers, he concluded that the time had come to push missile defenses that featured space-based lasers. His efforts won for Lockheed a series of studies sponsored by the military and carried out during the 1970s.[18]

By 1977 Hunter had concluded that lasers in space could produce a revolution in warfare by ending the long-standing dominance of offensive strategic weapons. As he put it:

> I suddenly realized that lasers are something we hadn't tried before. It may be decades before we understand the full implications of a speed of light interceptor, but there's one thing you know: the best interceptors are the fastest; and until Einstein is proven wrong, lasers are going to be the fastest interceptors. So if you build up to where they have enough pizzazz to hurt something, you better back off and seriously consider where these weapons will take you.[19]

This conclusion led Hunter to pull together his ideas on nuclear deterrence and strategic defense in the manuscript "Strategic Dynamics and Space-Laser Weaponry." Here he stated his view that America's strategic doctrine of mutual assured destruction was based upon the belief that the nuclear-tipped ICBM is the ultimate weapon against which no defense is possible. As a result, the United States had decided that its technology could no longer solve the problem posed by ICBMs and had "turned to psychology rather than physics, diplomacy rather than engineering, to protect the greatest technological power on the planet." Hunter disagreed with this position and argued that "high energy lasers are proliferating, and space transportation is about to become sufficiently economical that, if it is used to place such lasers in space, an effective defense against even massive ballistic missile exchanges . . . is, indeed, possible."[20]

Hunter could not understand those who wanted to make space a sanctuary from war, calling this a "cruel, genocidal hoax." He wanted to force any possible future nuclear war far out into space by deploying space forces "capable of dominating or at least strongly upsetting the opposing earth-bound strategic force balance." The means of bringing about this fundamental shift in the strategic situation between the superpowers was the deployment of a constellation of space-based, laser-armed battle stations, each protected by its own armor. The key characteristic of such a station would be the capability of its laser weapon to destroy ICBMs during their boost phase.[21]

Hunter believed that the qualities of a laser made it a revolutionary weapon. As already noted, in his eyes, laser weapons possessed the ultimate "muzzle velocity"—the velocity of light, or 50,000 times the speed of a rocket interceptor. Here, Hunter thought, was a counter to the great velocity of the ballistic missile that had thwarted defenses since the first V-2 attack against England. The speed of the laser beam and its narrow concentration of power made possible pinpoint accuracy, which in turn meant that it could be used with limited risks. A mistake with a nuclear weapon could mean the destruction of an entire city; a mistake with a laser would be the equivalent of one with a conventional rifle or light cannon. Because of this low risk, Hunter concluded that lasers could be used without human intervention.[22]

SENATOR WALLOP AND THE "GANG OF FOUR"

Although Hunter's Halloween paper was not published, it was circulated among his friends and colleagues and it set in motion a chain of events that eventually brought Hunter to the attention of Senator Malcolm Wallop. Wallop had become one of the Senate's staunchest supporters of strategic defense at the beginning of his first term when he discovered that the United States was defenseless against ballistic missiles despite heavy expenditures each year for defense.[23]

Soon after taking his seat, Wallop was appointed to the Senate Intel-

Soon after being elected to his first term, Senator Malcolm Wallop (R-Wyo.) began to wonder why the United States was spending billions of dollars each year on defenses that did not defend the nation. From his vantage point on the Senate Intelligence Committee he became familiar with the sophisticated pointing and tracking technology associated with intelligence satellites and became convinced that this technology indicated that space-based lasers could form the foundation of effective missile defenses. Much of his technical advice was provided by Maxwell Hunter. (Courtesy Senator Malcolm Wallop)

ligence Committee. To assist with his committee duties, he added Dr. Angelo Codevilla to his staff. Working together closely, these two men learned about Soviet strategic defense efforts and became intimately familiar with details of the Soviet strategic build-up that threatened to make U.S. ICBMs vulnerable to a Soviet first strike. At the same time, they also gained knowledge of the advanced technologies (optical, pointing, and tracking) associated with the national technical means of intelligence gathering. Furthermore, they became aware of the progress the United States had made in detecting Soviet missile launches, distinguishing between the various types of Soviet missiles, and predicting where these missiles would return to earth. As Wallop and Codevilla learned more about advanced technology and the strategic balance between the United States and the Soviet Union, they became displeased with America's reliance on offensive strategic systems to deter nuclear war. By the summer of 1978 they had concluded that the United States should develop missile defenses and began to search government and industry for others who shared their views.[24]

About this time, Hunter happened to be in Washington to attend a symposium on strategic defense. He had been invited to the conference because a copy of his Halloween paper had found its way to John Morse, a former under secretary of defense for international security affairs, who recommended that Hunter be invited to the symposium being organized by Robert Pfaltzgraff and Jacquelyn Davis of the Institute for Foreign Policy Analysis (IFPA). From Hunter's standpoint, the conference itself was unremarkable. However, after the symposium Hunter was invited to have dinner with Pfaltzgraff and Davis, who happened to bring Codevilla with them. Codevilla discussed missile defenses with Hunter, was excited by Hunter's ideas, and secured a copy of his paper. Somewhat later, Codevilla introduced Hunter to Wallop.[25]

This meeting was fortuitous. Although Wallop and Codevilla were convinced that the United States should develop missile defenses and were aware of many of the technical advances that would contribute to effective defenses, they did not know how to integrate the technology into an effective system. Hunter's constellation of laser-armed, space-based battle stations was just what they needed. Another of Hunter's important contributions was that he was able to identify for Wallop and Codevilla the organizations and people who could provide more concrete information on America's efforts to develop missile defenses.

In November 1978 Wallop visited the army's missile defense center at Huntsville, Alabama, in an effort to find out what was being done with ballistic missile defenses. Before his trip, Hunter advised Wallop of the areas he should explore while at Huntsville. Wallop found that the army had made significant advances in the power of its computers and had been doing experimental work on intercept techniques (the army was planning its homing overlay experiment at this time) and had been investigating the way a laser might be used to destroy an ICBM in its boost phase. These latter investigations indicated that a laser could destroy a booster without having to remain fixed on the missile long enough to burn through its skin. If this conclusion turned out to be valid, considerably less energy would be required to destroy a booster than had been thought previously. While at Huntsville, Wallop

also met Major General Stewart Meyer, the army's BMD program manager. Meyer and others informed Wallop that America's ABM program
was being impeded by national policies designed to assure that the
United States did not violate the ABM Treaty. He was also informed
that elements of the army and air force were opposed to missile defense
programs because of vested interests in established concepts and
weapon systems.[26]

Armed with this information, Wallop returned to Washington and
continued his investigation into BMD. He found that several other agencies, including DARPA, were studying the possible use of lasers to destroy ICBMs in their boost phase. Wallop also began a vigorous effort to
persuade other members of Congress and national leaders about what
could and should be done with ballistic missile defenses.[27] Wallop succeeded in sparking a limited amount of interest in his fellow senators.
Chief among these were Ernest Hollings (D-S.C.) and Howell Heflin (D-
Ala). Heflin held a series of small hearings in his subcommittee of the
Senate Commerce Committee in December 1979. However, Wallop believed this was not enough. He had to widen the number of senators interested in and informed about the issues of ballistic missile defense.
Since he had no formal committee position that would allow him to organize hearings, he decided to use informal briefings by representatives of industry to gain support for developing and deploying a missile
defense system. These briefings would be put together on a voluntary
basis and were to be attended by any senators and staffers who were interested in ABM matters.[28]

When Wallop approached the heads of various aerospace companies,
they refused to become involved for fear their participation in any such
initiative in Congress might upset officials in other branches of the
government. He then asked Hunter if he would develop the briefing.
Hunter also was reluctant to do so because his experience with the Department of Defense led him to believe that DOD officials would see
such a briefing by representatives of industry as an effort to bring congressional pressure to bear to secure the initiation of a new missile defense program. As an alternative, Hunter suggested that Codevilla attempt to find a source of briefings within DOD, for there was
considerable work being done on missile defense there.[29]

Codevilla, joined by Quentin C. Crommelin, Jr., a staff assistant to
Senator Harry F. Byrd, Jr. (I-Va.), did as Hunter recommended and began to work with DOD officials Alan Pike and Douglas Tanimoto. However, they could not secure a briefing that would indicate specifically
what capabilities could be developed within a given time frame. As a

result, Codevilla and Crommelin began pressuring Hunter to develop a briefing that could be used to gain support on Capitol Hill for a new ballistic missile defense program. Finally industry leaders grudgingly allowed Hunter to assemble a team of industry experts on a voluntary basis and prepare a briefing that could be used to educate members of Congress on the state of the art in missile defenses. The briefers were told to make it clear that their briefing was the work of private citizens and did not reflect the views of the companies for whom the individuals worked.[30]

Hunter recruited a team of leading experts in the key technical areas that would be involved in developing a missile defense system using space-based directed energy weapons. The team's expert on chemical lasers was Dr. Joseph Miller of TRW Incorporated. Dr. Norbert Schnog of Perkin-Elmer was the group's expert on optics. The team was rounded out by Dr. Gerald A. Ouellette of the Charles Stark Draper Laboratory, who provided expertise in the area of pointing and tracking technology. Hunter himself was the expert on integrating the components into a missile defense system. Together Hunter and his colleagues came to be known as the "gang of four."[31]

The briefing put together by Hunter's team focused on using lasers to thwart an attack by SS-18s. It concluded that a constellation of eighteen laser-equipped battle stations, organized into three rings and orbiting at an altitude of 1,087 miles, could defend U.S. MINUTEMAN missiles against the SS-18 threat. Such a defense system would cost about $10 billion with about one-third of this going for research and development.[32]

The battle stations would be assembled in space with their components being transported into orbit by the space shuttle. The core of a station—its laser and battle management systems—could be placed in orbit with a single shuttle mission. The laser itself would be between 19 and 27 feet long and weigh approximately 37,400 pounds. Placing the fuel packages for the laser in orbit would require one or two more shuttle missions. This amount of fuel would permit the battle station to engage a Soviet attacking force for fifteen to eighteen minutes. Each kill would require from ten to twenty seconds of irradiation time, depending on the flight profile of the missile being attacked.[33]

A DOD evaluation of this scheme concluded that it could be effective against an attack by as many as one thousand Soviet ballistic missiles. However, this would require a constellation of twenty-five battle stations as opposed to the eighteen proposed by the gang of four. The DOD system would be able to destroy Soviet ICBMs and SLBMs at the rate of about one per second using a 5-megawatt laser in conjunction with a 4-meter mirror.[34]

Under the auspices of Wallop, the briefing was given on several occasions to senators and staffers. The first version of the briefing was presented on 12 October 1979 to eleven congressional staffers, including Codevilla, Crommelin, Frank Gaffney (staff of Senator Jackson), Svenn Kramer (staff of Senator John G. Tower [R-Tex.]), and Ronald Lehman II (staff of the Senate Armed Services Committee). The briefing was generally well received, although some suggestions for changes were offered.[35]

On 27 November, a second version of the briefing was given to ten staffers, seven of whom had attended the earlier session. Two days later, it was given again, this time to DARPA officials, including Tanimoto and Pike; on 30 November, the presentation was given to Senators Wallop, Tower, John W. Warner (R-Va.), and Jake Garn (R-Utah). According to Hunter, the senators "all seemed intrigued, and may well consider doing something, if they can figure out what." Overall, Hunter thought that interest in "an early deployment of space lasers [was] spreading beyond all expectations. It is obviously driven by a perceived American weakness." If this trend continued, Hunter concluded, "we're headed for a replay of the early days of ballistic missiles, with all the turmoil and opportunities."[36]

Another group of senators received the briefing at a luncheon on 5 December. Senators Jackson, Hollings, Wallop, Warner, Daniel P. Moynihan (D-N.Y.), Harrison Schmitt (R-N.M.), William S. Cohen (R-Me.), and Roger W. Jepsen (R-Ia.) attended. The briefing lasted one and a half hours, yet only two of the senators left early.[37]

As Hunter had feared, the briefing upset some members of the DOD. In fact, these officials were "so rankled" that they pressured "those companies funded under laser contracts to keep members of the briefing team out of Washington."[38] Nevertheless, the briefing does seem to have been part of the reason some senators supported additional funding for space applications of lasers in 1980. Wallop proposed an amendment to the authorization bill that would have added $160 million to the $68 million already planned for this area, and Garn proposed adding $60 million. The Senate had "served notice on the Pentagon in the Fiscal 1981 authorization hearings that it wants the space-based laser weapons development accelerated."[39]

THE SENATOR AND THE CANDIDATE

By the summer of 1979, Malcolm Wallop's thinking on strategic defense and his knowledge of the technologies involved had advanced to the point where he felt confident an ABM system could be built that would overcome what was perhaps the major anti-ABM argument used in the two to three years before the signing of the 1972 ABM treaty. Specifically, Wallop believed that defensive technologies had matured enough that it was now cheaper to deploy an ABM system than to overcome the system by merely adding warheads to an offensive force.[40]

Wallop stated this view in a manuscript intended for publication in *Strategic Review*, a leading defense journal published by Arthur G. B. Metcalf's United States Strategic Institute. Before publication the draft article had been sent for comments to several people, including Hunter and Reagan, candidate for the Republican presidential nomination. Both men responded—Hunter with suggested changes and Reagan with supportive remarks.[41]

Wallop's article was published in the fall 1979 edition of *Strategic Review*. In it, Wallop noted that decisions shaping the U.S. strategic force structure in the 1970s and 1980s were made in the 1960s based on the assumption that the Soviets would be content to achieve numerical parity with the United States and would not pursue qualitative improvements that would give them a first strike capability. According to Wallop, these assumptions had proven wrong so that by the time Wallop wrote this article there was "broad agreement in the U.S. strategic community that a small portion of the Soviet missile force is capable of destroying nearly all American land-based missiles in their silos, thereby blunting the United States' capability to inflict retaliatory destruction upon Soviet society." Wallop argued that ABM technology had matured to the extent that it promised to provide a means of defeating ballistic missiles and ending the so-called balance of terror. It was time to abandon the concept of offensive-based deterrence and "turn our attention to the realistic task of affording maximal protection for our society in the event of conflict." In short, it was time to begin developing a ballistic missile defense system.[42]

Wallop believed that the key to deploying an effective missile defense was the use of laser weapons in space, and he described the main elements of such a system. It would include the laser, a mirror for focusing the laser, sensors to pick up targets, computers to develop target tracks, a mechanism for pointing the laser beam, and a communications system to tie tracking and aiming subsystems together. Wallop believed that such a system, composed of about twenty-five laser battle stations (an expression he probably picked up from Hunter) in orbits 800 miles above the earth, could be effective against a Soviet attack and could be in place by the mid-1980s.[43]

With this capability now within reach, Wallop considered it inexcusable that those charged by the Constitution with defending the United States would spend $120 billion for a defense that did not defend. In his view, these officials should be pushing vigorously for a system that "might minimize the catastrophe of war [and] save millions of lives." Given Soviet strategic superiority, the United States must not lose the opportunity to develop an effective ABM system. "Assured Protection would be preferable to Assured Destruction."[44]

About the time Wallop's article was published, he had an opportunity to present his views in person to Reagan when Reagan, accompanied by Senator Paul Laxalt (R-Nev.), visited Nevada on a campaign trip. Wallop joined the two in Las Vegas, and they retired to Laxalt's campsite near Marlette Lake in the Sierra Nevada Mountains. When Wallop presented his ideas about missile defenses, Reagan "seemed quite interested." He advised Reagan that because of advances in defensive technology a strategic defense system could be built that the Soviets could not easily and cheaply overcome by simply adding warheads to their nuclear force structure. Wallop went on to explain the advantage to be gained by basing the new defensive system in space; from this "high ground" the system's lasers would be able to destroy enemy missiles in the boost phase before they dispensed their warheads and decoys. The ability to kill in the boost phase, thereby destroying several warheads with one shot, was the feature that promised to make a new ABM system so much more efficient and effective than the earlier ground-based approach. The idea of a new strategic system that was designed to save lives rather than threaten them appealed to Reagan.[45]

A PRESIDENT FAVORABLY DISPOSED
TOWARD STRATEGIC DEFENSE

Reagan's meeting with Wallop was only one of the factors that made him an advocate of ballistic missile defenses. He had long been interested in strategic weaponry; soon after being elected governor of California in 1967, he had visited the Lawrence Livermore National Laboratory at the invitation of Edward Teller. During his visit, Reagan was briefed on the activities of the Livermore Laboratory, which was involved in preparations for a series of nuclear tests in the Aleutian Islands that were related to the SPARTAN missile program. These tests were to determine the kill effects of a nuclear explosion on missile warheads.[46]

By the time he ran against Gerald Ford in the Republican primary of 1976, Reagan had developed a strong dislike for the concept of offense-based nuclear deterrence, which had become the accepted American strategic doctrine while McNamara was secretary of defense. Reagan compared this doctrine to a situation in which two men attempt to control each other by pointing a cocked and loaded gun at the other's head. If either flinched, they both would die.[47]

During the summer of 1979 as Reagan was preparing for the 1980 presidential campaign, several experiences deepened his displeasure with America's deterrence doctrine and indicated to him that ballistic missile defenses offered a possible alternative to what he considered the insanity of mutual assured destruction. One of these experiences came at the end of July 1979 when Reagan visited the North American Air Defense Command (NORAD) command post deep under Cheyenne Mountain near Colorado Springs. During his visit Reagan witnessed a demonstration of the tracking and display capabilities of the center. Few who watch this demonstration are unmoved as the simulated tracks of missile warheads appear at the top of the display screen and progress rapidly toward theoretical targets in the United States. The impact of the demonstration on Reagan was intensified by his discussions with General James E. Hill, NORAD commander. Wasn't there anything the United States could do to stop the progress of these warheads, Reagan wanted to know. No, replied Hill. Furthermore, Hill continued, even the Cheyenne Mountain center was not likely to survive an attack, for it had been built to withstand a 5-megaton blast, and a Soviet SS-18 missile was capable of delivering a 25-megaton warhead that could "blow away" the NORAD command post. Reagan was sobered by the implications of what he saw and heard. On the plane back to California that evening, he and his aide Martin Anderson talked about the terrible vulnerability of the United States.[48]

Soon after returning to California, Anderson set to work drafting a campaign memorandum that would establish Reagan's position on strategic defense for the upcoming presidential campaign, coordinating his proposal with other key campaign advisers. This memorandum noted that the United States was becoming perilously vulnerable to Soviet nuclear forces and that this situation had produced a sense of unease throughout the country. Because of his reputation as a hawk, it would be politically unwise of Reagan to advocate a large expansion of U.S. offensive forces. However, the development of a ballistic missile defense system as a means of overcoming the nation's vulnerability might have widespread appeal since it concentrated "on making sure that enemy missiles never strike U.S. soil." The memorandum went on to say that such a defensive system would have the additional advantage of providing protection against an accidental missile attack.[49]

It was also in the summer of 1979 that Reagan added Daniel O. Graham to his campaign staff. As noted earlier, Graham had worked with Richard Pipes on the CIA Team B exercise and was by this time becoming a strong advocate for ballistic missile defenses. Graham's ideas on this subject began to coalesce in 1979 while he was writing a book with the help of Angelo Codevilla. Contrary to what its title promised in the context of post-1983 America, *Shall America Be Defended?* contains little information about missile defenses. Graham's thesis was that acceptance of mutual assured destruction by important U.S. officials had resulted in a national security policy that left America essentially defenseless in the event of nuclear war. Under the influence of MAD, the American government had negotiated arms agreements that worked largely to constrain U.S. strategic force development while leaving the Soviets free to pursue their goal of strategic superiority. If achieved, strategic superiority would allow the Soviet Union to win a nuclear war by first disarming the United States and then imposing its will on America.[50]

In his collaboration with Graham, Codevilla had advocated more emphasis on missile defenses to include the use of lasers. Graham, however, was still thinking more in terms of defending the United States with a civil defense system and a strategic nuclear force that could destroy Soviet military targets. As a result, he mentioned strategic defenses only occasionally in *Shall America Be Defended?* For example, noting that the SALT I agreements had allowed the Soviets to halt the deployment of a very promising U.S. ABM system and thereby to constrain America's technical superiority, Graham described how a two-tiered BMD system could be used with a deceptive basing mode for the MX missile to make it virtually impossible for the Soviets to achieve a successful first strike. Graham believed that strategic stability would be enhanced if the United States and Soviet Union deployed strategic defenses and reduced their offensive force structures. In only one place does he mention laser weapons in their strategic defense context.[51]

About the time Graham's book was published, he began the work that led directly to the establishment of his High Frontier organization and the development of a full-blown concept of strategic defense. Over time, Graham drew several people into his efforts to conceptualize a strategic defense system. Included in this group were John Morse; Dr. Peter Glazer of Arthur D. Little Company; Arnold Kramish, a physicist who worked on the first atomic bomb; Fred W. Redding, Jr.; and Robert Richardson. Graham's appointment to Reagan's campaign staff encouraged him to refine his concept of strategic defense, and by the end of 1979 he had concluded that the technological basis for a strategic defense system was near at hand and that the system would most likely take the form of a space vehicle that would serve as a "garage" for kinetic kill vehicles. Once developed, an effective strategic defense system would then serve as the basis for an alternative to the doctrine of mutual assured destruction. Graham would soon have the opportunity to inform the future president of his conclusions.[52]

In February 1980 the focus of the Republican primary campaign shifted to Nashua, New Hampshire, a town of eighty thousand people located near the point where the Merrimack River crosses the New Hampshire–Massachusetts border.[53] On 23 February this picturesque New England town was the scene of a debate between Republican presidential hopefuls. While Reagan had turned the corner in his New Hampshire campaign with a victory in another debate three days earlier at Manchester, the Nashua debate provided the "wildest and most memorable moments of the 1980 election campaign." George Bush had wanted to turn the debate into a head-to-head meeting between him and Reagan by excluding other Republican hopefuls from the event. Reagan strongly objected to Bush's plan and was making his position known during the debate when the moderator, Jon Breen, editor of the *Nashua Telegraph*, which was sponsoring the debate, tried to silence Reagan by cutting off his microphone. Reagan reportedly won the campaign, not to mention the debate, when he angrily responded: "I paid for this microphone, Mr. Green [*sic*]!"[54]

As dramatic as the actual debate was, the most important event with regard to ballistic missile defenses took place the day before in the Nashua motel where the Reagan entourage was resting and preparing for the debate. By this time, Graham was far enough along in his thinking to brief Reagan on his concept of strategic defense. As the general spoke, Reagan listened attentively and took some notes.[55]

Later, the Republicans shaped a platform that reflected Reagan's strategic views. For one thing, it stated that Republicans "reject the mutual-assured-destruction (MAD) strategy of the Carter Administration which limits the President during crises to a Hobson's choice between mass mutual suicide and surrender." Furthermore, a plank in the platform called for the "vigorous research and development of an effective anti-ballistic missile system, such as is already at hand in the Soviet Union, as well as more modern ABM technologies."[56]

In spite of the platform plank and the attention given ballistic missile defense by Reagan and his campaign staff, BMD was not a major issue in the presidential campaign of 1980. While key staff members such as Edwin Meese III and Richard V. Allen supported a new ABM initiative, other advisers, especially Michael K. Deaver and John Sears, believed it would not be wise to make missile defenses a major campaign issue. Such a proposal could complicate the campaign by making Reagan vulnerable to "demagogic attacks from his Democratic opponent."[57]

Following a successful election campaign, Reagan began his presidency as an optimist not worn down by the years of bureaucratic fighting that are often required in Washington to accomplish even the smallest of goals. When criticized for thinking the answers to problems were simple, he replied: "They *are* simple . . . There just aren't easy ones."[58] Here was a man who would look at a problem and say it could be solved regardless of what tired bureaucrats might think.

Upon taking office in January 1981, Reagan and his administration "faced a tangle of economic problems almost as difficult as those of the 1930s. . . . [I]nflation, interest rates, and the projected federal deficit stood at nearly record highs, and unemployment was 7.4 percent."[59] As a result, issues like strategic defense were pushed to the back burner as the new administration concentrated on getting its domestic and economic programs under way.[60]

However, the issue of ballistic missile defense was far from dead. From outside the government, General Graham continued to push for the establishment of an ABM program. As we shall see in the next chapter, the efforts of Graham and his allies began to impinge on the Reagan staff in the summer of 1981. Furthermore, several Reagan advisers who had favored a missile defense program during the campaign were appointed to top White House positions, and in the fall of 1981, with the administration's economic program under way, these advisers began discussing missile defenses during morning staff meetings that were chaired by White House counsel Edwin Meese, who was responsible for the development of policy.[61]

The principals at these meetings were Allen, Reagan's national security adviser; Anderson, White House adviser on economic and domestic matters; and Edwin Harper, an assistant to Reagan who was also deputy director of the Office of Management and Budget. Meese, Anderson, and Allen, at least, had been convinced for some time of the political wisdom of a new ABM program. They had been persuaded by people such as Edward Teller and Daniel Graham that missile defenses were technically feasible. These staffers soon acquired their own technical adviser by inviting Dr. George A. Keyworth, Reagan's science adviser, to join their meetings.[62]

A POLICY VOID

While the Reagan administration concentrated on economic issues, an intragovernmental debate continued over U.S. policy regarding missile defense. Moreover, the situation seems to have become increasingly chaotic, for the collapse of the SALT process at the end of the Carter presidency created a policy void that had yet to be filled. Complicating the situation further was the fact that directed energy weapons in space was an issue on which there was no consensus—the issue polarized both policy makers and technical experts. "No two studies seem to agree on the level of technology or on the requirement for national strategy and policy in developing directed energy weapons."[63] Yet space-based directed energy weapons were the devices upon which many supporters of ballistic missile defenses pinned most of their hopes. Before developments could be pushed more rapidly, a clear national policy was needed. According to one Pentagon official: "The overriding issue is not technology progress but U.S. space warfare doctrine. We are not at the point where Billy Mitchell was in 1921, but we can't go any faster without political and financial support."[64]

Evidence that the Reagan administration was not yet prepared to fill this policy void was provided in January and February 1981 by Caspar Weinberger whom Reagan had designated as his secretary of defense. Just as Weinberger was about to assume his duties, Hedrick Smith reported in the *New York Times* that Weinberger did not believe the renewal of the ABM Treaty was a foregone conclusion. Weinberger noted that the Reagan administration wanted to consider all the ways it might achieve "the kind of deterrence we need." To protect American ICBMs that were becoming vulnerable to a Soviet first strike, the United States might want to consider a more extensive deployment of missile defenses than was permitted by the 1972 ABM Treaty and the related protocol of 1974. "We want to give thought to the effectiveness of protecting—and thereby adding—to [sic] the deterrent that we now have," Weinberger said. One option was to develop a BMD system based upon "later technology." Weinberger supplied no details regarding possible plans to deploy an ABM system.[65]

Three weeks later, Senator William Proxmire (D-Wis.) tried to start a public discussion of the issues raised by LoADS when he asked Tower on the floor of the Senate if LoADS would be required to support the MX basing mode and if so, what were the implications for the ABM Treaty. When Tower declined to answer, Proxmire addressed the same questions in writing to Weinberger during his confirmation hearings for secretary of defense. Weinberger answered in writing: "I think we must look very carefully at ABM technology. An effective ABM system may be needed in the event the Soviets increase substantially the number of their hard target-kill capable warheads. If we were to achieve a significant breakthrough in the ABM area, we might—after extensive study—be able to deploy MX in fixed silos protected by ABM."[66]

Still another indication of the existence of an ABM policy void may be seen in actions being contemplated by the National Security Council in the spring of 1981. At this time the NSC was reported to be considering a major study of ballistic missile defenses that would be conducted under its own auspices. "White House policy decisions on programs, national objectives, and the level of commitment" were expected to flow from this study.[67]

By its nature, bureaucracy is possessed of great inertia, and this characteristic is exacerbated in the absence of a guiding policy and consensus. In the BMD policy vacuum of the early 1980s, the government bureaucracy was grinding to a halt or at best moving at a glacial speed with regard to actions on missile defenses. This was unacceptable to national leaders like Malcolm Wallop who believed the United States was in the midst of a major strategic crisis, and they attempted to jolt the bureaucracy into activity.[68]

Wallop criticized DOD for its recent tendency "to drag out innovation, to be terribly careful, to study problems to death"; he gave the MX missile program as an example. The United States started working on the MX missile about the same time the Soviets had started their SS-18 missile, which was fully deployed in 1980. In addition to the normal, cautious tendencies that marked DOD consideration of new weaponry, laser weapons were being resisted because of a commitment to the doctrine of mutual assured destruction, this in spite of what Wallop considered solid evidence that the Soviets were preparing to fight, survive, and win a nuclear war. According to the Wyoming senator, "[Soviet] programs in ABMs and lasers are several times as big as ours. It makes no sense for us to persist in our foolish concentration on spending money to kill Russians while wholly neglecting preparations to save American lives in the event of war."[69]

Wallop drummed on what he thought was the absurdness of mutual assured destruction, which was preventing the United States from the vigorous pursuit of ballistic missile defenses. As he put it: ". . .[W]e are at a crossroads in this country. We have spent money, dollar after dollar and billions and billions, for weapons whose only consequence is to kill people. Now we have within our capability the possibility of developing weapons whose only real role in the world is to kill the things that kill people."[70]

The cause of Wallop's displeasure was the slow progress being made in the air force program for space-based high-energy lasers. In arguing that the air force should push the development of these devices more vigorously, Wallop noted that Senators Schmitt and Tower had been advised by President Reagan of his interest in the development of laser weapons. Schmitt, a former astronaut, thoroughly supported Wallop's efforts with the air force and stated that Reagan's interest was stimulated by the possible use of these devices in a BMD role. Schmitt stated further that the president fully understood that a technological revolution was afoot that would make available new strategic options. "In the not-too-distant future, [these options would] make weapons of mass destruction obsolete . . . [and] provide a strategic policy option based on the principle of protection of human beings rather than their mass destruction."[71]

Schmitt saw space as the key to the future in much the same way as other advocates of space-based defenses. Just as the drama of the *Pax Britannia* had been played out on the oceans of the world, the future of civilization would be shaped by events in space. As he put it: "The new dramas of our times will be played out in three dimensions in space. While there is great national defense opportunity there, if we ignore the civilized application of space for commercial use we may lose the race after all. We must compete in space on all fronts."[72]

Wallop and Schmitt were joined by Tower and Warner in their efforts to push the air force into a more active R&D program for lasers. These senators succeeded in adding $30 million to the FY 1982 air force budget for the development of space-based high-energy lasers. According to Wallop, the goal of these senators was to create in the air force a constituency for lasers that might become the basis of a space-based defense against ICBMs. Specifically, language in their bill required the air force to establish a program office for airborne and spaceborne lasers and work toward an early demonstration of high-energy lasers in earth orbit. If the air force did not vigorously pursue this laser research, Wallop threatened to have the program shifted to army control. There was also some support for establishing a new military service to take responsibility for space operations, since none of the established services was showing adequate interest. One reason no service wished to become the patron of space weaponry was the fear that these expensive systems would consume resources that could be used for purposes the services considered more important.[73]

The reluctance of the air force to take a vigorous role in missile defenses is indicative of the type of bureaucratic inertia that would have to be overcome to initiate a new missile defense program. This inertia, along with the economic problems faced by the Reagan administration, help explain why no major missile initiative emerged during the first months of Reagan's presidency. Another problem was the absence of an overarching vision that could unite and give direction to such an initiative. In the spring of 1981, one man put forward a broad concept that bid fair to fill this void.

Part Four
Strategic Crisis,
Presidential Response

Conservative Republican Presidents (moderates or liberals need not apply) may be able to open doors to China and secure support for arms control treaties yet be unable to sustain a significant or even stable growth in military spending.

By contrast, liberal or moderate Democratic Presidents may be able to secure support for strategic and conventional modernization (few questioned the need for the MX, Stealth aircraft, Trident submarine, or a Rapid Deployment Force under Jimmy Carter) but will be less able to obtain ratification of arms control treaties.
                                    —*Senator William S. Cohen, December 1982*[1]

Ronald Reagan was a shrewd politician who understood the importance of timing. He was convinced as early as July 1979 that the United States should be defended against missile attacks, yet he did not push this issue in his election campaign for fear of intensifying his image as a Cold War hawk. During the first two years of his presidency, in spite of his belief in missile defenses and the steady importuning of friends and advisers who favored such defenses, he continued to bide his time as he pushed the modernization of America's strategic nuclear forces.

Perhaps the strongest and most persistent advocacy for missile defenses resulted from an alliance between General Daniel Graham and Karl R. Bendetsen. Beginning in the spring and summer of 1981, these two men and the private organizations they led kept steady pressure on the White House to make the deployment of missile defenses a top national priority. Their efforts were reinforced in late 1982 by support for ballistic missile defenses among members of the National Security Council staff, principally Robert C. McFarlane.

Still, Reagan was not prepared to push a new missile defense program until December 1982 when his efforts to modernize U.S. strategic forces were tripped up by the rejection of his dense pack basing plan for the MX missile. Even then he would not pursue such a program without the full support of the Joint Chiefs of Staff whose split vote had crippled the dense pack plan. In early 1983 the JCS adopted a position advanced by Admiral James D. Watkins that called for the development of missile defenses that would become the basis for a new concept of deterrence with greater emphasis on strategic defense. When this unanimous position was briefed to Reagan on 11 February 1983, he knew the time was right for a new strategic initiative. For the next month and a half it was Reagan who steadily pushed his staff to develop the missile defense concept that he presented to the nation in a televised speech on 23 March 1983.

CHAPTER SEVEN

The High Frontier

Bureaucracies are designed to execute, not to conceive.
                                        —*Henry Kissinger, 1957*[1]

DANIEL GRAHAM AND THE ORIGINS OF THE HIGH FRONTIER

Daniel O. Graham had been nicknamed "little dog" by his West Point classmates, a moniker that was derived from his initials and reflective of the fact that he was even then a hard-driving, determined man. By the spring of 1981, Graham and an informal staff had developed a new national strategy that included plans for missile defenses, and Graham was ready to sell it. Members of Reagan's administration had scarcely settled into their new offices when Graham began banging on their doors.

Among the first to receive a call was Edwin Meese, now serving as counselor to the president. Through Meese, Graham secured a meeting with Reagan on 17 February 1981. He advised the president that he had developed further the concept of defense about which he had briefed the president at Nashua and wished to present the idea to Secretary of Defense Caspar Weinberger. A meeting with Weinberger was arranged, and Graham briefed him on the new strategy. But Weinberger had just assumed his new duties and was in the middle of a host of briefings on a wide variety of defense issues and was not especially impressed with Graham's ideas. Weinberger simply asked Graham to keep him advised of any progress he might make in refining his ideas.[2]

Graham also managed to see the new secretary of state, Alexander M. Haig, Jr., and brief him on space-based missile defenses. Graham's briefing may have influenced a State Department study initiated by Haig, who asked for a review of ABM technology (including space-based lasers) and the political and military implications of an ABM system. This investigation was completed in early 1981 by Richard R. Burt, director of politicomilitary affairs at the State Department. The study concluded that attacking ICBMs during their boost phase posed daunting political and technical problems, since this approach to missile defense would require an almost immediate response on the part of the defense and leave little time for the national command authorities to become involved. Such problems made it unlikely that an effective missile defense system could be developed before the end of the twentieth century.[3]

The ideas Graham presented in his briefings to government officials were probably similar to those in an article he had published in the spring 1981 edition of *Strategic Review*. This article drew together a number of the arguments that had been advanced by those favoring a new American missile defense program and laid out a course of action the United States might follow to recapture the strategic initiative from the Soviet Union.[4]

Graham began the article by stating that the Peace through Strength Resolution of the House of Representatives (1980) and the expanded defense budget of the first year of the Reagan presidency, though commendable, were not enough to make up for the years in which the United States had inadequately supported its military forces. Because of this neglect, the Soviets were simply too far ahead in many areas and had too large a production base for America to regain a position of security by trying to produce more of the weapons that were common to the arsenals of both countries.[5]

The strategic balance between the superpowers was of special concern to Graham, and he chose to illustrate the difficulties the United States faced by comparing the state of the Soviet ICBM program with that of America. The Soviets, Graham noted, had far more ICBMs than the United States, and Soviet missiles had greater throw-weights. As the Soviets MIRVed their missiles and improved the accuracy of their warheads, they would achieve a first strike capability against U.S. ICBMs. To prevent this, the United States could build and deploy more missiles, but that would pose two problems. First, the American people

Daniel O. Graham, a West Pointer, had risen to the rank of three-star general when he served as the director of the Defense Intelligence Agency in the first half of the 1970s. After resigning this post in protest over the firing of Secretary of Defense James Schlesinger, he became a campaign adviser to Ronald Reagan. By 1981 he was convinced the United States had to have a strong space program, including missile defenses, to keep the Soviets from dominating space and gaining control of world affairs. He teamed up with Karl R. Bendetsen to form a committee of influential Republicans that recommended a new missile defense program to President Reagan. (Courtesy General Daniel O. Graham)

were unlikely to condone such measures. Second, the United States would lose such a competition, as the Soviets had five operational ICBM assembly lines and the United States had none.[6]

This meant that America could not solve its defense problems by merely pursuing traditional approaches to national security, which Graham lumped under the rubric of the "incremental" or "much-more-of-the-same" approach—adding funds to previously approved but underfunded programs. Instead, the United States should pursue a new strategy that entailed expanding American military forces while searching for ways of "harnessing innovativeness and American technological assets to the pursuit of the 'high ground' of military capabilities." Graham believed that the heart of this new strategy should be the development of space-based defenses. He advanced several arguments in support of this view. First, space operations required extremely sophisticated systems and high technology was America's forte. Second, the competition with the Soviets in strategic arms was where the high technology approach offered the greatest prospect of pay-off.[7]

In further support of his position, Graham pointed to the "enormous advantages" gained by nations that were the first to move into new media with military power, as in the case of those nations that made early use of the airplane to develop a military capability in the air. Graham believed that the time was right for the United States to seize the high ground of space, the next domain for human endeavors. Already, several important activities such as communications were well along in the move to space. Furthermore, "the most impressive means for projecting military power globally," the ballistic missile, passes through space enroute to its target. The rivalry between the United States and the Soviet Union would impel America increasingly into a competition with the Soviets for dominance in space.[8]

Additionally, by moving into space with a defensive system, the United States could greatly complicate the calculations of Soviet strategic analysts when it came to deciding if a first strike was feasible. Graham admitted that no defensive system could ever be perfect, but perfection was unnecessary. Once a defensive system was in place, an attacker could never know which of his warheads would be destroyed and thus which targets would be left undamaged. This meant that the attacker could never be assured of destroying an enemy's retaliatory force. "Such uncertainty is the essence of deterrence," according to Graham.[9]

A defensive system that could provide this uncertainty would consist of a number of manned space cruisers capable of extensive maneuvering and armed with either lasers or projectile-firing weapons. These cruisers could be orbited by a space shuttle or launch themselves into space after being dropped from a Boeing 747 aircraft flying at high altitude. The orbits of these vehicles would be designed to cover regions of space through which Soviet ICBMs were most likely to pass. In time of crisis, the number of space cruisers in orbit could be increased. These space fighters would receive controlling information from satellites in geostationary orbits over the Soviet Union. If the Soviets attacked, space cruisers would be expected to attack Soviet missiles during their boost phase.[10]

To ensure broader dissemination of these ideas, Graham published an almost identical version of his *Strategic Review* article in the May-June 1981 edition of *Signal Magazine*, and an abbreviated discussion of his new strategy appeared in the November edition of *Officer*.[11] Graham also sent a version of his paper to Frank R. Barnett whose National Strategy Information Center specialized in presenting information on defense topics at national security forums offered six or seven times a year. About three hundred national leaders representing Congress, industry, DOD, and the news media normally attended these forums.[12]

Barnett was so impressed with Graham's paper that he invited him to address a forum in May at the Army-Navy Country Club in Arlington. In the audience was Karl R. Bendetsen, a former under secretary of the army and member of the board of directors of the National Strategy Information Center. After Graham's presentation, Barnett invited Bendetsen and Graham to join him for dinner. Graham and Bendetsen discussed the importance of taking the actions outlined in Graham's concept, and before the evening was over, the two had formed an alliance to see that this concept became national policy.[13]

There were two facets to this alliance. First, Graham needed money for the detailed technical study that was necessary to flesh out the concept. Such a study would take up to four months to complete and cost $250,000. Bendetsen agreed to assist in the fund-raising efforts, and he and Graham worked energetically to secure the necessary donations. After Graham sent letters describing his plans to several prominent people, including Joseph Coors and William A. Wilson (both friends and long-time supporters of Reagan) and Richard Scaife of the Scaife Family Charitable Trust, Bendetsen followed up by asking Meese to call these people and recommend they make donations to the High Frontier project, the name adopted for this enterprise. At the end of

July 1981, Meese agreed to call five prospective donors. One of the first donations received was $15,000 from Champion International Corporation (Bendetsen was a retired CEO of this company). However, it was a donation of $100,000 by Gus A. Buder, Jr., a wealthy St. Louis lawyer, that essentially got the project off and running.[14]

As the donors were being lined up, it became apparent that the High Frontier staff would have to have an institutional home in a nonprofit organization so that the donors could receive tax benefits. For some time Graham had been affiliated with the American Security Council Foundation (ASCF). Through its president, John M. Fisher, Graham worked out an arrangement that would allow the High Frontier project to operate under the aegis of ASCF's Wedemeyer Strategy Center, a "publicly supported, IRS 501(c)(3) education and research organization" that was part of Fisher's foundation.[15]

KARL R. BENDETSEN AND
THE HIGH FRONTIER PANEL

The second facet of the Bendetsen-Graham alliance was the former's agreement to form a blue ribbon committee, the High Frontier Panel, to oversee the study effort and ensure that the completed study received a hearing in the Reagan administration that hopefully would lead to the concept becoming official government policy. Recruitment of the panel was essentially complete by the middle of August 1981. Among those Bendetsen selected for the panel were several top Republican supporters, each of whom was known and respected by the president.[16]

Joseph Coors was president of the Adolph Coors Company of Golden, Colorado, and a long-time political supporter and friend of Ronald Reagan. He also held a master's degree in chemical engineering from Cornell University and took pride in his ability to understand technical problems such as those posed by developing a defense against ballistic missiles. He was happy to accept Bendetsen's invitation to serve on the High Frontier Panel.[17]

Jaquelin H. Hume, chairman of Ampco Foods, was a successful California businessman and active supporter of the Republican party. He was also a close friend of Reagan whom he had met in 1965 when Reagan was running for governor of California. Bendetsen met Hume through the Bohemian Club of San Francisco, an all-male club whose membership included a number of influential national leaders.[18]

Karl R. Bendetsen, a former under secretary of the army, heard General Graham speak on missile defenses at a forum sponsored by Frank Barnett. Bendetsen was so impressed that he teamed up with Graham in an effort to convince the Reagan administration to make the vigorous pursuit of missile defenses a part of U.S. national policy. Bendetsen assembled a panel of influential Republicans that vetted Graham's concept. In January 1982 Bendetsen led a delegation of panel members to the White House where he briefed President Reagan on the panel's recommendation for a major new missile defense program. (Courtesy Karl R. Bendetsen)

Hume's connection with Meese, another prominent member of the Bohemian Club, was a major reason Bendetsen wanted Hume on the High Frontier Panel. Through Hume, Bendetsen could assure the High Frontier Panel of easy access to Meese; and through Meese, Reagan's powerful White House counselor, the panel would have access to the president.[19]

Also serving on the panel was William Wilson, who had been a friend of Reagan since the early 1960s when Wilson and his wife had met the Reagans during a dinner party at the home of a mutual friend. The friendship between the Wilsons and Reagans developed through their mutual interest in breeding and riding horses. In 1981 President Reagan appointed Wilson special envoy to the Holy See. When full diplomatic relations were restored with the papacy, Wilson became the first U.S. ambassador to the Vatican since 1867 when Congress severed relations with the papal state.[20]

Another member of the Bendetsen committee was Dr. Edward Teller, a renowned physicist who had helped develop the first atomic bomb and who later played a vital role in developing America's first hydrogen bomb. Teller also had been a driving force behind the founding of the Lawrence Livermore National Laboratory and was active from the beginning in its program. Additionally, he had been involved in various ways with ballistic missile defense since the 1960s. While Teller was serving on the panel, one of his protégés, Lowell Wood, was leading LLNL's project on the X-ray laser, which Teller was following closely.[21]

This project, code-named EXCALIBUR, was an important conceptual breakthrough from the standpoint of ballistic missile defense. After the X-ray laser was demonstrated in principle through experiments conducted by LLNL personnel, it convinced some people that directed energy technology had advanced to the point where it could shift ascendancy in the strategic nuclear realm from the offense to the defense. This was because EXCALIBUR promised the capability to destroy a large number of ICBMs during the boost phase of their flight. Those that leaked through the first defensive line formed by the X-ray lasers would be cleaned up by less powerful chemical lasers. EXCALIBUR excited Teller, and he in turn excited others by explaining the potential of lasers to revolutionize U.S. strategic doctrine.[22]

Although a detailed discussion of X-ray lasers appeared in the 23 February 1981 edition of *Aviation Week*, the government officially remained silent on the device until January 1983 when George Keyworth stated in a speech that the X-ray laser project was "one of the most important programs" in determining America's future defense posture.

Like Lowell Wood, Keyworth was a Teller protégé who had been strongly recommended by Teller for the position of presidential science adviser, an appointment Keyworth received in May 1981. Keyworth also served on the High Frontier Panel, although there was some difficulty at first when Bendetsen listed him on the official stationery as "White House Observer." Keyworth believed this was inappropriate and asked that his name be removed. Nevertheless, he continued to attend meetings of the panel or at least to send a representative.[23]

In addition to these major figures, several other people served briefly on the panel or played relatively minor roles in its activities. These included Dr. Edwin J. Feulner, Jr., president of the Heritage Foundation, a Washington-based public policy institution; Frank Barnett; and General Albert C. Wedemeyer, U.S. Army (Ret.).[24]

THE HIGH FRONTIER PANEL IN ACTION

The High Frontier Panel immediately established a working relationship with the White House. In July, Bendetsen met Meese several times in California where they discussed the High Frontier project. Then, on 28 July 1981, Bendetsen, Teller, and Graham met with Meese to discuss funding efforts. During this meeting, Meese wanted to know how the panel was to be funded and organized and asked for a definitive statement of its purpose. Bendetsen provided this information in a letter to Meese two days later. According to Bendetsen, his panel, supported by the High Frontier staff under the direction of Graham, was to develop "a coherent structure of strategic initiatives which modern technology and fiscal capabilities make feasible." These initiatives would

> include measures for exploitation of space; for assuring its continued availability to us. Space-borne ballistic missile defense and other defense systems which will make possible a break-away from the stultifying constraints and brooding menace of the Mutual Assured Destruction (MAD) syndrome will be put forward. A strategy of Assured Survival for ourselves and our allies would take its place. . . .
>
> The project would have unofficial status, outside of government. Those who participate will be required to use due care to avoid all publicity. If the ultimate recommendations submitted to you are approved, we believe they will present an historic opportunity for

the President to announce a bold, new initiative. Accordingly, premature publicity would be counter-productive.

Bendetsen stated that the High Frontier Panel would have its proposal ready for Meese by 30 November 1981.[25]

Bendetsen's efforts to schedule the panel's first meeting surfaced a dispute that had been festering for about two years between Daniel Graham and John Fisher over Graham's management of the High Frontier project. The situation degenerated to the point where Graham and Bendetsen began seeking another institutional home. On 14 September they initialed a memorandum of understanding with Feulner. The Heritage Foundation would establish a cost center for High Frontier and would charge this account only for direct costs associated with its support of the High Frontier study, which would be identified as a Heritage Foundation project when completed. Finally, to satisfy legal requirements for project oversight, Feulner was appointed a member of the blue ribbon panel Bendetsen had recruited. Fisher ended his ties with High Frontier by resigning from the panel on 30 September.[26]

While the arrangements were being completed with the Heritage Foundation, the panel continued its work. A second meeting was held on 9 September; by mid-September the panel had laid out an ambitious work plan with eight major areas of study. Each area was assigned to one of High Frontier's consulting experts. These experts reported to Graham, who acted as director of the study and served as a member of Bendetsen's committee. Progress reports were to be provided at meetings of the panel scheduled for 23 September and 7 and 20 October. The first draft of the full report was to be completed 3 November with approval of the final version of the report to come on 17 November. One week later, the panel planned to review the finished report and prepare a briefing based on it. The briefing was to be presented to Meese or Reagan on 1 December.[27]

With the panel's schedule now set, it was time to coordinate the plans with Meese and other White House advisers. On 14 September, Bendetsen, Graham, and Teller met in Meese's office with what was essentially Meese's policy staff—Richard Allen, Martin Anderson, and George Keyworth. According to Anderson, these men shared an enthusiasm for ballistic missile defenses and were convinced that an effective defense was technically and economically feasible.[28]

With a few minor exceptions, Bendetsen held the panel to the schedule he coordinated with the White House staff. On 12 October he met again with Meese and some of Meese's policy staff to report on the pan-

el's work and indicated that the panel was finding increasing support
for the idea of a new missile defense program in Congress, NASA, the air
force, DOD, and the CIA. There was also some discussion of calling the
new system the global ballistic missile defense (GBMD) system.[29]

A day-long meeting on 3 November was preceded by a two-hour classified briefing the evening before. Keyworth provided the facilities for
the evening meeting, which was held in the New Executive Office
Building. The following morning, Major General Meyer, who had
served as the army's BMD program manager between November 1977
and June 1979 before he retired, briefed the panel on ABM developments that were likely to occur in the near future. The panel also reviewed several other issues, including civil defense and the provisions
of the 1972 ABM Treaty. During an afternoon executive session chaired
by Bendetsen, panel members reviewed several chapters of the High
Frontier study and examined an outline of the briefing for Meese and
the president.[30]

From the afternoon executive session, a consensus on recommendations for the president emerged. Among the major points of agreement
was the idea that control of space could lead to control of the earth.
Since panel members believed the Soviets were driving for dominance
in space, America must do more in this arena. The top priority should
be developing a system for point defense against ICBMs. These systems
would first be fielded around America's own land-based ICBMs and then
deployed to protect the nation's fifty largest cities. Next would come a
layered defense system with the ability to destroy missiles in their
boost phase, a system that would protect U.S. allies as well as the
United States.[31]

During these early proceedings Hume was something of a doubting
Thomas, raising questions that were answered by Graham and Bendetsen. Among Hume's concerns were how the Soviets would react to U.S.
forces in space, the survivability of a space-based defense system if the
Soviets already had antisatellite weapons, the difficulty of fitting un-
tried elements together into a system and having all things work as
they should, and the apparently limited operational duration of Graham's space cruisers, which carried only one person.[32]

In spite of Hume's worries and other matters of disagreement, by the
end of November the panel had agreed on the contents of a memorandum that was to be presented to President Reagan. On 27 November
(Friday), Bendetsen and Graham briefed Secretary Weinberger on the
status of the High Frontier project. Later the same day, Bendetsen sent
Weinberger a copy of the latest version of the panel's paper for the pres-

ident, asking for an opportunity to discuss its contents on Saturday or Monday. On Tuesday, the two discussed the memorandum by phone. During the conversation, Bendetsen indicated his desire to have Weinberger present when the panel met with the president. The secretary indicated that he would like to attend the meeting, but it was not essential that he do so. Weinberger expressed disagreement only with the memorandum's recommendation that a task force be established to "select systems and formulate programs to implement the urgently required actions identified"; he did not think this was a good idea. The following day, Bendetsen completed coordination of the memorandum with panel members and called Meese to advise him that the panel had completed its work and was ready to report to the president. In a memorandum of the same day confirming the telephone conversation, Bendetsen advised Meese that Weinberger had received a copy of the memorandum and was fully aware of what the panel was recommending.[33]

In his effort to see Meese and ultimately the president, Bendetsen stayed in close contact with Ed Thomas, administrative assistant to Meese. However, the pressures of preparing the FY 1983 budget, the difficulties being encountered by Richard Allen, and a crisis in Poland consumed virtually all the time of the White House staff for the next two weeks. While waiting for his meeting with Meese, Bendetsen continued to review the situation concerning government programs on directed energy weapons and produced a four-page version of the panel's memorandum for the president. On 18 December he showed this abbreviated memorandum to Keyworth during a two-hour meeting. Keyworth agreed with the conclusions and recommendations of the longer memorandum. Also, since Bendetsen had learned that any memorandum going to the president could be no longer than a page and a half, the two men discussed ways to shorten the memorandum.[34]

Later in the day, Bendetsen made an appointment with Thomas to meet with him the next day (Saturday). Also, with the help of Frank Barnett, Bendetsen completed the page and a half version of the memorandum for the president and prepared a short hand-written note for Meese that he attached to the memorandum. In his note, Bendetsen explained that support for some form of strategic defense was growing in both parties in Congress. This support, Bendetsen wrote, "could overtake a presidential initiative which could be enormously popular."[35]

As scheduled, Bendetsen met with Thomas at 10:00 A.M. on Saturday. An hour and a half later, he met briefly with an extremely busy Meese and gave him a copy of the note and memorandum he had finished the evening before. Meese promised to read it the next day and said he would call Bendetsen the following week. The next day Bendetsen prepared a summary of the events of the past two weeks for members of the panel, advising them that they should not expect to see the president before the beginning of the new year. In fact, Bendetsen noted in a somewhat pessimistic tone, he was not sure that the panel would get to present its case to Reagan.[36]

During the first week of January 1982, Wilson and Hume were able to secure a White House agreement for the president to meet with representatives of the High Frontier Panel. On Thursday, 7 January, in the midst of a business meeting in New York City, Bendetsen received a call from Thomas advising him that four members of the panel were to meet the president the next day at 2:00 P.M. for fifteen minutes.[37]

The meeting began on schedule in the Oval Office and lasted five to ten minutes longer than planned. Bendetsen was accompanied by Coors and Hume (Wilson was supposed to have attended but was scheduled to return to Rome that afternoon and could not make the meeting). The president was accompanied by Edwin Meese, James Baker, William Clark, Martin Anderson, and George Keyworth. Bendetsen gave a brief presentation based on the short memorandum he had prepared and handed a copy of the memorandum to Reagan.[38]

The memorandum began by stating that the United States could not hope to match Soviet strategic offensive and conventional forces even if the nation were placed on a war footing. Moreover, there were "strong indications" that the Soviets were about to deploy "powerful directed energy weapons" in space that would allow them to dominate space and the earth. The president was urged to appoint an advisory systems selection task force to choose defensive systems for development and take other actions to ensure the United States had a defense against Soviet weapons. Once this step was completed, a special managerial structure similar to the one used in the Manhattan Project should be established to implement the recommendations of the task force. This course of action would allow the United States to end its reliance on mutual assured destruction and adopt a doctrine of "assured survival." The memorandum also advised the president that the course of action recommended was compatible with the 1972 ABM Treaty, which allowed either party to the treaty to withdraw after giving six months' notice if it believed its "supreme interests" were endangered.[39]

Bendetsen's presentation was followed by a discussion on the special committee and management procedures the panel advocated. Bendetsen stressed the need for urgency in proceeding with the program the High Frontier Panel was recommending. He also stressed the "indispensability of special management arrangements which would remove from regular channels of the departments and agencies the recommended projects."[40]

Bendetsen was optimistic about the outcome of the meeting with the president. He specifically mentioned that he was confident "George Keyworth, the President's Science Adviser, thinks well of our proposals."[41] This was not the case. Three days after the panel met with President Reagan, Meese held a management meeting of his staff. Among those attending were Anderson, Thomas, Keyworth, and Admiral James W. ("Bud") Nance, an assistant to William Clark, Reagan's national security adviser. Keyworth and Nance expressed misgivings about the ideas of the High Frontier Panel, which they thought involved some "very difficult technical aspects." As a result, Keyworth and Nance thought the White House should proceed slowly regarding the panel's recommendations. These two men were directed to examine possible responses and report back to Meese.[42]

Keyworth's role in these events is something of an enigma. Before becoming the president's science adviser, he had worked since 1968 as a physicist at the Los Alamos National Laboratory where he became director of the Physics Division. In his years at the laboratory, he had been involved in the laser fusion program and in nuclear testing in Nevada. Los Alamos personnel had been working on ballistic missile defense projects when Keyworth started work at the laboratory, and they were still at work on BMD problems when he left to join Reagan's staff. Keyworth believed that a missile defense system posed very difficult problems. An ABM system would be expensive to build and very vulnerable if placed in space. As a result, he was skeptical about the feasibility of missile defenses when he came to Washington.[43]

Keyworth's skepticism was upsetting to members of Congress who favored a renewed effort to develop a missile defense system. In November 1981 Senator Wallop sent a letter to White House Chief of Staff James Baker, urging that Keyworth be fired because of his lack of support for a ballistic missile defense system and for stating that the idea of developing a missile defense using DEWs "fundamentally frightened" him.[44]

Bendetsen had reason to know this, for his files contain a copy of an article showing that as late as September 1981 Keyworth opposed using space-based lasers for missile defenses. According to this article, Keyworth had taken note of the strong support for missile defenses in Congress and stated: "It's an area, in my opinion, where there has been a definite lack of expert involvement and, I would say, there have been a lot of unrealistic arguments made for" speeding up the program. To this, Keyworth is supposed to have added:

People don't realize that shooting down a satellite is not too tough. . . . But the really meaningful thing is to shoot down a missile in the boost phase. That is a formidable task and the technology is not in hand today. I would claim that self-pronounced laser experts who claim that it is something that we are a few years away from doing are plain not supported by the scientific and engineering communities. It is nothing better than speculation, and I think it unsound speculation and I have considerable experience in this area.

These statements were made while Keyworth was announcing plans for a Reagan administration review of U.S. space policy that had been originated by Richard Allen and would consider military as well as civilian aspects of the space program.[45]

In spite of his obvious reservations about the feasibility of defending against ballistic missiles, Keyworth had served since September 1981 as White House liaison with the High Frontier Panel and somehow had conveyed to Bendetsen that he supported its goals. Moreover, Keyworth would continue to confer with Bendetsen until the president's March 1983 speech, although there are reasons to believe that Keyworth did not support a major strategic defense program until it was apparent that the president himself was committed to such an undertaking.

SCHISM

The euphoria among panel members following the meeting with President Reagan was punctured by a schism that had begun to unfold in early December. Although the immediate cause of the split was an announcement by General Graham that he intended to publish the study completed under the auspices of the panel, there had been other points of contention virtually from the beginning of the panel's work. For one thing, though Graham had planned to exploit some advanced technology in his High Frontier defensive system, he stressed the use of off-shelf technology to allow the swiftest fielding of the least expensive defense system. Graham's insistence on the earliest possible deployment led some panel members to believe that he was too rigidly committed to "a very specific global ballistic missile defense system." Most members of the panel considered Graham's concept too confining and preferred a more open-ended approach in which the panel would make only general recommendations to the president, including one that called for Reagan to appoint a special board to determine specific system requirements and R&D tasks to restructure the nation's strategic forces to support a defense-oriented strategic doctrine.[46]

Furthermore, at least one specific high technology element in Graham's concept caused considerable tension among panel members: the solar power satellite (SPS). Graham's thinking centered around the economic development of space. Since he believed that SPS promised to be very profitable, it was a lynch-pin element in his vision for the High Frontier project.[47] Teller did not share Graham's enthusiasm. He advised Bendetsen in early September 1981 that Graham was overly optimistic about the power production, cost, and time of availability of SPS. In response to Teller's criticism, Graham advised Bendetsen bluntly that Teller would have to accept the SPS as part of the High Frontier concept or leave the panel. At the same time, Graham indicated that he did not believe that Teller would abandon the panel over the SPS issue. From Bendetsen's perspective, the entire matter was a nonissue, for he recognized that the panel's recommendations to the president would be too general to permit discussion of specific components.[48] Another point of contention between Graham and Teller concerned the space-lift capacity of the United States. Teller did not believe the United States had enough capacity to orbit the equipment that would make up Graham's space-based defense system.[49]

Also, Teller advocated a greater role for X-ray lasers than the others were willing to countenance. This technology needed considerably more work before it could be effective, and Teller wanted the Bendetsen group to assist him in gaining the additional funding needed to push its development. Other panel members opposed this idea for at least two reasons. Graham criticized the system because it would be unable to defend itself. If attacked, a space-based X-ray laser would have to destroy itself or be destroyed; this meant that it was strategically useless. Graham and others on the panel also objected to Teller's system because of its reliance on a nuclear explosion to produce the X-ray lasing. The idea of using nuclear weapons in space was unacceptable from a political standpoint.[50]

All of these were specific issues that could be resolved through compromises among panel members. However, when Graham made clear his intention to publish the High Frontier study, he raised an issue upon which there could be no compromise. Since Bendetsen's 30 No-

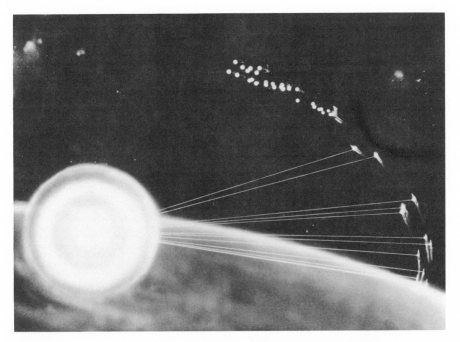

The operational concept for an X-ray laser called for the detonation of a small nuclear charge that would produce lasing in metal rods that could be aimed at individual targets. In the short time before the device destroyed itself, it would produce enough energy, concentrated in its laser beams, to destroy a large number of warheads. This artist's visualization shows the split second in which the nuclear blast and concomitant lasing occur. (Lawrence Livermore National Laboratory)

vember 1981 memorandum to Meese, the panel had been committed to working in private and avoiding publicity. This commitment notwithstanding, Graham was a man used to publicizing his views. From the outset, he had followed a publicist's approach where his own views were concerned, putting forward his arguments for a new U.S. strategy in as many public forums as possible. On the other hand, the existence and work of the High Frontier Panel was kept very quiet, which Bendetsen clearly preferred. The panel was working to develop a concept to present to the president, who was to be free to use the concept as he saw fit. This policy and the rationale behind it were detailed in a set of rules drafted for Bendetsen by Graham and sent to "all participants in Project High Frontier." According to this document, members of the panel were interested in a *Reagan* initiative, not one attributed to *us*. Secondly, we wish not to tip off potential naysayers in and out of government to make it easier to erect obstacles. Therefore all participants must keep our activities and findings within the circle. Publicity must await a Presidential decision one way or the other on our proposals. There is already a fairly high degree of press interest in defense options, especially space options. While the more prominent members of the team may not be able to avoid comment on space options totally, there must be no mention in the press of the make-up of the team, its views, or its genesis, in particular the interest of high Administration officials.[51]

Not surprisingly then, when Graham announced that he would publish the full High Frontier study, he unleashed a maelstrom of protest from panel members. The trouble started in early December 1981 with a letter from Graham to Bendetsen in which the former first made clear his intention to publish a report on the work of his staff. Although Graham had "no serious reservations" about the recommendations the panel would make to the president and his staff, he believed that the two short summaries prepared for this purpose did not adequately cover the complex concepts generated by Graham's staff of thirty consultants. This coverage would require a longer, more detailed report that would have to be published, for Graham had "a legal obligation to some donors (and a moral obligation to all of them) to prepare an end-product, a public document." With Bendetsen's concurrence, the foreword of the published report would "associate the panel with the general thrust of High Frontier concepts" but make no claims that the panel approved the entire published study.[52]

Graham also advised Bendetsen that in addition to the report, the High Frontier staff was preparing a publicity campaign designed to support a presidential announcement of a strategic program based upon the panel's recommendations. This campaign would include a half-hour television documentary, press releases, appearances on talk shows, and speeches in all major cities. Graham made one concession to the panel's requirement for secrecy. He and his staff would "hold our fire as requested to avoid stealing thunder" from the president, but he hinted strongly that this vow of public silence would extend only until the president's State of the Union Address scheduled for 21 January. If the president had not responded positively to the panel's suggestions by that time, he probably would not respond at all.[53]

As part of Graham's effort to prepare the foreword that would credit the High Frontier Panel for its work, he asked panel members for photographs and biographical information. When Jaquelin Hume received the request, he was most upset and immediately contacted Bendetsen and reminded him that a specific prerequisite for his service was that he would not be identified in any way with the work of the panel. Moreover, the value of the panel to the president would be "substantially reduced" by any publicity. Therefore, if publicity was planned, Hume would immediately resign from the panel.[54]

Bendetsen was also upset with Graham and tried to persuade him not to publish the report. He argued that there was no way to separate the High Frontier Panel from the work of Graham's staff. Therefore, Graham should publish nothing until he had the concurrence of all members of the panel. Bendetsen also chided Graham for even preparing a publicity campaign before the president had time to respond publicly to the recommendations the panel planned to make to him. Such actions risked a leak that could undermine the work of the panel. He specifically disagreed with Graham's view that the president would be able to respond to the panel's recommendations by the time of the State of the Union Address.[55]

At Bendetsen's request, Graham addressed Hume's concerns. His letter was conciliatory but not submissive. He assured Hume that nothing would be published before the president had an opportunity to respond to the panel's recommendations and that no panel member would be named in a publication without that member's consent. Nevertheless, he made it clear that he was going to publish the High Frontier study: "We will publish our Project Report at some juncture. I am legally bound to do so by accepting over a quarter million dollars in . . . tax-free donations. This must by law be used for 'public education.' Thus there can be no question of not publishing at all."[56]

Graham sent copies of this letter to all members of the panel and continued to maintain that he had a legal obligation to publish a report in spite of strong urgings to the contrary from panel members. Bendetsen's appeals were among the strongest of these. He had been an attorney before becoming a corporate executive and now advanced legal arguments as to why Graham was not obligated to publish a report. He reiterated that Graham could not publish without the consent of all members of the panel, adding that Graham would also need the permission of the Heritage Foundation. Moreover, during his meeting with the president, Bendetsen had promised him that all members of the panel were committed to secrecy until the president made a decision, at which time panel members would support that decision. If the president rejected the recommendations of the panel, its members were pledged to remain silent. In a similar vein, Teller asked Graham to assure him that "no further thought or affirmative steps toward any publication" would be taken before panel members had time to consider the issue, for the appearance of a public document "would have most unfortunate consequences and could well compromise, if not greatly diminish, what might otherwise have been the benefits of a dramatic Presidential initiative." Hume told Graham that he was "strongly opposed to any publicity about the panel, its members, its work, or its conclusions." The sole purpose of the panel was "to develop recommendations which might be useful to the President." Finally, Wilson informed Graham that he agreed with Bendetsen because of the power of Bendetsen's arguments against publishing and because of the "sensitive nature of some of the material."[57]

By March 1982, when the High Frontier study was published, Bendetsen was thoroughly disillusioned with Graham. In a letter to John Fisher, he wrote: "I have traversed an exceedingly painful series of subsequent events in which Dan Graham, in another role which I had not before observed, carried forward with his own unilateral objectives. His actions have shocked a majority of the members of the High Frontier Panel."[58]

GRAHAM GOES IT ALONE

In early 1982, Graham was perfectly prepared to pursue his own goals regardless of what other panel members thought. He was convinced that if the case for the High Frontier concept was not made to the public, the Washington bureaucracy would strangle the infant idea in its cradle. Furthermore, Graham was quite miffed that he had not been included in the meeting with the president on 8 January. His final answer to the calls for silence was made clear in early February with the announcement in *Air Force Magazine* that the High Frontier study was about to be made public. The story noted that the project had been "aided by the ready access to the White House of some of its politically prominent members" and presented a general description of the global ballistic missile defense system that was a central feature of the High Frontier program. The article also described criticism of the proposal from the Pentagon and "Congressional defense experts." After reporting the High Frontier cost estimate for the system ($5.2987 billion), the article stated:

Defense Department analyses suggest that, not counting ancillary C^3 and other support equipment or operational and life-cycle costs, that figure would be $300 billion, and that the underlying technology is "one vugraph deep" and unencumbered by practical engineering considerations or the laws of physics. Congressional defense experts, nevertheless, are concerned that "Project High Frontier" will turn into a successful media event and weaken support for such "mundane" components of the administration's strategic force modernization package as a survivably based MX and the D-5 SLBM.[59]

About the same time, as if to underscore his intentions to publish, Graham sent Bendetsen an advance copy of his High Frontier study.[60]

In fact, Graham's determination to publicize the High Frontier concept should not have surprised Bendetsen and his panel. From the beginning, Graham had played the role of outspoken public advocate for High Frontier ideas and had done so more or less continuously and independently of Bendetsen's efforts with the Reagan administration. His article in the spring 1981 *Strategic Review* and his subsequent presentation before a meeting sponsored by Frank Barnett's National Strategy Information Center had brought Graham and High Frontier to Bendetsen's attention. The précis of Graham's concept that appeared in the November 1981 edition of *Officer* called on President Reagan to take advantage of a historic opportunity to use America's high technology for a bold move into space that could shift the world away from mutual assured destruction to a world dominated by "assured survival."[61]

Even as he argued with Bendetsen about whether or not to publish the High Frontier study, Graham was continuing his independent stumping for the project. Shortly after the panel's meeting with the president on 8 January 1982, Washington was gripped by one of its worst winter storms in years. The snow started the morning of January 13 and had the city tied in knots by the afternoon. As always, there were numerous automobile accidents around the metropolitan area. At 4:00 P.M an Air Florida jetliner with over seventy people on board took off from National Airport in the blinding snowstorm. Because of improper de-icing, it was unable to climb and struck the northbound span of the Fourteenth Street bridge, killing all but a few people on the plane. National Airport was closed until 8:00 P.M. Thirty minutes after the aircraft accident, there was a major derailment of a Washington Metro subway train near the Federal Triangle in downtown Washington.

Three people were killed, and two of the Metro system's lines were blocked for several hours.[62]

Before the snowstorm started, Harry Goldie, Boeing's "top aerospace engineer," arrived in Washington. Unknown to Graham, Boeing had assigned Goldie to head up a team to evaluate Graham's concept of missile defense, and Goldie had come to Washington to brief him on the results of the study. During the briefing, which took place the morning of 13 January, Goldie advised Graham of his conclusion that with minor adjustments Graham's system could destroy up to 95 percent of the ICBM force the Soviets could launch against the United States. The Boeing study was a breath of fresh air to Graham; the Pentagon's strong opposition to his ideas was beginning to discourage the High Frontier staff. Graham immediately asked if Goldie would be willing to brief Keyworth and Dr. Richard DeLauer, under secretary of defense for research and engineering. Goldie agreed.[63]

As a veteran of the Washington bureaucratic mill, Graham knew the snowstorm raging over the city that day would play havoc with the schedules of government leaders. People could neither get into nor out of the city. Some officials would be unwilling to travel about Washington due to hazardous road conditions. This meant openings in calendars that ordinarily would be filled for a week or even several weeks ahead. The storm created a window of opportunity, and Graham took advantage of it. He quickly secured meetings with Keyworth and DeLauer, and Goldie, accompanied by Graham, briefed both men. Later events indicate that Goldie's briefing did not convince either man of the efficacy of ballistic missile defenses.[64]

Graham met again with Keyworth on 8 February, the same day he sent a prepublication copy of *High Frontier* to Bendetsen. James Jenkins of Meese's office was also present. Graham gave Jenkins a copy of the same document and explained his timetable for publication. Neither Keyworth nor Jenkins expressed opposition to Graham's plans.[65] This was just after *Air Force Magazine* had announced the pending publication of the study.

A month later, *High Frontier: A New National Strategy* was published. It was essentially the same study Graham and his staff had prepared under the supervision of Bendetsen's panel and constituted the full, detailed conceptual underpinning for the short briefing paper the panel delivered to the White House. In response to the preferences of panel members, Graham did not mention their activities. In the foreword, he did thank Bendetsen for his support of the High Frontier pro-

ject but made no reference to Bendetsen's role as chairman of the High
Frontier Panel.[66]

In *High Frontier*, Graham and his staff argued that the West faced a
strategic crisis that had both an economic and a military dimension.
Where the latter was concerned, growing Soviet military power was
threatening to undermine the West's ability to deter nuclear war and
restrain Soviet aggressiveness. This dangerous military situation was
coupled with a Soviet drive to achieve economic hegemony by dominating space. Once the Soviets controlled space, they could dominate its
commercialization just as the Europeans had dominated international
commerce in the nineteenth century.[67]

The solution to both facets of this strategic crisis was a bold new
strategy based on an exploitation of space that would produce a syner-
gistic relationship between military and commercial activities similar
to that which developed in the early modern period when Europeans
used their navies and merchant fleets to control world trade. The commercialization of space would entail cooperation between the government and the private sector to develop the infrastructure that would be
required for the economic development of space. Once in place, this infrastructure would support commercial enterprises and the government activities needed to protect these enterprises. The cost of the infrastructure and government operations would be offset by the jobs,
wealth, and tax revenues generated by economic activities in space. By
the year 2010, space ventures could add as many as 3.8 million jobs to
the U.S. economy and generate tax revenues of $40 billion. Total reve-
nues from "industries in orbit" could represent from 4 to 6 percent of
America's gross national product.[68]

Given the world's insatiable appetite for energy, power production
would play a major role in the economic development of space and
promised to be one of the most lucrative of space industries. The *High
Frontier* study called for power to be produced by solar power satellites.
These satellites would be composed of a huge solar array and a trans-
mitter that would beam the power to earth via microwaves. The satellite's antenna would be 3,000 feet in diameter and would transmit to an
elliptical antenna on earth that was 5 miles long and 4 miles wide.
Such a system would produce 5,000 megawatts of power and deliver 1.6
trillion kilowatts over a forty-year period. As an example of the demand
that such a technology would meet, the report stated that by 2010 In-
dia could use seventy-five of these satellite systems.[69]

Eventually, cooperation in space between government and industry
would contribute to the development of a defense against ballistic mis-

siles, and such a defense was the best Western response to growing Soviet military power. *High Frontier* called for the deployment, in phases, of a multi-tiered missile defense system. Because of the gravity of the strategic situation in 1982 and the fact that it would be some time before high technology space systems could be used to defend the United States, the study recommended the immediate development of a terminal defense system in which a number of "swarmjet" launchers would be deployed to protect hardened ICBMs. Each launcher would hold five hundred to one thousand small projectiles that would be fired in a shotgunlike blast to destroy an attacking warhead at a range of about 4,000 feet. This phase of the missile defense system could be completed within two to three years.[70]

The second stage of the defense would be a global ballistic missile defense system that could defend the United States and its allies. The GMBD would be a network of over four hundred orbiting space "trucks," each carrying between forty and forty-five kill vehicles controlled by their mother vehicles. The orbits of the trucks would permit them to attack Soviet ICBMs during their boost, postboost, and late midcourse phases. Depending on national priorities, this network of trucks could be deployed in five to six years at a cost of $12.6 billion. Improved infrared sensors would be added later to enhance the performance of the GMBD. This improvement would cost about $5 billion and could be deployed in about eight years.[71]

In several years, High Frontier's BMD system could be improved still further with the addition of high performance spaceplanes that would cost less than $500 million apiece. These manned vehicles would perform such tasks as inspecting objects in space, defending satellites and space stations, and retrieving satellites. The study also discussed possible improvement of the GMBD by the addition of ground-based lasers operating through space-based pointing systems. However, Graham and his colleagues were not particularly sanguine regarding the role of directed energy weapons in missile defenses. Although DEWs showed promise in the laboratory and possessed the potential to change the world's balance of power, operational weapons of this kind were too far in the future "to meet the urgencies of the High Frontier study." The United States should support a vigorous R&D program to ensure against a Soviet breakthrough in the area of DEWs but should not stake the future of its own missile defense program on such a breakthrough. All the requirements of High Frontier's multi-tiered defense could be met without a breakthrough in beam weaponry or in any other technical area.[72]

From the standpoint of national security, the wisdom of Graham's "bold new strategy" was that it would allow America to take advantage of its superiority in high technology to turn a strategic flank of the Soviet Union. The United States no longer had the industrial base to out-produce the Soviets where weapons based on conventional technology were concerned. On the other hand, in space, America's strong base in high technology would give it a decisive edge.

Our best hope is to change our strategy and to move the key competition into a technological arena where we have the advantage.

A bold and rapid entry into space, if announced and initiated now, would end-run the Soviets in the eyes of the world and move the contest into a new arena where we could exploit the technological advantages we hold. This is far preferable to pursuing a numbers contest here on Earth, which will be difficult if not impossible for us to win.[73]

An effective defense against ballistic missiles would go beyond restoring the strategic balance between the United States and the Soviet Union; it would also provide the basis for a shift away from the doctrine of mutual assured destruction to one of assured survival. Such a shift in doctrine could inspire Western peoples to renew their flagging commitment to defense.[74] Overall, then, the High Frontier project was nothing less than an effort to create a new grand strategy for the West. In the eyes of Graham and his colleagues, this strategy promised to revitalize the economies of the West while revolutionizing and rejuvenating its defenses.

The publication of *High Frontier* produced a number of opportunities for publicity. About the time the study came out, the *Washington Post* carried a story describing the concept as a "10-year, $50 billion project [that] could reduce a Soviet attack 'by 95 percent or better.'" The article reported the opinions of Pentagon officials who had read the study and believed it contained some solid information as well as "Star Wars stuff."[75] In the second half of 1982, several journals carried discussions of High Frontier concepts and interviews with Graham. *Defense Science 2000+* printed the entire fifteen-page summary that introduces *High Frontier*.[76] *Government Executive* published a speech Graham had given in February at Hillsdale College, Hillsdale, Michigan, in which he outlined the High Frontier concept.[77] And in October, *Defense Electronics* carried an interview in which Graham discussed the multitiered defense system and explained what it meant to turn a strategic flank of the Soviet Union by moving energetically into space.[78]

THE PANEL CONTINUES ITS WORK IN PRIVATE

While Graham was publicly pushing the High Frontier concept, Bendetsen and members of his panel kept silent as they waited for the president to announce the beginning of the program they had recommended to him. In the wake of their January meeting with Reagan, members of the panel believed that he would move swiftly on their recommendations and that the publicity Graham threatened to generate would undermine the resulting presidential initiative. The president himself encouraged this view by advising Bendetsen that he had spoken to Meese, Keyworth, and Weinberger about "following up" on the panel's recommendations. Reagan assured Bendetsen that "we will be moving ahead rapidly with the next phase of this effort."[79] But as several weeks slipped by with no apparent White House action, panel members began to believe that their efforts to win swift government action on the High Frontier program were being undermined by opposition within the Reagan administration. They also had second thoughts about the panel's policy of eschewing publicity.

One of the first hints of trouble came in mid-February when Hume attempted to call William Clark to find out what was being done on the panel's recommendations. He was unable to reach Clark and spoke instead to Bud Nance, deputy assistant to the president for national security affairs. Although Nance advised him that the White House planned to appoint a "blue ribbon task force" as recommended by the panel, Hume concluded from this conversation that "nothing concrete" had been done since the meeting with the president a month earlier. He recommended that Bendetsen also call the White House in an effort "to keep ABM on the front burner."[80]

Toward the end of February another indication of trouble reached Bendetsen. This was a memorandum reporting the results of Graham's 8 February meeting with James Jenkins and George Keyworth. In addition to indicating that these White House staffers expressed no opposition to Graham's publication plans, it reported that a presidential decision on a strategic defense program was still months away. Keyworth had been directed to develop a strategic defense program of his own, and his timetable called for completion of this effort near the end of 1982.[81]

Still panel members held to their vow of silence and continued their efforts to rein in Graham. Following the publicity generated by the publication of Graham's *High Frontier*, Ambassador Wilson chided Graham for pulling the rug from under the panel's efforts and alerting the Soviet Union to what U.S. leaders might be thinking. Graham defended his publicity campaign by stating that the published report had generated a positive response in Congress and the bureaucracy. He also reminded Wilson of the panel's own concerns that prompt action was required on their recommendations to the president. As Graham put it: "I think it is the propitious time for the Administration to cut across the parade ground and get in front of the parade we are creating."[82]

A month later, there was still no indication of any definite White House action on the panel's recommendations and panel members began to look for ways to energize the Reagan administration. At the end of April, Hume sent Bendetsen a copy of the March 1982 *Washington Report*, which contained an article by Representative Ken Kramer (R-Colo.). In this article, Kramer called for the establishment of a space command and the deployment of military space systems that could defend the U.S. homeland. Kramer's phraseology was reminiscent of Graham's *High Frontier*. In the letter that accompanied the copy of Kramer's article, Hume said he did not believe the White House was going to act on their recommendations and asked Bendetsen if they should not support Kramer in an effort "to build a fire under the Administration?" In his response, Bendetsen said that he shared Hume's "disappointment concerning what appears to be total inaction with respect to our urgent recommendations" of 8 January and indicated that he would be happy to join Hume in "any well considered effort to 'build a fire under the administration.'"[83]

In early May, Bendetsen and Hume received identical letters from Keyworth; here was an indication that their phone calls and Graham's publication of *High Frontier* might have broken the White House logjam blocking action on a missile defense initiative. "Now that the *High Frontier* report has been disseminated," Keyworth wrote, "I want to make you aware of some action we are taking that is commensurate with the conclusions of that study." For one thing, a panel of the White House Science Council had been established "to urgently examine the issue of new military technology." The panel was headed by Dr. Edward Frieman, vice president of Science Applications Incorporated, and included Edward Teller, David Packard, Solomon J. Buchsbaum, Harold M. Agnew, Robert Hunter, William A. Wierenberg, Gregory Canavan, and Charles Townes. The first focus of the Frieman Committee, Keyworth said, would be "non-conventional weapons, including potential space-based ballistic missile defense systems."[84]

Although this committee concluded that technology was not likely to offer President Reagan any major new options in the strategic realm, it did note that lasers showed considerable promise as missile defense weapons. Moreover, Teller was able to persuade the group to recommend further study of the X-ray laser. Also highlighted by the committee was the development of an "adjustable beam-directing mirror" that could compensate for turbulence in the atmosphere while focusing a laser beam on a target. These mirrors were composed of "compensating actuators" that could be moved rapidly to change the shape of the mirror, thereby making small, rapid changes in the direction of the beam.[85]

Keyworth later claimed that the Frieman Committee's findings on atmospheric compensation constituted a turning point in his thinking about strategic defense. As a former official of the Los Alamos National Laboratory and a member of the White House staff, he had been wrestling for some time with the problem of strategic force modernization. This included considering the role of strategic defense in national security. His major objection to using lasers in a missile defense system was that the lasers would have to be placed in space because without the ability to compensate for the effects of the atmosphere, a laser beam would be dispersed by the air and lose its destructive power. If they were placed in orbit to overcome the atmospheric problem, they would be vulnerable to Soviet antisatellite weapons. With the new compensating mirror, the heavy and expensive part of a laser could be left on the ground where it could be defended and easily maintained. Now Keyworth began to believe that lasers might be used to develop a defense that could at least improve the survivability of America's ICBMs, thereby making a Soviet first strike more problematic and therefore less likely.[86] Nevertheless, Keyworth still harbored doubts about the feasibility of ballistic missile defenses.

Both Hume and Bendetsen considered Keyworth's science committee a response to their proposal that the president appoint a blue ribbon panel to initiate a national strategic defense program. According to Hume, Keyworth's committee was "exactly what we recommended." Bendetsen was a little more cautious in his appraisal, saying only that "this panel was established in a somewhat modified response to the recommendation we submitted to the president for the appointment of a Systems Selection Task Force."[87]

Between May and October, Bendetsen queried White House staff members who had attended the 8 January meeting with the president about what action was being taken on the panel's recommendations to the president. During this time, there were indications that the Reagan government was working on a space policy that would include provisions for missile defenses. However, these indications and what he learned from the White House staff did not reassure Bendetsen, who continued to believe that the administration had not really responded adequately to the panel's recommendations. As a result, he decided in early October to reconvene the High Frontier Panel to consider a new initiative that might "prod" the government into action.[88]

The other panel members were agreeable, and the meeting took place on 21 December in the board of directors room of Northrop Corporation in Los Angeles. In addition to the regular panel members (Bendetsen, Coors, Hume, Wilson, and Teller), two other people attended: George Keyworth and Wesley Glenn Campbell, a director of the Hoover Institution and member of the President's Foreign Intelligence Advisory Board, who was invited at the suggestion of Teller.[89]

During the meeting, the panel agreed to provide the White House with draft remarks for inclusion in the president's 1983 State of the Union Address. As with the position paper provided the president a year earlier, Bendetsen took the lead in preparing the comments the president was supposed to use in announcing plans for the United States to deploy a missile defense. Bendetsen's State of the Union insert started with remarks about the tremendous technical advances of recent years, noting that *Time* magazine had just selected the home computer for its Man of the Year award. It then stated that breakthroughs in classified areas of research and development would soon place at America's disposal the means to defend itself against nuclear attacks. The insert called for the nation to deploy an ABM system to defend the MX missiles in whatever basing mode they were deployed. This would be the first step away from the doctrine of mutual assured destruction and would be followed by an expansion and improvement of the missile defense system to protect the nation's cities against nuclear warheads. This expansion of the system would complete the transition from the "anachronistic doctrine of MAD" to a doctrine of assured survival.[90]

At the end of December, Bendetsen sent copies of the proposed insert to those who had attended the Northrop meeting. He received several suggested changes from Teller, who considered the draft too long and did not like Bendetsen's reference to classified areas of research. President Reagan, Teller wrote, "has been criticized for overemphasizing secrecy." Therefore, such a reference in a Reagan State of the Union Address could be "counterproductive." Teller rewrote the first part of the insert, eliminating its references to classified research.[91] Bendetsen also sent copies of the suggested insert to Keyworth and Anthony Dolan (Reagan's speech writer) in the hope that they would see that the panel's comments were inserted in the president's State of the Union Address. However, these efforts were for naught, as other members of the White House staff would not allow the insert to be used.[92]

Nevertheless, by this time the stage was set for a major new presidential initiative in national strategy. The president disliked the prevailing U.S. strategic doctrine of assured destruction and had heard from several sources that advances in technology meant that defense against ballistic missiles was becoming feasible. Furthermore, from some of his oldest and most trusted friends he had received strong recommendations for a policy initiative that would not only provide a defense against ballistic missiles but also offer the nation the prospect of shifting away from mutual assured destruction to assured survival. In early 1983 Reagan's professional military advisers added their voices to the chorus calling for a shift in national strategy.

CHAPTER EIGHT

The Presidential Decision

An invasion of an army can be resisted, but not an idea whose time has come.

—*Victor Hugo,* Histoire d'un crime, *1852[1]*

On Tuesday, I think, I called Jay Keyworth, who was Science Adviser to the President whom I had not yet brought into the picture. I asked him to come over and see me. He did and was a little bowled over with the suddenness of it, but he said he agreed that it was an idea whose time had come.

—*Robert C. McFarlane, 15 September 1987[2]*

The focus of Bendetsen's recommended remarks for the State of the Union Address indicates a connection between the effort to find an acceptable basing mode for the MX missile and the resurgence of ballistic missile defense during the Reagan administration. This indication is strengthened by the fact that the basing mode crisis was the catalyst that induced the JCS and other important national security advisers to support a renewed effort to develop defenses against ballistic missiles.

According to several conservative leaders, the SALT process had failed to produce adequate restrictions on Soviet offensive strategic forces. As a result, in the early 1980s the Soviets were on the verge of achieving a first strike capability against America's ICBMs. In spite of such dire assessments, when the Reagan presidency began, the United States had no plans to defend its existing missiles and had not begun fielding the

MX missile, which was supposed to offset gains in Soviet offensive power.

The search for a secure and politically acceptable basing mode for the MX missile had stretched across three presidencies by the time it came to a head at the end of 1982. Finding such a basing mode proved to be a wrenching experience for the Reagan administration. It brought key officials face-to-face with the fact that it would be exceedingly difficult to generate political support for any attempt to upgrade America's offensive deterrent force despite steady improvements in the Soviet ICBM fleet.

In a sense, the MX basing issue represents what Thomas S. Kuhn has referred to as a paradigm crisis in his classic work, *The Structure of Scientific Revolutions*.[3] The old pattern of thinking about strategic nuclear systems and how to deter nuclear war seemed to be breaking down as the United States failed to reach a national consensus on a response to improving Soviet strategic forces. This experience opened a number of minds to the idea that it was time for a fundamental reevaluation of America's strategic policies to include reviewing the role strategic defense might play in assuring the continued deterrence of nuclear war. One of those with a sense of this crisis and its implications for American strategic policy was President Reagan.[4]

THE MX MISSILE DURING
THE CARTER ADMINISTRATION

Although the need for a missile to replace the MINUTEMAN had been recognized in the 1960s, it was not until 1971 that the Strategic Air Command established the actual operational requirements for what became the MX missile. In planning for the MX, the air force considered several basing options but by early 1976 had come to favor some form of multiple-shelter basing mode with the MX deployed in MINUTEMAN silos until a permanent basing mode could be established.[5]

During the Carter administration, it became apparent that the United States would have to field a new strategic missile. In August 1978 Secretary of Defense Harold Brown convinced President Carter that deployment of the MX was dictated by improvements in the accuracy of Soviet MIRVs. But while Carter agreed to proceed with development of the MX, he did not select a specific basing mode for the missile until 7 September 1979 when he announced that the MX would be deployed in a deceptive basing mode. Under this scheme, each of two

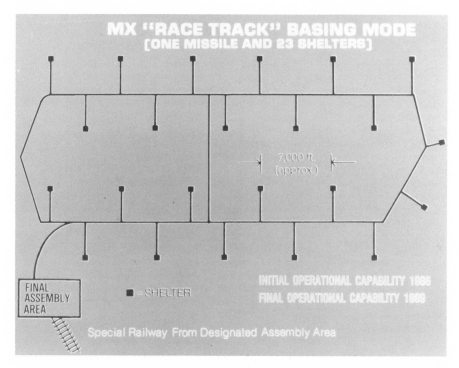

This diagram shows the layout of a "race track" complex that would support a single MX missile. If the United States had deployed the MX missile in this basing mode, two hundred of these complexes would have been constructed in the southwestern United States. (Photo 342-KE-70574, National Archives)

hundred MX missiles would be based in a complex of twenty-three shelters, with the missile being shuttled between the shelters in such a way that the Soviets could not know the missile's location. Each shelter complex would cover about 25 square miles and ideally would be placed in a valley so it would be isolated from other shelter complexes. The entire MX force would be deployed in a remote desert area in Nevada and Utah.[6]

Carter's plan, known as the multiple protective shelter (MPS) system, generated opposition in the Southwest. In February 1980, Senators Orrin Hatch (R) and Jake Garn of Utah and Paul Laxalt and Howard F. Cannon (D) of Nevada protested against the basing mode in a letter to President Carter. They noted that there was strong opposition to the proposed basing mode in Congress and in the states where the missiles would be located because of the extensive social and environmental ef-

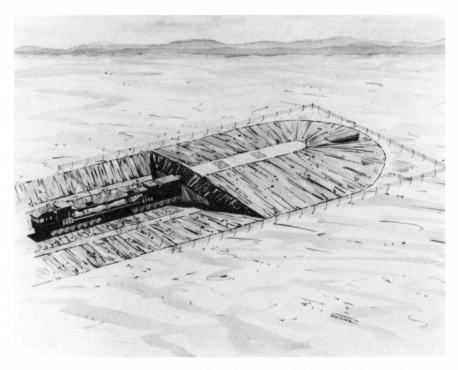

This artist's drawing shows one of the twenty-three horizontal shelters that would make up each race track complex. The transporter shown at the entrance of the shelter would have been used to shuffle an MX missile between the shelters to create uncertainty in the minds of Soviet strategic analysts attempting to target U.S. ICBMs. The two squares in the top of the shelter were ports that could be opened when Soviet satellites passed overhead so that the Soviets could confirm that the total number of MX missiles deployed did not exceed the number allowed under arms control agreements. Of course, the missiles would have to be moved as soon as the confirmation process was completed. (Photo 342-KE-71570, National Archives)

fects expected from the MX deployment. The senators called for Carter to abandon MX and develop a new missile that could be based in some mode other than the MPS. Nevertheless, Carter stood by his decision and stated that the MPS basing mode was "the best solution to the ICBM vulnerability problem."[7]

Opposition to the basing plan continued through the summer of 1980 and was reflected in two proposals for anti–MX missile planks in the Democratic National Convention in New York. After a special appeal from President Carter to convention delegates, the two proposals were defeated.[8]

In spite of this opposition, Carter was able to secure passage of a bill providing $1.5 billion in FY 1981 for the MX missile based in the MPS mode. This measure also provided for the study of a "split basing" mode where only part of the MX missile force would be deployed in the Great Basin of the Southwest. The bill did stipulate that the study of a split basing alternative was not to delay the operational date of the MX system. Furthermore, if split basing was found by the air force not to be feasible, all the missiles could be placed in the Great Basin. This measure was signed into law on 8 September 1980.[9]

As deployment activities began, the MX missile became a major national issue. It was widely covered in national newspapers, journals, and on national television shows such as "The MacNeil-Lehrer Report," "60 Minutes," and "Bill Moyers' Journal." Several small citizens groups opposed to deployment in the Great Basin were formed in the Southwest. These groups were supported by larger national organizations such as SANE, Friends of the Earth, and the Union of Concerned Scientists.[10]

In Utah, Governor Scott M. Matheson and state government strongly opposed the deployment on environmental grounds and because of the effects the project might have on the state's economy. Furthermore, on 5 May 1981 the leadership of the Mormon church announced its opposition to the MX deployment. President Spencer Kimball and two other elders of the church attacked the nuclear arms race and the decision to base the MX in the Southwest. This placed a disproportionate share of the burden for nuclear war on one part of the country. From this point on, the statements of Utah's political leaders consistently indicated opposition to the MPS deployment in the Southwest.[11]

In Nevada the opposition to the MX deployment was considerably weaker. Although Governor Robert List was cooperative with air force officials working to get the MX base structure started, he expressed serious concern about the project in a letter to President Carter. In early November 1980 List advised Secretary of Defense Brown that he and Governor Matheson were committed to supporting the MX deployment, but that they intended to conduct studies to ensure that social, economic, and environmental damage was minimized.[12]

On 1 December 1980 the air force released its draft environmental impact statement (EIS). It was a massive document of nineteen hundred pages that cost $17 million to complete. It was thoroughly scrutinized by the Nevada government in a review program established by List. This involved an examination of the EIS by thirty-one different state teams, which involved the work of 387 people. In the end, the review teams concluded that the air force EIS was fundamentally flawed. Of special concern was the inability of the air force to specify how much land the MX system would require.[13]

THE MX AND REAGAN'S
STRATEGIC MODERNIZATION PROGRAM

The battle over the MX and its basing mode was part of the backdrop of the 1980 election campaign, and it continued into Reagan's first term in office. During the campaign, candidate Ronald Reagan expressed reservations about the MPS basing mode. His concerns were intensified by the fact that the MX issue had polarized the people of Utah and Nevada by the time he took office. Moreover, the MX had become a particularly nettlesome issue in Congress where the opposition included conservative senators and representatives whose votes were needed to implement Reagan's budgetary plans. It is not surprising then that President Reagan decided to reevaluate the issue of MX basing before committing himself to a course of action. Accordingly, in March he appointed a panel of fifteen distinguished Americans to review the basing mode decision. The committee was chaired by Charles Townes, inventor of the laser and professor of physics at the University of California, Berkeley. Other members of the panel included General Bernard Schriever, who had headed the crash program to develop the first U.S. ICBM, and Lieutenant General Brent Scowcroft, who had served as President Ford's national security adviser.[14]

The commission was scheduled to complete its work by 1 July 1981. However, Townes and his colleagues became divided and deadlocked over whether to recommend a deep underground basing (DUB) mode or a continuous patrol aircraft (CPA) basing mode. As a result, the commission failed to reach a decision and later in the summer recommended basing one hundred of the new missiles in hardened silos until a permanent basing mode could be selected.[15]

On 2 October 1981 President Reagan announced his plan for modernizing America's strategic forces. The plan would cost $180 billion over a six-year period and called for resurrecting the B-1 bomber that President Carter had deleted. Also, in line with the recommendations of the Townes Commission, Reagan canceled the MPS deployment in the Southwest and directed the Department of Defense to base a limited number of MX missiles in superhardened TITAN or MINUTEMAN silos while continuing the search for an acceptable permanent basing mode.

This would involve considering both the CPA and DUB modes. Although this decision did not completely resolve the problem of ICBM vulnerability, Reagan wanted to get the nation started with some deployment of the MX to end "the decade-long pattern of postponement, vacillation and delay" that had marked America's effort to modernize its strategic arsenal. Reagan promised to select a permanent basing mode by early 1984.[16]

The White House announcement also indicated that the United States would continue to push research and development work on ballistic missile defenses, including the development of a space-based defense against ICBM warheads. Missile defenses were discussed in two contexts. First, an ABM system might be deployed as an adjunct to the MX missile to counter the growing vulnerability of American ICBMs. Second, ballistic missile defenses were mentioned in the context of "strategic defense," which included civil defense and air defenses against attacking air-breathing systems.[17] Furthermore, during the conference at which Reagan announced the general provisions of his strategic program, Secretary Weinberger mentioned missile defenses as a possible long-range solution to the problem of ICBM vulnerability.[18] However, Weinberger indicated that ABM technology was not yet capable of providing an adequate defense. In spite of these discussions, the *Washington Post* reported that Reagan's modernization plan went against the recommendations of the Defense Science Board, which had favored the MPS system supported by an antiballistic missile system.[19]

In keeping with the president's announcement of 2 October, at the end of December, Weinberger ordered the army and air force to work together to integrate missile defenses into consideration of a permanent basing mode for the MX, with the army providing the expertise on missile defenses and the air force providing the knowledge of ICBM basing concepts. Regarding the interim basing mode, the air force chose to place the MXs in MINUTEMAN silos because the layout of MINUTEMAN fields was more compatible with defensive schemes.[20]

About this same time, Congress responded to the president's new basing mode policy with an appropriations bill that was essentially a vote of no confidence. It limited to 5 percent the amount of MX R&D funds that could be spent on the development of super-hardened silos and required a decision on the permanent basing mode by 1 July 1983, six months earlier than Reagan had proposed for this decision.[21]

As 1981 came to a close, the Reagan administration faced a situation in Congress best described as byzantine. Liberals could be expected to support various positions on the MX project in the hope that these might delay the program and help them kill it later. Conservatives might oppose a basing mode because they did not believe it would solve the vulnerability problem or because it was what their constituents demanded. This situation was further aggravated by earlier disagreements between members of DOD and elements in ACDA and the State Department.[22]

Nor was this all. In fact, national support for strategic modernization was tenuous. The MPS proposal had produced widespread opposition to a major strategic system in a part of the country that usually supported a strong defense program. Additionally, the Reagan administration was encountering opposition from elements of the freeze movement, which actively opposed deploying the MX in the MPS mode. The "broad objectives" of this movement compelled it "to oppose any new weapon in the nuclear arsenal."[23]

Further dissatisfaction with Reagan's decision on the MX manifested itself at the end of March 1982 when the Senate Armed Services Committee voted to withhold all funding for the MX deployment until the Reagan administration decided on a permanent basing mode. Moreover, the committee encouraged Defense Secretary Weinberger to ensure that the decision was made by 1 December 1982, a date that would advance by another seven months the decision time already set by Congress.[24]

Two months later, a new basing concept surfaced. This was the defendable modular array basing system (dense pack), which was under study in the Office of the Secretary of Defense. Soon after the new basing mode surfaced, Weinberger directed the army to develop an ABM design that was compatible with it. The army's candidate for this mission was LoADS, with which the army had planned to defend the MX since 1979. In 1982 the name LoADS was changed to SENTRY.[25]

In the meantime, Reagan's interim basing mode proposal was not being well received in Congress. To begin with, the decision had been taken with such speed that Reagan's aides did not have time to win the support of key elements within DOD. Furthermore, the air force did not have sufficient time to prepare a defense of the Reagan decision before being required to appear before Congress. As a result, DOD testimony in support of the president's position was unconvincing. Things became worse as it was understood that the interim basing mode would not solve the problem of ICBM vulnerability in spite of its considerable expense. On 19 July 1982, faced with the likelihood that Congress would reject his interim silo basing concept, Reagan abandoned this plan and announced he would select a permanent basing mode by 1 December

1982 as requested by the Senate Armed Services Committee. By this time, "it was beginning to appear as if no basing mode could ever appeal to the disparate factions in Congress, and that the new weapon project was doomed."[26]

On 22 November the Reagan administration announced the president's decision to deploy the MX missile, now designated PEACE-KEEPER, in the dense pack configuration at Francis E. Warren Air Force Base in southeastern Wyoming. In a prepared statement issued by the White House, Reagan seemed to be at pains to assure the Soviets that the MX was a decidedly measured U.S. response designed to offset Soviet strategic advantages and encourage the Soviets to negotiate strategic arms reductions. At the same time, if they failed to respond, the Soviets could expect the United States to pursue one or both of two options: field more MX missiles or deploy a missile defense system.[27]

With regard to the latter option, the White House statement first assured the Soviets that the United States preferred to adhere to the ABM Treaty and did not intend to field even the minimum system allowed under the provisions of the treaty. However, the statement continued, "we plan to continue research on ballistic missile defense technology—the kind of smart, highly accurate, hopefully nonnuclear, weapons that utilize the microelectronic and other advanced technologies *in which we excel* [italics added]."[28] The last four words seem to have been a warning that if the MX deployment failed to bring the Soviets to the bargaining table, the United States would escalate the strategic arms competition into the realm of high technology where America would possess a decided advantage.

The new basing mode had two things to recommend it. First, it was much more acceptable politically in that it would affect only 10 to 15 square miles of territory already controlled by DOD. This meant that it would have minimal impact on the local environment. As a result, it was quickly endorsed by the governor of Wyoming, Edward Herschler, and other local officials.[29] Second, it seemed to offer a solution to the problem of ICBM vulnerability. The idea behind the dense pack system was that all the missiles would be based in a long, narrow strip of land so small that the Soviets could not place enough warheads in the area to destroy the missiles before most of them could be fired. The factor limiting the rate at which Soviet warheads could strike the dense pack complex was the phenomenon of fratricide, the fact that a nuclear warhead going off near another warhead might destroy the second warhead. Thus, if the Soviets tried to saturate the area where the MX missiles were based, the detonations of the early warheads would form a protective barrier for the missile field. Furthermore, any attempt to pin down the American missiles in their field with a systematic barrage of warheads would deplete the Soviet nuclear missile force.[30]

In spite of its apparent theoretical soundness, the new concept was savaged. Foes of the MX argued that the second strike capability of the United States was still sufficient to deter a Soviet attack. Therefore, fielding the MX with its hard-target kill capability would be destabilizing since it would give the United States a first strike capability. Opponents also pointed out that the dense pack mode would involve the construction of new silos, which was a violation of the SALT I and II agreements.[31]

Perhaps the greatest damage to dense pack was done within the government itself. First, Reagan had again suddenly announced a strategic decision. Theoretically, making the announcement just after a congressional election would have precluded hearings on the issue until the new Congress convened, giving DOD time to prepare its defense of the system. However, Congress moved swiftly to conduct hearings on the dense pack decision. As a result, "the Pentagon was confronted with the problem of selling an extremely complex and bizarre theoretical concept to an already highly suspicious group of legislators without a reliable data base, and with only a week to do so."[32]

Even more damning was the opposition to the concept that surfaced in the JCS. The army doubted the fratricide phenomenon could be used to protect the closely spaced missiles. These doubts could not be dispelled without test data, and the required testing was prohibited by the 1963 Nuclear Test Ban Treaty. The navy did not believe that silos could be hardened to the level called for in the dense pack plan. On 7 December, the day before General John W. Vessey announced the JCS split on the MX, the House of Representatives had voted 245 to 176 to eliminate $988 million to begin procurement of one hundred MX missiles. When Vessey announced the following day that three of five Joint Chiefs wanted to delay proceeding with the program until "technical uncertainties" could be resolved, support for the new basing mode was further eroded.[33]

Thus, as 1982 was ending, U.S. strategic policy was in disarray. While the MIRVing of SS-18s and improvements in the accuracy of Soviet warheads fed growing concern about the vulnerability of U.S. MINUTEMAN missiles, the executive and legislative branches of the government were finding it impossible to agree on a suitable U.S. response. Three previous administrations and now Reagan's had considered over thirty different basing modes for the MX, and still there was no consensus. As the United States continued to grope for a solution to the co-nundrum of ICBM vulnerability, frustration welled to the surface in statements of conservatives like Alabama's Republican legislator Jack Edwards, who said: "I am supposed to be one of the hawks on the [House Appropriations C]ommittee, I guess, but I swear the more I sit here and listen to this, the more I wonder what in the world we are up to." Even Barry Goldwater was fed up with the MX issue and indicated that he would try to kill the program. "I'm not one of those freeze-the-nuke nuts," Goldwater declared, "but I think we have enough."[34]

Because of congressional opposition to dense pack, the Reagan ad-ministration appointed another blue ribbon commission to examine the basing mode problem: the President's Commission on Strategic Forces, chaired by Brent Scowcroft. It was not to deliver its report until April 1983.[35] By that time, President Reagan would have announced a new strategic initiative aimed at placing American deterrence strategy on a fundamentally different footing.

THE NATIONAL SECURITY COUNCIL
AND STRATEGIC DEFENSE

The plight of the MX was particularly worrisome for Robert Mc-Farlane. When he had served Ford as special assistant for national se-curity affairs, the United States was already developing this missile, which was to have an initial operational capability (IOC) in 1983. Over five years later in 1982, McFarlane was Reagan's deputy assistant for national security affairs, and the United States still had not taken de-cisive action on the MX. The IOC for the MX was now projected to be 1986. This situation and the seeming inability of the United States to respond meant to McFarlane that "the United States faced a military crisis; our deterrent force was badly out of balance with the Soviet force, and we needed to compensate for that militarily."[36]

The problem was not one of technology, but rather of political will. In McFarlane's view, "The politics of deploying ICBMs in the United States was becoming too difficult."[37] Of particular concern to McFarlane was the nuclear freeze movement, which seemed to be gaining strength in the summer and fall of 1982.

Throughout the nuclear age, the vast majority of the American people maintained a relatively stable attitude toward nuclear weapons. Although having strong reservations about these weapons, they gener-ally saw them as essential for the preservation of peace and the prevention of nuclear war. Americans favored arms talks with the Soviets but opposed any agreement that might place the United States at a disadvantage.[38] This "resigned ambiguity" was disrupted by several events between 1979 and 1982. These included the collapse of the Shah's government in Iran and the ensuing hostage crisis, the Soviet invasion of Afghanistan, and the East-West confrontation over intermediate-range ballistic missiles in Europe. The anxiety created by these events was intensified by careless statements from officials in the Reagan administration indicating that the American government might be too cavalier about the prospect of nuclear war.[39]

Although this heightened anxiety did not represent a fundamental shift in the basic attitudes of the American people, it did manifest itself in increased public support for the freeze movement. In the November 1982 election, freeze propositions passed in eight of the nine states voting on this issue and in several cities and counties.[40] McFarlane believed that there were sound arguments against the goals of this movement, but there were just too few people willing and able to present these arguments in the face of widespread freeze support. Therefore, McFarlane believed it was important for the Reagan government to "find a way to outflank the freeze movement." Such a move could redound to the advantage of the Reagan administration by offering a means of gaining congressional support for Reagan's defense program.[41]

Additionally, McFarlane understood that Reagan wanted to reduce strategic weapons and believed that the United States had to develop some strategic system that could be used to draw the Soviets into strategic arms negotiations. Given the lack of consensus that kept hamstringing efforts to deploy the MX, other strategic options such as missile defense had to be explored. McFarlane realized that the earlier SAFEGUARD system had faced technical limitations that made it largely ineffective, but "by 1982 people who were good scientists and engineers began to say that technology had advanced to where it was time to reconsider missile defense."[42]

The superiority of American technology was another reason for beginning a major development program for ballistic missile defense, which is highly dependent on sophisticated equipment, concepts, and software. If the United States undertook such a program, it could force the U.S.-Soviet strategic competition into the realm of high technology where McFarlane was confident the United States would prevail.[43]

For these reasons McFarlane had concluded by the fall of 1982 that ballistic missile defense might offer the United States a way out of its strategic conundrum. While Reagan was on a campaign visit to New York, the issue of the nuclear freeze movement surfaced during a discussion with a local official and concern was expressed that the freeze movement might undermine President Reagan's defense build-up. McFarlane later informed Reagan that he was working on a concept that might outflank the freeze movement while also solving the problem of the nuclear imbalance and improving the negotiating position of the United States in strategic arms talks. Furthermore, McFarlane expected to have the concept fully developed by the beginning of 1983. The president encouraged him to pursue his solution and report on his work in January.[44]

About this time McFarlane discovered that Admiral John M. Poindexter, military assistant to NSC adviser William Clark, was having similar thoughts regarding the strategic situation of the United States. In the fall of 1982 Poindexter had come "to see the handwriting on the wall in terms of a general feeling in the population of the United States that there wasn't any way that we could compete with the Soviets in building strategic offensive systems." Poindexter concluded that a strategic defense system would be popular with the American people while providing "a disincentive to the Soviets to produce offensive systems and an incentive for them to initiate a nuclear pact." Based upon his knowledge of the technology involved, Poindexter had doubts about the technical feasibility of a new missile defense system. Nevertheless, given the strategic crisis the United States faced, he believed it "completely reasonable" to investigate the possibility of developing an effective system.[45]

Poindexter and McFarlane agreed that the NSC staff should begin studying this matter. As a result, Poindexter tasked Richard Boverie, an air force general who headed the defense portion of the NSC staff, to put his section to work on the concept of missile defense with the idea of later having "a brainstorming session about what the possibilities might be." This session was held in the NSC situation room and was attended by Poindexter, Boverie, air force colonel Robert Linhard, and Alton G. Keel, Jr., who had been assistant secretary of the air force for research and development. From this meeting, there emerged a consensus that it was time to place more emphasis on strategic defense and that the technology had progressed to the point where it was worth "a concerted effort" to develop missile defenses. Nevertheless, Keel was not optimistic about the technology involved and believed that even if feasible an effective missile defense was still far in the future.[46]

While McFarlane and the NSC staff were developing their position on strategic defense, the Joint Chiefs of Staff were involved in their own review of the strategic problems confronting the United States. The leading figure in the JCS effort was the chief of naval operations (CNO), James Watkins. The story of Watkins's role in the JCS review begins in mid-1982.

INTO THE "STRATEGIC VALLEY OF DEATH"

When Watkins assumed his duties as CNO on 30 June 1982, DOD and the Reagan administration were in the midst of the MX missile crisis. On 19 July 1982 President Reagan canceled his decision on the interim basing mode (the MX in MINUTEMAN silos) and announced that his administration would have a permanent basing mode selected by 1 December 1982.[47] The difficulties the administration was having with the MX signaled Watkins that the United States was in trouble strategically. In his words: "We were reaching a point where we were losing our hat, ass, and overcoat at Geneva. We had no bargaining chip, no strength, with which to negotiate. The Soviets could just sit at Geneva and watch us throw away all of our chips right here in Washington. That's one reason I wanted to influence the Joint Chiefs of Staff, so I worked hard. . . . I felt so strongly that we were heading into a strategic valley of death.[48]

What Watkins meant by "working hard" was essentially to take the lead in a JCS review of the strategic issues revolving around the MX missile. This review consisted of over forty executive meetings of the chiefs during which the strategic situation of the United States and the long-range prospects for technical developments were thoroughly examined. This effort involved briefings on a number of key issues, such as the activities of the Soviet Union; U.S. efforts to develop an antisatellite capability; the army's ABM program, which included schemes for protecting ICBM silos; and other advanced technology programs. To support him in this undertaking, Watkins called upon the Theater and Strategic Nuclear Warfare Division (OP-65) of the CNO's staff, using members of this agency (especially Captain Linton F. Brooks) as something of a special staff to prepare briefings and position papers to help him think through the problems associated with the quest for a secure basing mode for the MX missile.[49]

After several months of working with his staff, Watkins decided there was no variation of the MX basing mode that offered the United States a way out of the "strategic valley of death." Continuing the

Between the summer of 1982 and February 1983, the Joint Chiefs met in executive session over forty times to consider the issues raised by the growing vulnerability of the U.S. ICBM force. From these deliberations there emerged a unanimous agreement that America's response to the crisis should include an expanded missile defense program. Without the full support of the JCS, it is unlikely that President Reagan would have proposed a new missile defense effort. Shown in this photograph from right to left are Admiral James D. Watkins, chief of Naval Operations; General Edward C. Meyer, chief of staff, U.S. Army; General John W. Vessey, Jr., U.S. Army, chairman of the Joint Chiefs; General Robert H. Barrow, commandant of the Marine Corps; and General Charles A. Gabriel, chief of staff, U.S. Air Force. (JCS History Office)

quest for a safe basing mode was like flying into a blind canyon. With their superiority in heavy ICBMs, the Soviets could easily defeat any basing mode the United States might select. At the same time, each new basing mode would be taking the United States deeper and deeper into the gorge. The Americans would encounter the end of the canyon when it was too late to select another strategic option. In Watkins's mind, the basing mode exercise was tantamount to competing with the Soviet Union where it was strongest (land-based ICBMs) and the United States weakest. Since America's forte was high technology, instead of pursuing the same old solutions to the vulnerability crisis, Watkins believed America should turn to its superior technology for a new answer.[50]

As Watkins was grappling with the technical problems of maintaining America's ability to deter nuclear war, his thinking was also being affected by the efforts of America's Catholic bishops to develop a pastoral letter on war and peace. In addition to being the navy's top professional officer, Watkins was a devout Catholic. As a result, he was acutely aware that any pronouncement by the bishops on the moral issues of war and peace would have profound implications for national defense in a country where over fifty million people profess Roman Catholicism. Depending on its final form, the pastoral letter could pose a serious challenge to the nation's ability to deter nuclear war.[51]

The Challenge of Peace: God's Promise and Our Response, the formal title of the pastoral letter, grew out of a general reevaluation of American values that started in the 1960s. The increase in the size of nuclear arsenals, combined with the Vietnam war, assured that issues of war and peace would be central to this reexamination. With the end of the Vietnam war, the focus of Catholic concern came increasingly to fall on issues of nuclear arms and strategic deterrence.[52]

The election of Reagan, who had promised to strengthen U.S. military forces, stimulated further interest among Catholics in a review of American policies regarding nuclear weapons. Moreover, by 1981 there had emerged within the hierarchy of the Catholic church "a very visible and vocal segment" that opposed "the arms race and American nuclear policy." In October 1981, twenty-nine bishops publicly stated that it was immoral to possess nuclear weapons.[53]

During the November 1980 National Conference of Catholic Bishops (NCCB), the growing concern of some Catholics with war and peace issues resulted in a motion for the conference to address these issues in a pastoral letter. In response to these sentiments, Archbishop John Roach, president of the NCCB, appointed a committee under Archbishop Joseph Bernardin of Chicago to prepare a draft pastoral letter for consideration by the conference. Bernardin, along with Father J. Bryan Hehir, a member of the committee's staff, were the dominant influences in drafting the letter.[54]

Bernardin's committee began to conduct hearings in July 1981, and presented a draft to the bishops about the time Watkins assumed his duties as CNO. A second draft was ready in time for consideration by the NCCB at its meeting in November 1982. Amendments were offered and plans made to bring the revised document before a special session of the conference in May 1983 for final review and approval. The public effects of these activities were felt long before the conference of 1983, for the committee's work was widely reported in the news media just as the power of the freeze movement was cresting. The bishops' questioning of U.S. defense policy reinforced the freeze movement, which in turn added emphasis to the activities surrounding the pastoral letter.[55]

In the late summer of 1982, Watkins was disturbed to hear from the navy's chief of chaplains that news of the bishops' work was causing sailors and officers to leave because they believed that service in the navy was no longer compatible with a moral life. This situation prompted Watkins to speak out strongly on the morality of nuclear deterrence and service in the navy. The commencement ceremony at Marymount College in Arlington, Virginia, provided a public platform for his views.[56]

Watkins's commencement address was intended as much for those serving in the navy as for the graduates of Marymount. The admiral made it clear that nuclear weapons as well as deterrence were moral from his perspective. Placing the national policy of deterrence squarely in the centuries-old Catholic tradition of just war, he told his audience on 22 August that "faced with an obvious and overt threat of military aggression, a nation has the right—and its leaders have the concomitant moral obligation—to maintain its own military strength at the level necessary to *deter* war. In such circumstances, the possession of military strength per se, provided always that that strength is not itself used for aggressive purposes, is *not* inherently evil but is, rather, a positive good."[57]

Later in the address, Watkins quoted words of the Vatican II Council that obviously were intended to reassure officers and sailors that their service in the U.S. Navy was morally acceptable: "All those who enter military service in loyalty to their country should look upon themselves as custodians of the security and freedom of their fellow countrymen. . . . When they carry out their duty properly, they are contributing to the maintenance of peace."[58] Toward the end of his remarks, he specifically addressed the issue of nuclear weapons:

> [Nuclear] weapons, terrible and terrifying as they might be if used for the wrong purposes, do exist—just as, and because, the threat exists. *That* is the reality with which I must deal. It is my responsibility to deal with it, in a world in which good and evil also both exist—a world where my options are anything but clear. I may not always be happy about or comfortable with the usually limited options available to me. *But I do have the responsibility for choosing between those options, and I must make those choices as a moral man.*[59]

Although Watkins had no personal qualms about the morality of nuclear deterrence, he was concerned about the effect of the bishops' activities on navy personnel. Moreover, these events signaled Watkins that national support for offensive strategic deterrence was declining.

This situation was being exacerbated by the effort to find a safe basing mode for the MX, an exercise that Watkins had concluded was doomed to failure.[60] Clearly, it was time to consider a new departure. But what should it be?

Watkins may have received an important hint concerning the answer to this question just two weeks after the announcement of the JCS split over the dense pack basing mode. Apparently, the Joint Chiefs met with the president on 22 December. Information on this meeting is extremely sketchy, but evidently the purpose of the session was to discuss strategic issues. Among the items on the agenda was a briefing by the air force on strategic systems, both offensive and defensive. The broad purpose of this meeting may have been to consider strategic options in the wake of the collapse of the dense pack basing initiative. At one point in the meeting, perhaps after the air force had completed its briefing on strategic systems, President Reagan is reported to have asked: "What if we began to move away from our total reliance on offense to deter a nuclear attack and moved toward a relatively greater reliance on defense?"[61] If President Reagan made this remark, it apparently had little effect on Watkins's thinking. Not until 10 January 1983 when national security adviser William Clark notified the Joint Chiefs that they would meet with the president on 11 February did the admiral begin the process that made him an advocate of strategic defense.[62]

During the February meeting, the Joint Chiefs would be expected to present their positions on three issues: TRIAD, the MX, and associated basing modes. This meant that in a few weeks Watkins would have to present his recommendations on the U.S. strategic force structure to the president. His participation in the lengthy JCS review of strategic issues had convinced him of the bankruptcy of the search for a secure basing mode for the MX and exposed him to information on DOD's ABM and antisatellite (ASAT) programs. Furthermore, he suspected that the commitment of the American people to offensive nuclear deterrence was on the wane. Yet he had no concrete suggestions for revising the force structure, nor could he suggest a replacement for the prevailing concept of nuclear deterrence based on offensive systems. Then, on 20 January, Watkins had lunch with a group of high-level advisers that included Edward Teller. Teller talked about the possibilities for missile defense offered by new developments in technology. Specifically, he discussed EXCALIBUR and its use in a "pop-up" mode wherein it would be launched into space from a submarine to defend against a Soviet ICBM attack.[63]

Teller's remarks made a deep impression on the admiral because of Teller's reputation and because of Watkins's faith in the possibilities of future technology. Moreover, what Teller said more or less confirmed what Watkins had been hearing in JCS briefings on strategic technologies and in discussions with his own R&D advisers.[64] During the luncheon, Teller told Watkins that he was in the same state of frustration he had experienced earlier when trying to convince U.S. leaders that it was necessary to develop the hydrogen bomb. Teller was aware of what the Soviets were doing in their ABM program and was convinced that the United States should be pushing ballistic missile defenses aggressively. As Teller spoke, he seemed to shake with excitement, and his vibrations reminded Watkins of an engineering problem he had been required to solve at the Naval Postgraduate School. This problem required students to find the resonant frequency of a reed, knowing that the vibration of the reed is greatest at its resonant frequency. When Teller talked of the possibilities of strategic defense, he seemed to vibrate like a reed responding to its resonant frequency. Watkins realized that placing nuclear weapons in space was politically impossible, but his discussion with Teller "convinced him that strategic defenses offered a way to use the resources of American technology to move beyond the sterile debate over MX basing modes in the short term" and, in the long term, to shift toward a form of deterrence that might be more palatable to the American people.[65]

Watkins pressed Teller for more information on ABM technology. Could a power source for a terrestrial laser be made small enough to fit in this room, Watkins asked? Yes, responded Teller; it would perhaps be a bit longer. Then lasers could be installed aboard submarines, Watkins noted, and stationed under the Arctic ice off the coast of the Eurasian land mass. In case of an attack, the submarines could surface through the ice and attack Soviet ICBMs by bouncing the beams of their lasers off space-based mirrors that would direct the laser beams onto the Soviet missiles. Could the national laboratories produce the technologies that would make ballistic missile defenses feasible within twenty years, Watkins inquired? Unquestionably, responded Teller. Watkins then asked specifically if the United States could accomplish detection, boost-phase intercept, and battle management within that twenty-year period? Yes, Teller replied.[66]

Now Watkins knew what he would recommend to the president in February. He directed his staff "to develop, on a close hold basis, a very brief [five-minute] presentation which would offer a vision of strategic defense as a way out of the MX debate." There followed a series of meetings in the "sea cabin" (the CNO's Pentagon office) in which Captain Brooks and Admiral W. J. Holland (head of OP-65) presented various "drafts" of the five-minute briefing for Watkins's approval. He repeatedly rejected their proposals without being able to give specific reasons for doing so. When his staff officers sought hints from him as to what he wanted from them in the next draft, he would reply: I'm not quite sure, but I'll know it when I see it. During the week of 24 January, Brooks and Holland finally found the proper balance and wording. The main points of this paper were that the United States should quit looking for a complex basing mode for the MX missile, deploy a small number of MXs in MINUTEMAN silos, and start developing a strategic defense that would provide the basis for a shift "to a long term strategy based on strategic defense." Such a change in strategy "is both militarily and morally sound."[67]

As Watkins often did in cases of major policy matters like this, he turned to the CNO's Executive Panel (CEP) for a review of his position. The CEP is an advisory panel constituted under the Federal Advisory Commission Act to provide policy advice to the CNO. It is composed of distinguished citizens, both in and out of government, and is supported by a small full-time staff of naval officers.[68]

On 2 February, Watkins discussed with selected members of the CEP the position he had worked out with Holland and Brooks. Although the CEP supported Watkins's recommendations that the United States use strategic defense as a means to offset the growing vulnerability of American ICBMs, it advised him to proceed cautiously. CEP members noted that the technical problem of building a strategic defense system was comparable to that of the Apollo program in the 1960s, and they did not believe that the nation was ready for this kind of challenge where missile defenses were concerned.[69]

A week remained before the Joint Chiefs were scheduled to meet with the president, and still they had no common position on the issues they were expected to address. Knowing this, Watkins advised Vessey that he had a position he would like presented to the president. Vessey then arranged for a 5 February meeting of the JCS at which Watkins gave his views. The meeting, another executive session of the Joint Chiefs, took place in Vessey's office. By the time of the meeting, both Vessey and air force chief of staff General Charles A. Gabriel were particularly worried by the collapse of the dense pack plan. Additionally, Vessey had long supported the army's ballistic missile defense program and had come to have "moral and military qualms about deterrence." As a result, these two officers were especially open to suggestions for a new strategic initiative. After hearing the CNO's briefing, the chiefs agreed that this should be the position the JCS presented to the president and that General Vessey would give the briefing.[70]

When the Joint Chiefs approached Secretary Weinberger with their position, they found that he was opposed to their proposal. However, as was his practice in matters such as this, he believed that the president should hear the views of the Joint Chiefs and he agreed that Vessey would present their position to the president that Friday.[71]

While these events were occurring, Watkins had informally discussed with McFarlane and Poindexter what was transpiring, advising McFarlane that he favored some role for missile defense in America's strategic policies. In the interest of supporting his own efforts to make the development of strategic defenses a national goal, McFarlane encouraged Watkins to cultivate a consensus among the Joint Chiefs on this issue, for as McFarlane put it: if the chiefs were "all over the lot on this issue, there's not a chance in the world he [Reagan] would support a missile defense program." Indeed, given the effect of the recent JCS split over the dense pack basing mode, it would have been virtually unthinkable for the president to launch a major missile defense program without the complete support of the chiefs.[72]

The day of 11 February dawned cold and snowy. By noon when the meeting with President Reagan began, the road conditions were so bad that the Joint Chiefs had to use four-wheel-drive vehicles for their trip to the White House. The hour-and-a-half-long meeting started with Secretary Weinberger presenting his recommendations on the MX missile. He then stated that the Joint Chiefs had a different view that he believed the president should hear.[73]

Vessey then delivered a broad thirty-minute briefing that was based on the views presented by Watkins and included some of the phrases the admiral had used in briefing the JCS. After this, each of the Joint Chiefs was given an opportunity to speak, and Watkins strongly supported the position Vessey had presented. Since McFarlane had a good idea what the JCS would recommend, he was prepared to exploit this opportunity to push the president toward a decision to develop a ballistic missile defense capability. When Watkins finished, McFarlane interjected: "Mr. President, this is very, very important. For thirty-seven years we have relied on offensive deterrence based on the threat of nuclear counterattack with surviving forces because there has been no alternative. But now for the first time in history what we are hearing here is that there might be another way which would enable you to defeat an attack by defending against it and over time relying less on nuclear weapons."[74]

The president indicated that he understood the significance of the JCS position. Furthermore, to be sure the position was unanimous, he asked each officer in turn if he agreed. Each confirmed that he believed it was time to explore the possibilities offered by strategic defenses. The president then informed the Joint Chiefs that he was very interested in what they had recommended and asked them to work diligently to develop a missile defense proposal and report the results of their work as soon as possible. Moreover, with his sensitivity to politically effective rhetoric, he took special note of one particular expression used by Vessey, an expression he had picked up from the briefing Watkins had presented earlier to the JCS: "Wouldn't it be better to protect the American people rather than avenge them." Reagan liked this phrase very much and remarked: "Don't lose those words."[75]

As the meeting was breaking up about 1:30 P.M., McFarlane sought to ensure that the Joint Chiefs understood that they had "really struck a responsive chord" with the president. He told each of them that he expected them to develop a thorough report advising the president of an appropriate approach to take in developing a missile defense capability.[76]

ANNOUNCING A NEW NATIONAL POLICY

Following the 11 February meeting, McFarlane charged General Boverie, Colonel Linhard, and Raymond Pollock with developing a general program for strategic defenses that would project a funding level to develop the technologies that would be involved in a missile defense system. They were to work quietly with the JCS and its staff and bring no one else in on the project at this stage, not even the president's science adviser, Keyworth. There was some interaction with technically qualified people in industry such as former director of defense research and engineering Dr. John Foster, who was with TRW Incorporated in early 1983. There was also contact with the national laboratories.[77]

At this time, McFarlane believed the president would not expect a report until after the Scowcroft Commission completed its work in April. But a month after his meeting with the Joint Chiefs, President Reagan began to prod Clark and McFarlane to speed up their work.[78]

About the middle of March the president again indicated his desire to have the strategic defense proposal completed quickly. Congress was

"Don't lose those words" was Reagan's response when in the course of a brief-ing to the president on 11 February 1983 General John Vessey, chairman of the Joint Chiefs, asked the rhetorical question: "Wouldn't it be better to protect the American people rather than avenge them?" These words originated in a brief-ing that Chief of Naval Operations Admiral James D. Watkins had given ear-lier to the Joint Chiefs. In this photograph Watkins, at the extreme left, seems to be talking to President Reagan (second from the right). To Reagan's left is Sec-retary of Defense Caspar Weinberger; on Reagan's right is National Security Adviser Robert C. McFarlane. To Watkins's left are General Edward C. Meyer, chief of staff, U.S. Army; General Vessey; General Robert H. Barrow, comman-dant of the Marine Corps; and General Charles A. Gabriel, chief of staff, U.S. Air Force. (Photo C12954-28, Presidential Libraries Branch, National Ar-chives)

about to begin its work on authorizations for DOD, and Reagan was wor-ried about the state of his defense program. He wanted to give a major speech on defense issues in which he could "break something new." Specifically, he wanted to provide the nation with something reassur-ing that might stem the momentum of the freeze movement. Mc-Farlane passed this message to the JCS and at the same time put Linhard and Pollock to work on the main body of a speech dealing with general defense matters. McFarlane was to write the portion of the speech dealing with strategic defense and then coordinate it with Sec-retary of Defense Weinberger.[79]

By this time, McFarlane had come to suspect that some other force or influence was pushing the president. He suspected that the president's political advisers (Baker, Meese, and Deaver) were encouraging Reagan to take some action to outflank the freeze movement.[80] Perhaps it was

Reagan's own sense of the crisis his administration was facing in strategic policy that led him to push McFarlane on the missile defense concept.[81] Or maybe the president was responding to the importuning of Bendetsen and the High Frontier Panel. Whatever the president's motivation, he was clearly pushing his immediate staff for a policy initiative pertaining to strategic defenses.

The weekend before the president's speech, McFarlane wrote the portion that would present Reagan's vision of strategic defense. On Saturday, 19 March, McFarlane brought George Keyworth into the inner circle that knew of the impending announcement. He broke the news to Keyworth gradually, first asking him what he would think if the president wished to introduce some new options into the strategic arena. Keyworth placed this question in the context of his own involvement with Reagan's strategic modernization program and thought that McFarlane was probably talking about something like stealth technology or a new basing mode for the MX. Keyworth began discussing some of the possible options that might be considered, including some of the ideas his science council advisory committee had developed. The discussion finally worked around to the matter of missile defense, and McFarlane asked Keyworth what he would think if President Reagan announced a major national commitment to develop a missile defense system. At first Keyworth was "dumbfounded," but then he "blurted out" what the science council had revealed regarding atmospheric compensation technology. "If there ever was an exciting time to take a look [at missile defense]," Keyworth said, "now is it."[82] Since Keyworth did not realize the scope of the missile defense program the president would propose, McFarlane handed him a copy of the insert he had drafted, complete with crossed-out words, for apparently McFarlane himself had typed the draft. According to Keyworth, as he left McFarlane's office, the latter indicated that the president would not propose the new ABM defense program without Keyworth's concurrence.[83]

Keyworth was not supposed to show the speech to anyone, but he felt compelled to discuss its implications with two trusted colleagues: Victor H. Reis, who worked for Keyworth, and Solomon Buchsbaum, chairman of the science council Keyworth had convened to investigate technologies with strategic military significance. Reis was opposed to the initiative and apparently resigned his position in Keyworth's office because of his conflict with Keyworth over this issue. It may have been because of Reis's opposition that Keyworth began to have "cold feet" regarding the proposed presidential initiative and informed McFarlane of his misgivings. After a thirty-minute pep talk from McFarlane, Keyworth's faith was restored and he never again had "any compunction about strategic defense."[84]

While Keyworth was reviewing the speech insert and making some suggested changes, McFarlane began to inform key government officials about the pending policy announcement and handled the objections raised by at least some of those notified. General Scowcroft noted that it would be very difficult to develop a missile defense and expressed "real misgivings" about the proposal. On the other hand, McFarlane also contacted John Foster, who believed the new departure was sensible and noted that there had been important progress on missile defense technologies. Some of the strongest opposition came from the State Department where the principal concern was how the announcement would affect relations with America's allies. Richard Perle of DOD, who was in Europe at the time, also opposed the new initiative on the same ground as the State Department.[85]

Meanwhile, McFarlane continued to work on the insert, advising the other speech writers to compose the main body of the speech and a conclusion, leaving space for a five-minute insert. During this time, he probably also received suggested changes from Keyworth. He then sent a draft of the strategic defense insert by courier to Weinberger. Although Weinberger expressed some misgivings because the president's proposal would cause a certain amount of upheaval in the military services and among U.S. allies, he was generally favorably disposed toward it.[86]

As the night of the speech approached, last-minute preparations had to be completed. For one thing, messages had to be drafted from the president to NATO's heads of state assuring them that the new missile defense initiative did not mean that the United States was abandoning its commitments to NATO.[87]

Furthermore, to provide a possible source of favorable comment on the president's announcement, McFarlane and Keyworth planned a dinner for cabinet members, past secretaries of state and defense, and representatives of the scientific community. Those attending included Secretary of State George Shultz, Henry Kissinger, James Schlesinger, and Edward Teller. The affair took place in the East Room of the White House. Before dinner, McFarlane and Keyworth briefed the guests on what the president would say. After dinner, a large-screen television was turned on and the group watched the president give his speech from the Oval Office.[88]

In his speech that evening, President Reagan announced his belief that defensive technologies had advanced to where the United States could hope to prevent nuclear aggression by developing a defensive system that would save lives rather than avenge them. He realized that this would be a "formidable technical task"; it could "take years, even decades, of effort on many fronts" to produce a new missile defense system. However, it was clearly time to begin, so the president called upon the American "scientific community who gave us nuclear weapons to turn their great talents to the cause of mankind and world peace; to give us the means of rendering these nuclear weapons impotent and obsolete." The effort Reagan envisioned was to be consistent with U.S. obligations under the ABM Treaty and would begin with the establishment of "a comprehensive and intensive effort to define a long-term research and development program" to find a defense against nuclear-tipped ballistic missiles.[89]

Epilogue:
Triumph and Transition

During the next 10 years, the U.S. objective is a radical reduction in the power of existing and planned offensive nuclear arms, as well as the stabilization of the relationship between offensive and defensive nuclear arms, whether on earth or in space. We are even now looking forward to a period of transition to a more stable world, with greatly reduced levels of nuclear arms and an enhanced ability to deter war based upon an increasing contribution of non-nuclear defenses against offensive nuclear arms. This period of transition could lead to the eventual elimination of all nuclear arms, both offensive and defensive. A world free of nuclear arms is an ultimate objective to which we, the Soviet Union, and all other nations can agree.

—Paul H. Nitze, 20 February 1985[1]

The world situation has changed dramatically since President Reagan announced his decision to launch the Strategic Defense Initiative. This was and continues to be one of the most controversial presidential decisions in American history, yet arguably it was a wise one. Its emphasis on high technology to offset a Soviet advantage in nuclear-tipped ballistic missiles was squarely in an American strategic tradition that stretches back to World War II and beyond.

In 1953 Dwight Eisenhower had set out a grand strategy for the United States that was based on three basic tenets. First, maintain military forces that are sufficient to protect the interests of the United States and its allies and if necessary to inflict massive damage on the Soviet Union through a retaliatory nuclear stike. Second, preserve "a sound, strong and growing economy, capable of providing through the operation of free institutions" the required military forces "over the long pull." And third, maintain "morale and free institutions and the willingness of the U.S. people to support the measures necessary for national security."[2] In short, America would use its high technology nuclear forces to compensate for Soviet advantages in conventional military power.

Thirty years later, the willingness of the American people to support offensive strategic deterrence seemed to be faltering. The need for a new American ICBM had been recognized in the late 1960s; but thirty basing modes and over ten years later, the United States still had not found a safe and politically acceptable way to deploy the MX missile. Moreover, the freeze movement and the pastoral letter that was being prepared by the Catholic bishops pointed toward a growing unease with mutual assured destruction. On the other hand, the Soviet Union seemed to be moving along in stride. The steadily improving quality of Soviet nuclear forces which had worried every secretary of defense from Melvin Laird to Caspar Weinberger now threatened to give the Soviets a first strike capability.[3]

Under these conditions, SDI may be seen as giving the United States a second wind in the critical home stretch of the Cold War. SDI immediately seized the strategic initiative for the United States and forced the Soviet Union into a responsive mode both militarily and diplomatically. Moreover, in promising a new, defensive-based strategy, it defused the freeze movement and provided a new focus around which a political consensus could form, however fragile and brief it might prove to be. And "in a democracy," Senator Albert Gore, Jr. (D-Tenn.), has reminded us, "consensus is itself a strategic asset."[4]

By the time the consensus had begun to dissipate, the Soviets were back at the arms control bargaining table, impelled by their concern over SDI and their desire to squelch this program as they had done earlier with SAFEGUARD. The first fruit of these talks was the Intermediate Nuclear Forces (INF) Treaty signed in December 1987 by Ronald Reagan and Mikhail Gorbachev. This agreement has been hailed as the first treaty to eliminate an entire class of weapons. With the destruction of the last operational missiles in 1991, the only INF missiles left in the world are museum pieces such as the Soviet SS-20 and American PERSHING, which now stand alert in the National Air and Space Museum in Washington, D.C.[5]

Furthermore, by 1987 a vigorous SDI program was developing the high technologies required to support space-based defensive systems.

An energized and superior American technology base seemed on the verge of making important breakthroughs in the areas of sensors and high speed computers. These technologies promised to revolutionize warfare on the ground as well as in space. Soviet military and political leaders recognized that their technology base simply could not meet this challenge. With their economy already strained to maintain their massive conventional and strategic force structures and facing severe shortages of consumer goods, the Soviets were forced to undertake fundamental changes in their political and economic systems. The Cold War was over. Eisenhower's grand strategy had prevailed.[6]

The conclusion of this long-term competition with the Soviets brought with it a brief moment of exhilaration. There was talk of a "peace dividend" and even of the "end of history" brought about by the absolute triumph of Western liberalism.[7] This euphoria was cut short by the Persian Gulf war in which PATRIOT missiles completed the first intercepts of ballistic missiles under combat conditions. The "Age of 'Star Wars' " had begun, proclaimed the *Los Angeles Times*.[8]

In response to these new conditions, President George Bush announced in his 1991 State of the Union Address that the SDI program would be refocused to emphasize defense against limited attacks of up to two hundred warheads. Called GPALS—short for global protection against limited strikes—the refocused program would be composed of three elements: a theater system to protect friendly nations, allies, and deployed American forces; a national component that would protect the American people; and a space-based global system that could stop a small attack against virtually any point on the globe.

This downscaled version of Reagan's original concept received congressional approval as 1991 was drawing to a close. Included in the authorization and appropriation bills for FY 1992 was a provision calling for the deployment of a treaty-compliant, ground-based missile defense system by 1996 or as soon as technically feasible. Congress also called for the beginning of negotiations with the Soviets regarding modifications to the ABM Treaty that would permit expansion of this initial deployment beyond the one site allowed by the treaty.

These post-1983 events have been accompanied by a steady erosion of Soviet opposition to SDI and the emergence of Soviet interest in cooperative missile defense efforts. Reagan had offered to share SDI technology with the Soviets within a week of his original SDI speech and repeated the offer personally to Mikhail Gorbachev at the Geneva summit in 1985 and again at Reykjavik in 1986, but the Soviets were skeptical.[9] However, as the Bush administration was transforming the

SDI program into a limited protection system, the Soviets began to express interest in cooperating with the United States where missile defenses were concerned. In a July 1991 letter to the leaders of the G7 conference in London, Gorbachev mentioned a number of possible joint activities between the East and the West. One of these was the "development of joint ABM early warning systems to prevent unauthorized or terrorist operated launches of ballistic missiles." Since this letter was received, several other important Soviet officials have expressed further interest in cooperative missile defenses.[10]

Thus Ronald Reagan's Strategic Defense Initiative contributed significantly to the West's triumph in the Cold War. Moreover, there are indications that SDI as sustained and transformed by the Bush administration will play an important role in the peaceful transition to a more benign, post–Cold War era in which it may once again be better to defend people than to avenge them.

NOTES

PREFACE

1. Interview with Maxwell W. Hunter II, retired aerospace engineer, Washington, D.C., 29 October 1987, pp. 48–49. Earlier in his career, Hunter had a similar experience while he was involved with the U.S. space shuttle program.

2. Sir Walter Ralegh [sic], *The History of the World Treating of the Beginning and First Ages of the Same from the Creation unto . . . the Romans (Prevailing over All) Made Conquest of Asia and Macedon* (Edinburgh: Archibald Constable, 1820), p. lviii. For information about Raleigh's crime, see Will Durant and Ariel Durant, *The Story of Civilization*, Vol. 7: *The Age of Reason Begins: A History of European Civilization in the Period of Shakespeare, Bacon, Montaigne, Rembrandt, Galileo, and Descartes, 1558–1648* (New York: Simon and Schuster, 1961), p. 157.

PART ONE. DAWN OF THE MISSILE AGE

1. Strobe Talbott, *The Master of the Game: Paul Nitze and the Nuclear Peace* (New York: Alfred A. Knopf, 1988), p. 70.

CHAPTER ONE. THE ORIGINS OF MISSILE DEFENSES: FROM V-2 TO NIKE-X

1. Bernard Brodie, *Strategy in the Missile Age* (Princeton, N.J.: Princeton University Press, 1959), p. 202.

2. James McGovern, *Crossbow and Overcast* (New York: William Morrow,

1964), pp. 66–68, 83; Winston S. Churchill, *The Second World War*, Vol. 6: *Triumph and Tragedy* (New York: Bantam Books, 1953), pp. 44–45.

3. General Board, United States Forces, European Theater, Antiaircraft Artillery Section, "V-2 Rocket Attacks and Defense," Study 42, n.d. [late 1945 or early 1946], Document 502.101-42 in the Air Force Historical Research Center, Maxwell Air Force Base, Alabama (AFHRC), pp. 17–19; Ronald W. Clark, *War Winners* (London: Sidgwick and Jackson, 1979), p. 102; David Irving, *The Mare's Nest* (Boston: Little, Brown, 1965), p. 280. An excellent summary of the Allied effort against the V-2 is contained in W[illia]m S. Mark, Jr., Joseph P. D'Arezzo, R. A. Ranson, and G. D. Bagley, "Detection and Plotting of the V-2 (Big Ben) Missile as Developed in ETO," 4 July 1945, Document 142.0423-16 Jul.-Sep. 1945, AFHRC.

4. Report 237-45 of the United States Naval Technical Mission on Guided Missiles, quoted in General Board, "V-2 Rocket Attacks and Defense," pp. 4, 18.

5. Mark et al., "Detection and Plotting of the V-2," p. 65; General Board, "V-2 Rocket Attacks and Defense," pp. 18–19; Th[eodore] von Kármán, *Science, the Key to Air Supremacy*, Vol. 1 of U.S. Army Air Forces, Scientific Advisory Group, *Toward New Horizons: A Report to General of the Army H[enry] H. Arnold*, 12 vols. (Washington, D.C.: Headquarters Army Air Forces, December 1945), pp. 2–3, 13, 47–48, 74–75. Von Kármán noted that the future goal for "pilotless bombers" was to develop rocket-propelled intercontinental missiles and discussed the possibility of combining atomic bombs with such "pilotless bombers." He also discussed possible means of active defense against such weapons. Von Kármán believed that "adapting the target-seeking principle to winged rocket projectiles" offered hope of hitting missiles moving twice as fast as the speed of sound.

6. The reference here is to an extract of the report that is printed as an appendix in Ruth Jarrell and Mary T. Cagle, *History of the Plato Antimissile Missile System: 1952–1960* (Redstone Arsenal, Ala.: U.S. Army Ordnance Missile Command, 23 June 1961). At another point, the report mentions the possibility that the missile of the future would be guided by "self-contained 'memory' devices" (p. 111). Also, the report noted that since the aircraft and missiles of the future could be armed with atomic bombs, "no single airplane or bomb-carrying missile should be permitted to penetrate the defenses of a vital area" (p. 110).

7. Headquarters United States Air Force, Air Force Technical Committee, Wright-Patterson Air Force Base, Dayton, Ohio, *Semi-annual Progress Report of the Guided Missiles Program, Department of the Air Force (31 October 1949)*, Case No. 13-2, Report No. 10, pp. 49–51 (hereafter Air Force Technical Committee, *Progress Report, Oct. 49*). This document may be found in the Redstone Scientific Information Center (RSIC), Redstone Arsenal, Alabama. Over one hundred of the WIZARD studies are available in the RSIC. Examples of titles in the study series are "A Survey of Possible Uses of Electromagnetic Energy as a Defensive Weapon" (UMM-44, 30 Sept. 49); "Defense against Ballistic Missile Targets of the Intercontinental Class" (UMR-111, Vols. I and II, June 54); "Detection of Enemy Missiles by Infrared Radiation in the 6.3-Micron Water-Vapor Band" (UMM-45, 1 Mar. 50); and "A Survey of Early Warning and Tracking Radar" (UMM-68, Dec. 50). Additional information on WIZARD may be found in T. C. Tennant, *Survey of Guidance Systems*, Part 1: United States Missiles, 31 March 1957, pp. III-AC-1–III-AC-3. This document is also known as the Gilfil-

lan Report after Gilfillan Brothers of Los Angeles, the company that contracted with the U.S. Army to complete the survey.

8. Air Force Technical Committee, *Progress Report, Oct. 49*, pp. 54–56; Tennant, *Survey*, pp. III-AA-1–III-AA-7. THUMPER and WIZARD are also discussed in Max Rosenberg, *The Air Force and the National Guided Missile Program, 1944–1950* (Washington, D.C.: Headquarters United States Air Force, Historical Division Liaison Office, June 1964) (hereafter Rosenberg, *Guided Missile Program*), pp. 75–79.

9. Rosenberg, *Guided Missile Program*, pp. 80–83, 114–19; Ruth Currie-McDaniel, *The U.S. Army Strategic Defense Command: Its History and Role in the Strategic Defense Initiative*, 2d ed. (Huntsville, Ala.: U.S. Army Strategic Defense Command, January 1987), pp. 1–2; and Benson D. Adams, *Ballistic Missile Defense* (New York: American Elsevier Publishing Company, 1971), p. 27. In January 1958, Defense Secretary Neil McElroy directed the air force to continue that portion of the WIZARD program that related to things like radar and communications links and to ensure that they were compatible with the NIKE-ZEUS system.

10. Currie-McDaniel, *Army Strategic Defense Command*, pp. 1–2.

11. Bell Laboratories, ABM *Research and Development at Bell Laboratories: Project History, October 1975* (study completed for the United States Army Ballistic Missile Defense Systems Command under contract DAHC60-71-C-0005), Part I, pp. I–1, I-5–I-6 (hereafter Bell Labs, *ABM Project History*).

12. Ibid., Part I, pp. I-2–I-5.

13. Ibid., Part I, pp. I-5–I-6, I–11. Whether an ABM system provides terminal or area protection depends on the altitude at which it is capable of intercepting incoming warheads. In general, an area defense system is one that can intercept outside the atmosphere and therefore has the ability to protect a relatively large area. On the other hand, a system that intercepts warheads as they are re-entering the atmosphere covers a smaller area and is referred to as a terminal or point defense system.

14. Currie-McDaniel, *Strategic Defense Command*, p. 2; Bell Labs, ABM *Project History*, Part I, pp. I-12–I-20, Part II, pp. 1-21–1-22.

15. Paul H. Nitze, with Ann M. Smith and Steven L. Rearden, *From Hiroshima to Glasnost: At the Center of Decision—A Memoir* (New York: Grove Weidenfeld, 1989), p. 248; Ronald E. Powaski, *March to Armageddon: The United States and the Nuclear Arms Race, 1939 to the Present* (New York: Oxford University Press, 1987), pp. 49–50, 52–53, 61–64, 66.

16. Powaski, *March to Armageddon*, p. 65; Ernest J. Yanarella, *The Missile Defense Controversy: Strategy, Technology, and Politics, 1955–1972* (Lexington: University of Kentucky Press, 1977), pp. 28–29; Morton H. Halperin, "The Decision to Deploy the ABM: Bureaucratic and Domestic Politics in the Johnson Administration," *World Politics* 25 (October 1972): p. 67.

17. Michael H. Armacost, *The Politics of Weapons Innovation: The Thor-Jupiter Controversy* (New York: Columbia University Press, 1969), pp. 110–19.

18. The concepts of point defense and area defense were not defined with precision. One missile defense expert used horizontal range to distinguish between the two. He claimed that the maximum horizontal range for a point defense system was 200 miles. In another view, whether an ABM system provided terminal or area protection depended on the altitude at which its missiles could intercept incoming warheads. In general, an area defense system was one that could intercept outside the atmosphere and therefore had the ability to

protect a relatively large area. On the other hand, a system that intercepted warheads as they re-entered the atmosphere could cover only a relatively small area and was referred to as a terminal or point defense system.

19. Adams, *Ballistic Missile Defense*, p. 22; Yanarella, *Missile Defense*, pp. 29–31, 131. Adams quotes a definition of the difference between point and area defense which notes that these concepts "cannot be defined with precision." Maxwell W. Hunter II, a retired aerospace engineer who was involved in the development of defensive systems for decades, advised me that the maximum horizontal range for a point defense system was 200 miles. For more on Hunter, see note 13 above and Chapter 6.

20. Yanarella, *Missile Defense*, pp. 31–32, 35. This inconsistency in the air force position was not corrected until 1959, when Richard Horner, assistant secretary of the air force for R&D, told Congress that based on a study of WIZARD, defense was not cost effective. Money used for defense would be better spent by adding to offensive capability.

21. Adams, *Ballistic Missile Defense*, p. 34.

22. U.S. Executive Office of the President, Office of Defense Mobilization, Security Resources Panel of the Science Advisory Committee, *Deterrence and Survival in the Nuclear Age: Report to the President*, 7 November 1957, pp. 16–19, 39–40 (hereafter the Gaither Report). Gaither organized the panel in May 1957 and directed its efforts until September when he was forced to abandon his work for reasons of health (Gaither Report, p. 9). The Gaither Report was reprinted as a joint committee print in 1976 by the U.S. Congress' Joint Committee on Defense Production.

23. Neil H. McElroy to secretary of the air force, memorandum, "Program for Defense against the Intercontinental Ballistic Missile," 16 January 1958; Neil H. McElroy to Secretary of the Army, memorandum, "Program for Defense against the Intercontinental Ballistic Missile," 16 January 1958. A copy of each letter was printed in U.S. Congress, House, Committee on Armed Services, *Investigation of National Defense Missiles: Hearings before the Committee Pursuant to H. Res. 67*, 85th Cong., 2d sess., 1958, pp. 4196–97.

24. House, *Investigation of National Defense Missiles*, pp. 4772–73.

25. Ibid., pp. 4778–80.

26. Ibid., pp. 4786–95.

27. Ibid., pp. 4798–4800.

28. Thomas A. Sturm, *The USAF Scientific Advisory Board: Its First Twenty Years, 1944–1964*, Office of Air Force History Special Studies (Washington, D.C.: Government Printing Office, 1986; reprint of 1967 edition), pp. 81–82.

29. Ibid., pp. 80–81.

30. Ibid., pp. 82–83.

31. Ibid., pp. 83–84.

32. Adams, *Ballistic Missile Defense*, pp. 28–29, 33–34; Yanarella, *Missile Defense*, p. 60.

33. ARPA was established in 1958. Its name was changed to DARPA (Defense Advanced Research Projects Agency) in 1972.

34. U.S. Congress, House, Committee on Science and Technology, *United States Civilian Space Programs, 1958–1978: A Report Prepared for the Subcommittee on Space Science and Applications of the Committee on Science and Technology by the Science Policy Research Division of the Congressional Research Service of the Library of Congress*, Serial D, vol. 1, 97th Cong., 1st sess., January 1981, pp. 48, 52; Sidney G. Reed, Richard H. Van Atta, and Seymour J.

Deitchman, DARPA *Technical Accomplishments: An Historical Review of Selected DARPA Projects*, vol. 1, IDA Paper P-2192 (Alexandria, Va.: Institute for Defense Analyses, February 1990), p. 1; Herbert F. York, *Making Weapons, Talking Peace: A Physicist's Odyssey from Hiroshima to Geneva* (New York: Basic Books, 1987), pp. 136–43; House, *Investigation of National Defense Missiles*, p. 3991. ARPA was charged with temporary responsibility for guiding the U.S. space program while Congress and the president established a more permanent framework for the nation's space activities. With President Eisenhower's signing of the National Aeronautics and Space Act on July 29, 1958, ARPA's focus became advanced military space programs.

35. Reed et al., *DARPA Accomplishments*, pp. 1-1–1-8. For York's account of this episode, see *Making Weapons*, pp. 128–32.

36. Jerome B. Wiesner and Herbert F. York, "National Security and the Nuclear-Test Ban," *Scientific American* 211 (October 1964): 33–34; John Bosma, "Space and Strategic-Defense Reorientation: Project Defender," *Defense Science and Electronics* (September 1983): 60.

37. Bosma, "Project Defender," p. 61.

38. Ibid., pp. 61–62.

39. Ibid., p. 62.

40. Reed et al., *DARPA Accomplishments*, p. 6-1.

41. Adams, *Ballistic Missile Defense*, pp. 39, 44–45; Yanarella, *Missile Defense*, pp. 66–68, 72.

42. Bell Labs, ABM *Project History*, Part I, p. I-26. An example of a partial success is the intercept of 19 July 1962 when a ZEUS missile came within 2 kilometers of its target (an ATLAS D ICBM).

43. Ibid., Part II, pp. 2-1, 2-3; Adams, *Ballistic Missile Defense*, pp. 63–64; Yanarella, *Missile Defense*, pp. 79–80.

44. Yanarella, *Missile Defense*, pp. 82, 90; Bell Labs, ABM *Project History*, Part II, pp. 1-14–1-21, 2-1, 2-3.

45. Bell Labs, ABM *Project History*, Part II, p. 2-1.

46. Yanarella, *Missile Defense*, pp. 86–87; Adams, *Ballistic Missile Defense*, pp. 85–86.

47. Adams, *Ballistic Missile Defense*, pp. 85–86.

48. Fred Kaplan, *Wizards of Armageddon* (New York: Simon and Schuster, 1983), pp. 343–45; York, *Making Weapons*, pp. 176–77.

49. York, *Making Weapons*, pp. 141, 176–77.

50. Kaplan, *Wizards of Armageddon*, pp. 344–45.

51. "U.S. Expert Doubts Full ICBM Defense," *New York Times* (hereafter *NYT*), 17 February 1961, p. 9.

52. Walter Sullivan, "Spot Check Urged as Arms Control Solution," *NYT*, 6 January 1962, pp. 1, 4; George C. Wilson, "President, Dr. Bethe Differ over Usefulness of Anti-Missile Missile," *Aviation Week* (hereafter *AW*), 19 February 1962, p. 29. James R. Killian, *Sputnik, Scientists, and Eisenhower: A Memoir of the First Special Assistant to the President for Science and Technology* (Cambridge, Mass.: MIT Press, 1977), pp. 154–55, refers to Bethe as "one of the heroes of the long campaign that led to the limited test ban of 1963." The *AW* article quotes extensively from what apparently is the same speech reported in the *NYT* on 6 January.

53. Wiesner and York, "National Security and the Nuclear-Test Ban," pp. 27, 31–33, 35; Lawrence Freedman, *The Evolution of Nuclear Strategy* (New York: St. Martin's Press, 1983), pp. 252–53; Yanarella, *Missile Defense*, pp. 104–

6; Currie-McDaniel, *Strategic Defense Command*, p. 5; Adams, *Ballistic Missile Defense*, pp. 112–13.

54. Wiesner and York, "National Security and the Nuclear-Test Ban," pp. 33–35 (emphasis in original). For a critique of York and Wiesner's argument, see Hanson W. Baldwin, "Slow-Down in the Pentagon," *Foreign Affairs* 17 (January 1965): 263. Baldwin calls their views "simplistic."

55. Yanarella, *Missile Defense*, pp. 104–6; Currie-McDaniel, *Strategic Defense Command*, p. 5; Adams, *Ballistic Missile Defense*, pp. 112–13.

56. Yanarella, *Missile Defense*, pp. 105–6.

57. Freeman, *Nuclear Strategy*, pp. 245–56; Adams, *Ballistic Missile Defense*, pp. 108–9, 113; Yanarella, *Missile Defense*, pp. 110–14. The McNamara quotation is from Adams, *Ballistic Missile Defense*, p. 113.

58. Adams, *Ballistic Missile Defense*, pp. 108–10; Yanarella, *Missile Defense*, pp. 110–11. Freeman, *Nuclear Strategy*, p. 253, noted that there were basically two arguments against missile defenses: They are not technically feasible, and if one side decides to pursue missile defenses it will stimulate an arms race. Until 1966, McNamara used the first argument, but as technical progress was made, it lost much of its power.

CHAPTER TWO. FIELDING AN ABM SYSTEM: DECISION AND DEBATE

1. Quoted in John Newhouse, *War and Peace in the Nuclear Age* (New York: Alfred A. Knopf, 1989), p. 205.

2. *Congressional Record*, 91st Cong., 1st sess., 14 July 1969, 115: 19421.

3. Bell Labs, ABM *Project History*, Part I, pp. I-41, I-43, Part II, 2-10; Adams, *Ballistic Missile Defense*, p. 111; Yanarella, *Missile Defense*, pp. 113–14.

4. Adams, *Ballistic Missile Defense*, pp. 111–12, 115; Yanarella, *Missile Defense*, pp. 113–14.

5. Adams, *Ballistic Missile Defense*, pp. 127, 130; Yanarella, *Missile Defense*, pp. 114–16. In 1966, Lockheed Missiles and Space Company undertook a review of missile defense prospects that included revisiting BAMBI. Lockheed engineers considered lifting NIKE-ZEUS-type missiles into space using a Lockheed design for a space-shuttle-like vehicle called Starclipper. When it appeared that this would require orbiting too much weight, the engineers reviewed the possibility of placing lasers in orbit. Maxwell Hunter, the leader of this project, said the idea of space-based lasers was rejected at this time because "it seemed to me that it would not be credible." However, Hunter went on to say, "now, I had a feeling for laser possibilities." (Maxwell W. Hunter II, "Great Zeus!" 4 July 1987, personal paper, p. 6. Copy provided by Hunter.)

6. Adams, *Ballistic Missile Defense*, pp. 128–32.

7. Ibid., pp. 130–34.

8. Ibid., pp. 132–34.

9. Michael Getler, "Chinese Missile Shot Forcing Nike Choice," *Technology Week*, 7 November 1966, p. 13; Robert B. Semple, Jr., "McNamara Hints Soviet Deploys Antimissile Net," *NYT*, 11 November 1966, pp. 1, 19; "China Announces It Has Exploded a Hydrogen Bomb," *NYT*, 18 June 1967, p. 1. Getler describes the debate over how long it would take to achieve initial operational capability (IOC) with NIKE-X should a deployment decision be taken in 1967.

The announcement by the Chinese that they had successfully tested a nuclear-tipped guided missile touched off the debate.

10. David S. Yost, *Soviet Ballistic Missile Defense and the Western Alliance* (Cambridge, Mass.: Harvard University Press, 1988), pp. 25–26.

11. Ibid., p. 26.

12. Ibid., p. 27.

13. Ibid., pp. 27–28. Since these missiles do not appear to have been armed with nuclear warheads, there is a serious question about their effectiveness in the BMD role.

14. Ibid., pp. 28–29.

15. William Beecher, "The Antimissile Issue," *NYT*, 11 November 1966, p. 19.

16. Halperin, "Decision to Deploy," pp. 74–76; Yanarella, *Missile Defense*, pp. 123–25, 136–37, 141.

17. Michael Charlton, *The Star Wars History: From Deterrence to Defence: The American Strategic Debate* (London: BBC Publications, 1986), p. 4; Halperin, "Decision to Deploy," pp. 76, 83–86, 91; Yanarella, *Missile Defense*, p. 126.

18. Halperin, "Decision to Deploy," pp. 64–65; Adams, *Ballistic Missile Defense*, p. 145; Yanarella, *Missile Defense*, p. 118.

19. Halperin, "Decision to Deploy," p. 85; Yanarella, *Missile Defense*, pp. 124–25, 216(n7); John Newhouse, *Cold Dawn: The Story of SALT* (New York: Holt, Rinehart, and Winston, 1973), pp. 67, 89; Herbert F. York, *Race to Oblivion: A Participant's View of the Arms Race* (New York: Simon and Schuster, 1970), pp. 194–95. McNamara claimed in a speech in San Francisco on 18 September 1967 that this group unanimously agreed that an ABM system would not work; in that same speech he announced that the United States would deploy a thin ABM system against China (Robert S. McNamara, "Text of McNamara Speech on Anti-China Missile Defense and U.S. Nuclear Strategy," *NYT*, 19 September 1967, p. 18 [hereafter McNamara, "Anti-China Missile Defense"]). According to Gregg Herken, *Counsels of War*, expanded ed. (New York: Oxford University Press, 1987), p. 198, a majority of the science advisers at the 23 January meeting "specifically opposed the idea of a limited ABM system to counter the yet-to-appear missile threat from China." Herken also noted that the political motivation behind the SENTINEL deployment decision led Richard Garwin to charge that SENTINEL was an "anti-Republican" system rather than an "anti-Chinese" one. For Jerome Wiesner's views on the meeting with the president and McNamara's September 1967 speech, see "After the Pentagon Papers: Talk with Kistiakowsky, Wiesner," *Science* 174, (November 1971): p. 925. Wiesner felt that the scientists had rejected both the thick and thin ABM systems and that McNamara misused their advice, making it appear as if the scientists favored the thin program. Because of McNamara's announcement on the thin ABM system, Wiesner began to oppose missile defenses publicly and "stopped working within the government and started to work outside." He was convinced that the decision to deploy the thin system was strictly political. As he put it: "There was no rationale to justify the ABM that I could see, and I decided to see if this waste for political reasons could be stopped" (ibid., p. 927).

20. Adams, *Ballistic Missile Defense*, p. 152; Yanarella, *Missile Defense*, pp. 129–30.

21. Yanarella, *Missile Defense*, pp. 126–28.

22. Yanarella, *Missile Defense*, pp. 128–29.

23. Yanarella, *Missile Defense*, pp. 126–28.

24. Quoted in Adams, *Ballistic Missile Defense*, p. 154.

25. Newhouse, *War and Peace*, p. 205; Halperin, "Decision to Deploy," p. 87; Adams, *Ballistic Missile Defense*, p. 158. The principal account of the interaction between Johnson, Kosygin, and McNamara is McNamara's recollection of events as recounted by John Newhouse. Lawrence Freedman, *Nuclear Strategy*, p. 248, commented that "there was something of the lecturer in McNamara." This remark may give an insight into the way McNamara addressed Premier Kosygin on the ABM issue.

26. "China Announces It Has Exploded a Hydrogen Bomb," *NYT*, 18 June 1967, pp. 1, 3; McCandlish Phillips, "Kosygin Takes a Walk," *NYT*, 18 June 1967, p. 1; William Beecher, "Pressure in U.S. for Defense Seen," *NYT*, 18 June 1967, p. 2.

27. Halperin, "Decision to Deploy," p. 87.

28. Ibid., pp. 87–88; Yanarella, *Missile Defense*, pp. 129, 140.

29. McNamara, "Anti-China Missile Defense," p. 18.

30. Ibid., For information on the "unanimous" agreement of the group of scientists and technical advisers, see the discussion of McNamara's 23 January 1967 meeting above.

31. "United States Missile Defense Is Renamed Sentinel," *NYT*, 5 November 1967, p. 84; Yanarella, *Missile Defense*, pp. 140–41; Halperin, "Decision to Deploy," pp. 87–88.

32. McNamara, "Anti-China Missile Defense," p. 18.

33. Ibid., pp. 18–19.

34. "Visions of Star Wars: A NOVA/Frontline Special Report," No. 5008 (Boston: WGBH Foundation, 1986), p. 13. This is a transcript of a NOVA program that was originally broadcast on 22 April 1986.

35. Adams, *Ballistic Missile Defense*, pp. 180–86.

36. Yanarella, *Missile Defense*, p. 143; Powaski, *March to Armageddon*, pp. 123–26.

37. Yanarella, *Missile Defense*, pp. 131–32.

38. Anne Hessing Cahn, "American Scientists and the ABM: A Case Study in Controversy," in Albert Teich, ed., *Scientists and Public Affairs* (Cambridge, Mass.: MIT Press, 1974), pp. 53–55.

39. Ibid., pp. 56–57; Yanarella, *Missile Defense*, p. 149; Adams, *Ballistic Missile Defense*, pp. 185–87. Cahn argues that the scientists used the personal concerns of residents about the safety aspects of having missile sites close to their neighborhoods to generate support for their own opposition to SENTINEL, which was largely motivated by perceptions about an arms race. Cahn quotes one source as saying the intensity of the opposition to SENTINEL was generated by "good old American feelings about real estate." For an excellent discussion of the opposition to SENTINEL and SAFEGUARD, especially in the Boston area where the first two of seventeen SENTINEL sites were to be built, see Mary D. Anderson, *Annual Historical Summary of SAFEGUARD System Command* (1 July 1968–30 June 1969) (RCS CSHIS-6 [R2]), vol. 1, Narrative, 31 October 1968, pp. 244–80, Historical Office, U.S. Army Strategic Defense Command, Huntsville, Alabama.

40. Adams, *Ballistic Missile Defense*, pp. 187–91; Yanarella, *Missile Defense*, p. 144.

41. Robert B. Semple, Jr., "Nixon Staff Had Central Role in Missile Decision," *NYT*, 19 March 1969, p. 22 (hereafter Semple, "Missile Decision").

42. Ibid.

43. Ibid.; Richard Nixon, *Memoirs of Richard Nixon* (New York: Grosset and Dunlap, 1978), p. 370.

44. Semple, "Missile Decision," p. 22.

45. Richard M. Nixon, "The President's News Conference of March 14, 1969" and "Statement on Deployment of the Antiballistic Missile System, March 14, 1969," Documents 108 and 109, respectively, in *Public Papers of the Presidents of the United States, Containing the Public Messages, Speeches, and Statements of the President: Richard Nixon, 1969* (Washington, D.C.: Government Printing Office, 1971), pp. 208–19; Semple, "Missile Decision," p. 22; Bell Labs, ABM *Project History*, Part I, p. I-46; Adams, *Ballistic Missile Defense*, p. 200; Henry Kissinger, *White House Years* (Boston: Little, Brown, 1979), p. 209. For an account of how the SAFEGUARD name was selected, see Yanarella, *Missile Defense*, pp. 173–74.

46. Yanarella, *Missile Defense*, pp. 174–75. The Nixon quotation is found on p. 175.

47. Adams, *Ballistic Missile Defense*, p. 157; Yanarella, *Missile Defense*, p. 145.

48. Adams, *Ballistic Missile Defense*, p. 203; Yanarella, *Missile Defense*, pp. 144–45. For more details on the opposition to SENTINEL, see Yanarella, *Missile Defense*, pp. 149–55.

49. Daniel J. Kevles, *The Physicists: The History of a Scientific Community in Modern America* (New York: Vintage Books, 1977), pp. 406–7.

50. Ibid., p. 407.

51. Adams, *Ballistic Missile Defense*, p. 200; Yanarella, *Missile Defense*, pp. 176–77.

52. Adams, *Ballistic Missile Defense*, pp. 208–10, 213, 215, 217–18; Yanarella, *Missile Defense*, p. 146. The established organizations opposed to BMD were frequently scientific and academic associations.

53. Talbott, *Master of the Game*, p. 112.

54. Ibid., pp. 112–13. Wilson, Wolfowitz, and Perle, known as the "three musketeers," were protégés of Albert Wohlstetter, a leading defense analyst who had been at RAND during its early days.

55. Adams, *Ballistic Missile Defense*, pp. 192, 208–15.

56. "The Scale Tips against the ABM," *Newsweek* (hereafter *NW*), 21 July 1969, p. 25.

57. "Safeguard: Pro and Con," *NW*, 21 July 1969, pp. 26–27. Even Senator George Aiken (R-Vt.), who eventually voted against deployment, recognized that Nixon needed a strong Senate vote behind him as he began negotiations with the Soviets ("The ABM: Winners and Losers," *Washington Post* (hereafter *WP*), 7 August 1969, p. A16).

58. "Safeguard: Pro and Con," p. 27.

59. *Congressional Record*, 91st Cong., 1st sess., 9 July 1969, 115: 18895.

60. Ibid., 18908.

61. Ibid., 18910, 18915.

62. Ibid., 18922.

63. Ibid., 18922-23.

64. Ibid., 18923.

65. "Scale Tips against the ABM," pp. 25–26.

66. John W. Finney, "ABM Foes Set Back as Prouty Shifts to Support Nixon," *NYT*, 15 July 1969, p. A1; "Armaments: Plea for an Extra Button," *NW*, 28 July 1969, p. 39. Prouty's speech may be found in *Congressional Record*, 91st Cong., 1st sess., 14 July 1969, 115: 19420-23. The quoted material is from p. 19421.

67. "Woman Passenger Killed, Kennedy Escapes in Crash," *NYT*, 20 July 1969, pp. 1, 50; "ABM: Winning Isn't Everything," *NW*, 18 August 1969, pp. 20–21. President Nixon later wrote of this episode: "And when Teddy Kennedy's car went off a bridge at Chappaquiddick in July, the effectiveness of his leadership against the ABM was significantly reduced" (Nixon, *Memoirs*, pp. 417–18).

68. Richard L. Lyons, "Mrs. Smith Plays Key Role in Vote," *WP*, 7 August 1969, p. A12; "The Surprising Lady from Maine," *NW*, 18 August 1969, p. 21. The *Newsweek* article contains an error. It speaks of spending $751.9 million on SAFEGUARD research and development. This should read $759.1 million (see *Congressional Quarterly Almanac*, 91st Cong., 1st sess., 1969, p. 270).

69. Lyons, "Mrs. Smith," p. A12; "Lady from Maine," p. 21.

70. "Cry of Opposition Precedes Session," *WP*, 7 August 1969, p. A12; "Lady from Maine," p. 21; "Nixon Missile Plan Wins in Senate by a 51–50 Vote; House Approval Likely," *NYT*, 7 August 1969, p. 22.

71. "The Nation: Moving Ahead, Nixon Style," *Time*, 15 August 1969, p. 12; "Nixon Missile Plan Wins," pp. 1, 22; Spencer Rich, "ABM Wins Crucial Senate Test," *WP*, 7 August 1969, p. A1.

72. Rich, "ABM Wins," p. A12.

73. Chalmers M. Roberts, "The Close ABM Vote: A Victory or Defeat?" *WP*, 7 August 1969, p. A12; "Scale Tips against the ABM," p. 28; "Armaments: Plea for an Extra Button," p. 39; "ABM: Winning Isn't Everything," p. 22. With regard to SAFEGUARD as a symbol for those opposed to U.S. military policies, Richard Nixon, in his *Memoirs*, quoted columnist Stewart Alsop, who wrote that voting against ABM was "the liberals' way of getting back at the generals for Vietnam" (p. 416). Paul Nitze found the roots of the anti-ABM effort "in the country's disenchantment with the Vietnam war, in the widespread alienation from the government of former supporters of the nuclear defense program, and in the desire of many to wish away the problems of national security" (Nitze, *Hiroshima to Glasnost*, p. 294).

One indication of the attitude of scientists opposed to the ABM program may be found in the comments of George Kistiakowsky: "The proposals of these, I might call them 'hot-rod military' types, are not sacrosanct anymore. They are challenged, and the ABM debate was the first of these public debates" ("After the Pentagon Papers," p. 927).

74. Nixon, *Memoirs*, pp. 415–18.

PART TWO. THE SALT DECADE

1. "Kissinger Assesses the Moscow Summit and the Arms Race," 3 July 1974 (hereafter Kissinger, Press Conference, 3 July 1974), pp. 264–65 in Roger P. Labrie, ed., *SALT Hand Book: Key Documents and Issues, 1972–1979* (Washington, D.C.: American Enterprise Institute for Public Policy Research, 1979).

CHAPTER THREE. SALT I AND THE
INSTITUTIONALIZATION OF MAD

1. Kissinger, *White House Years*, p. 208.

2. Gerard Smith, *Doubletalk: The Story of the First Strategic Arms Limitations Talks* (Garden City, N.Y.: Doubleday, 1980), p. 148.

3. Richard M. Nixon, Inaugural Address, 20 January 1969, transcript in *NYT*, 21 January 1969, p. 21; Nixon, *Memoirs*, p. 416; Kissinger, *White House Years*, p. 132; Powaski, *March to Armageddon*, p. 128; Yanarella, *Missile Defense*, p. 181; Adams, *Ballistic Missile Defense*, pp. 189–90.

4. Kissinger, *White House Years*, pp. 138, 145; Richard Halloran, "U.S.-Soviet Talks on Missiles Open Nov. 17 in Helsinki," *NYT*, 26 October 1969, p. 1; William Beecher, "Some See Vote Spurring Arms Talks," *NYT*, 8 August 1969, p. 12; Powaski, *March to Armageddon*, pp. 133–44. The quoted material is from Kissinger, *White House Years*, pp. 138 and 145, respectively. Similar sentiments were reported in the Beecher article.

5. Kissinger, *White House Years*, pp. 149, 539–40, 798–99, 804, 806, 811–12, 1129; Newhouse, *Cold Dawn*, pp. 156–57, 168, 173; Smith, *Doubletalk*, p. 204. It may be possible to speak of a bargaining-chip mentality where the attitudes of some involved in these events are concerned. Those affected by this way of thinking would believe that since a BMD system really wouldn't be effective and would merely heat up the arms race, the concessions the Soviets might offer in return for an agreement by the United States to restrict or forego SAFEGUARD would be of little significance. The main objective of those guided by this line of thought would be to stop the deployment of ABM systems. This mind set may have affected some U.S. SALT negotiators who seemed at times more interested in limiting ABM systems than in gaining restrictions on Soviet ICBMs. For example, Gerard Smith's attitude toward ABM seems to have been ambivalent at best. An indication of his view might be this statement about the ABM Treaty: "It put an end to the expensive and unpopular U.S. ABM program." Smith comes across toward the end of *Doubletalk* as one who could see little or no value in defensive systems even though the Soviets seemed to have taken the prospective capabilities of an American ABM system quite seriously. For Smith's views on ABM, see *Doubletalk*, pp. 31, 147, 153, 156, 192, 204, 455–57, 460. SAFEGUARD was also opposed by elements of the American press, some members of the scientific and academic communities, and advocates of disarmament on the grounds that an American ABM would do nothing but intensify the arms race.

6. Newhouse, *Cold Dawn*, p. 185; Kissinger, *White House Years*, pp. 539–42, 810–11; Smith, *Doubletalk*, pp. 192, 205.

7. Smith, *Doubletalk*, pp. 75–107, especially pp. 86–87; Newhouse, *Cold Dawn*, p. 177; Kissinger, *White House Years*, pp. 149–50; Powaski, *March to Armageddon*, pp. 132–34; Nitze, *Hiroshima to Glasnost*, pp. 303–7.

8. Kissinger, *White House Years*, pp. 149–50; Newhouse, *War and Peace*, pp. 221–22; Newhouse, *Cold Dawn*, pp. 173, 177; Nitze, *Hiroshima to Glasnost*, p. 307; Smith, *Doubletalk*, pp. 88–89, 93–96. Discovering the desire of the Soviets to negotiate on ABM systems was enough by itself to make round one of the talks worthwhile in Smith's opinion (*Doubletalk*, p. 96). With regard to MIRVing, Smith pointed out that limitations on this emerging technology were not included in the paper "Illustrative Elements" that the U.S. delegation tabled on 24 November in an effort to get the first round of talks "down to

specifics." Smith commented in 1980 that this omission "must have told the Soviets something about the degree of U.S. interest in that major issue" (*Doubletalk* pp. 88–89). Newhouse, *War and Peace*, p. 222, pointed out that the Soviets did not mention MIRV either.

9. Newhouse, *Cold Dawn*, pp. 177, 182–83; Smith, *Doubletalk*, pp. 477–78; Kissinger, *White House Years*, pp. 541–42. For a fascinating account of the extremely high qualifications of the Soviet negotiating team, their careful preparations, and their tough, detail-oriented negotiating techniques, see Paul Nitze, "The Strategic Balance: Between Hope and Skepticism," *Foreign Policy* (Winter 1974–75): 141–44 (hereafter Nitze, "Between Hope and Skepticism"). Nitze believed that democratic societies are at a disadvantage when negotiating with the Soviets. In all fairness, it must be noted that the U.S. delegation was also composed of clearly outstanding people with a broad knowledge of strategic arms issues. Nitze himself made this point in his memoirs (*Hiroshima to Glasnost*, pp. 299–300; see also Smith, *Doubletalk*, pp. 38–43). In *Hiroshima to Glasnost*, Nitze made an interesting point that gives an insight into the conciliatory position taken by the U.S. delegation. Several American delegates approached the negotiations as a "non-zero-sum game in which both sides could profit from an agreement." Most of the Soviet negotiators, including their chief negotiator, Vladimir Semenov, were unfamiliar with American game theories and did not understand the concept of a non-zero-sum outcome. According to Nitze, Semenov "took the position that he was negotiating for the interests of his side alone and that it was up to the United States to protect its own interests" (*Hiroshima to Glasnost*, p. 301).

10. Kissinger, *White House Years*, pp. 539–42; Newhouse, *Cold Dawn*, p. 185. Nitze claims to have originated the U.S. negotiating position that would shift America's ABM program from silo defense to defense of the NCA (*Hiroshima to Glasnost*, p. 307). For a discussion of the different interest groups involved in arms control negotiations, see Talbott, *Master of the Game*, p. 117. He lists eight different sources of influence on negotiations and notes that no agency of the U.S. government "had a clear idea what it wanted out of SALT. Not surprisingly, the infighting over SALT was especially intense and chaotic." For a description of the communication problems between the U.S. SALT team and Washington, see Nitze, "Between Hope and Skepticism," pp. 144–45.

11. Newhouse, *Cold Dawn*, pp. 179–85; Kissinger, *White House Years*, p. 545. The quoted words are Kissinger's.

12. These were weapon systems like fighter aircraft and aircraft carrier planes that the United States considered tactical systems. Because these planes were capable of carrying nuclear weapons and could reach Soviet cities, the Russians wanted them included in SALT negotiations. The United States would not agree to this request because, for one thing, the basing and operation of these aircraft were tied to U.S. relations with its European allies.

13. Smith, *Doubletalk*, pp. 146–47.

14. The "front channel" refers to the normal lines of communication between a negotiating delegation and its government through which instructions are passed to the delegation and the delegation reports back to its government. In "back channel" communications, an additional link is established between special contacts for each government and only the absolute minimum number of people are involved. Throughout the remainder of the talks, whenever the formal negotiations became deadlocked, the Nixon administration would use

the back channel to resolve the disagreement and then leave it to the U.S. delegation to negotiate the details in the formal SALT talks. See Kissinger, *White House Years*, p. 1216, and Newhouse, *Cold Dawn*, p. 203.

15. Kissinger, *White House Years*, pp. 547–49; Smith, *Doubletalk*, p. 147. For a view of how communications were carried out in this back channel, see *White House Years*, pp. 806–10.

16. Kissinger, *White House Years*, pp. 548–49; Newhouse, *Cold Dawn*, pp. 186, 189–90.

17. William Beecher, "Expansion of ABM to 3D Missile Site Is Sought by Laird," *NYT*, 25 February 1970, pp. 1, 30; Adams, *Ballistic Missile Defense*, pp. 222–23.

18. Beecher, "Expansion of ABM," pp. 1, 30.

19. Adams, *Ballistic Missile Defense*, pp. 227–28; Newhouse, *Cold Dawn*, pp. 185, 187; Kissinger, *White House Years*, p. 547.

20. See Smith, *Doubletalk*, pp. 204–05, and Adams, *Ballistic Missile Defense*, pp. 228–31, for discussions of the situation faced by the Nixon administration with regard to the ABM issue.

21. Chalmers M. Roberts, "ABM Approval Urged to Curb Soviet Missiles," *WP*, 24 July 1970, p. A12; "Kissinger Declares ABM Key to Gains at Vienna Parley," *NYT*, 24 July 1970, p. 2; Kissinger, *White House Years*, p. 551; Newhouse, *Cold Dawn*, pp. 187–88; Nixon, *Memoirs*, 417.

22. John W. Finney, "Expansion of ABM Backed by Senate by 52-to-47 Vote," *NYT*, 13 August 1970, pp. 1, 12; Spencer Rich, "ABM Curb Beaten by Senate, 52 to 47," *WP*, 13 August 1970, pp. A1, A10. For commentary on this vote, see Chalmers M. Roberts, "ABM Vote Is Signal to Moscow," *WP*, 13 August 1970, p. A11.

23. Finney, "Expansion of ABM Backed by Senate," p. 12. For Smith's account of his efforts here, see *Doubletalk*, pp. 148–49. For Kissinger's views, see *White House Years*, p. 551.

24. Smith, *Doubletalk*, pp. 179–92; Powaski, *March to Armageddon*, p. 136.

25. Smith, *Doubletalk*, pp. 192–93.

26. Smith, *Doubletalk*, pp. 179, 193–98; Newhouse, *Cold Dawn*, pp. 193–94.

27. Smith, *Doubletalk*, p. 194; Newhouse, *Cold Dawn*, p. 193. Somewhat later, squabbles over America's negotiating position on ABM brought to light a slightly different aspect of this sense that the Americans were negotiating with themselves. Newhouse quoted one official as saying with bitterness: "We dissipate our energies negotiating between ourselves." (*Cold Dawn*, p. 231). Newhouse also reported that the White House had serious reservations about the reliability of the American delegation with regard to the faithful execution of instructions from Washington. Smith (*Doubletalk*, p. 259) noted that at times negotiating with Washington was more difficult than negotiating with the Soviets.

28. Kissinger, *White House Years*, pp. 811–13; Newhouse, *Cold Dawn*, pp. 197–200.

29. Newhouse, *Cold Dawn*, p. 198; Smith, *Doubletalk*, pp. 206–7; Kissinger, *White House Years*, pp. 811–12.

30. Kissinger, *White House Years*, pp. 811–12. The relevant passage reads: "On February 1, Senator Hubert Humphrey urged the Senate to freeze American ABM and MIRV programs. 'At no cost to ourselves,' Humphrey declared, 'and with absolute guarantee of our own security—we can stop our part of the nuclear arms race in response to actions already taken by the Soviet Union.'"

Smith (*Doubletalk*, pp. 206–7) admits that the halt in SS-9 deployments "looked like an indication of Soviet intention to curb the arms competition," but he does not mention what, if anything, he might have recommended to Nixon on the basis of the Soviet action.

31. Kissinger, *White House Years*, p. 811; Smith, *Doubletalk*, p. 207.

32. For a view of how the negotiations inched along in the back channel, see Kissinger, *White House Years*, pp. 813–18. All of these negotiations were carried out against a backdrop that included great pressure for the Nixon administration to accept Soviet offers. For example, Gerard Smith reported that during the winter of 1970-71 the Federation of American Scientists, a *NYT* editorial, and the Democratic Policy Council supported the Soviet position that would have separated an ABM agreement from an agreement limiting offensive arms. Smith also noted that Hubert Humphrey introduced a resolution in the Senate calling for Nixon to "first agree to ban or limit ABM deployments and then to negotiate offensive limitations" (*Doubletalk*, pp. 205–6).

33. This port is on the southern coast of Cuba. In the summer of 1970 the Soviets attempted to establish a submarine base there. After constructing several facilities, the Soviets dispatched to the port a flotilla of ships including a submarine tender. The crisis ended in early fall after some intense behind-the-scenes diplomacy. The Soviets stopped construction of their facilities and withdrew the submarine tender on 10 October. For details, see Kissinger, *White House Years*, pp. 632–52.

34. Kissinger, *White House Years*, pp. 810–15; Nixon, *Memoirs*, p. 523.

35. Smith, *Doubletalk*, p. 211; Newhouse, *Cold Dawn*, pp. 205–6; Kissinger, *White House Years*, pp. 813–15.

36. Newhouse, *Cold Dawn*, pp. 205–6; Kissinger, *White House Years*, p. 813. Smith viewed this change with incredulity. In his account of the SALT negotiations he compared the U.S. negotiations on ABM to a shell game in which the position on ABM favored by the United States was the pea the Soviets had to discover under the shells. Of the 11 March instructions, Smith wrote: "But this time we had three shells! 'This can't be serious,' was my reaction as I read that we were directed also to put to the USSR delegation a new concept for ABM control having 'equal status' with the alternative proposals already tabled" (*Doubletalk*, p. 211).

37. Kissinger, *White House Years*, pp. 810–16. The major quotation is from p. 816. See also Nixon, *Memoirs*, p. 523.

38. One of the carrots Nixon and Kissinger had used to encourage the Soviets to compromise on key SALT issues was a promise to expedite negotiations aimed at curtailing the activities in Berlin of the Federal Republic of Germany. In return for this, the Soviets made certain commitments regarding better Western access to Berlin, with this improved access being guaranteed by the Soviets. There was also talk of expanded trade between the United States and the Soviet Union. See Kissinger, *White House Years*, pp. 408, 802–3, 806–10.

39. Kissinger, *White House Years*, pp. 817–19. Smith's account of the overtures from Semenov may be found in *Doubletalk*, pp. 218–21. Whereas Kissinger gives 2 and 9 May for the pertinent meetings between Smith and Semenov, Smith specifies the date of the first meeting as 4 May (his fifty-seventh birthday) and the following Sunday, which would have been 9 May. Newhouse, *Cold Dawn*, pp. 214–15, specifies 4 and 9 May for the meetings and mentions a third meeting on 6 May.

40. Kissinger, *White House Years*, pp. 819–20; Newhouse, *Cold Dawn*, pp. 218–19.

41. Newhouse, *Cold Dawn*, pp. 218–25; Smith, *Doubletalk*, pp. 250–51. The quotation is from *Cold Dawn*, p. 225. Smith is rather critical of the aspect of the 20 May agreement dealing with simultaneity, saying essentially that the agreement did not resolve the issue of the sequence of offensive and defensive weapons talks.

42. Smith, *Doubletalk*, pp. 205, 214–16.

43. Ibid., pp. 250–51.

44. Ibid., pp. 254–55, 266. Smith felt very strongly that the United States made a grave mistake by not pushing for a complete ban on ABM systems. He pushed for and received authority to raise the question of a ban privately with his Soviet counterpart, Semenov. In Smith's eyes the Soviets responded positively. However, this initiative was ended when President Nixon wrote Smith on 12 August and explained why he thought the idea of a complete ban was detrimental to negotiations under way. For Smith's thinking on the ABM ban, see *Doubletalk*, pp. 256–57, 261; see pp. 485–86 for a copy of the Nixon letter. See also Newhouse, *Cold Dawn*, pp. 226–27.

45. Newhouse, *Cold Dawn*, pp. 226–27.

46. Ibid., pp. 227–30. As already indicated in note 44 above, Gerard Smith favored a complete ban on ABM (*Doubletalk*, p. 256).

47. Newhouse, *Cold Dawn*, pp. 232–33; Smith, *Doubletalk*, pp. 267–68.

48. Newhouse, *Cold Dawn*, pp. 235–36.

49. Smith, *Doubletalk*, pp. 192, 317; Newhouse, *Cold Dawn*, pp. 236–37. Newhouse also reported that Soviet military men became "steadily more enamored of the American hard-site concept for defending ICBMs" (p. 237).

50. Newhouse, *Cold Dawn*, pp. 237–40.

51. Ibid., p. 241.

52. Ibid., pp. 224–25, 241–42. As a further precautionary measure, only four copies of NSDM 158 supposedly left the White House. These copies went to Richard Helms at the CIA, Secretary of State William Rogers, Secretary of Defense Melvin Laird, and Gerard Smith.

53. Ibid., pp. 242, 244. For details of Kissinger's negotiations with the Soviets in March and April, see Kissinger, *White House Years*, pp. 1129–31, 1137, 1148–50.

54. Newhouse, *Cold Dawn*, pp. 245–47. For interesting details on some of the "horse trading" required to gain U.S. Navy acceptance of the Soviet numbers on submarines and SLBMs, see ibid., pp. 245–46.

55. Smith, *Doubletalk*, pp. 301–18, 387–88; Nitze, *Hiroshima to Glasnost*, pp. 315–21; Newhouse, *Cold Dawn*, pp. 248–49. Nitze, apparently, was a leader in the effort to include radar limitations in the ABM Treaty. In the dispute over what constituted an ABM-capable radar, the United States wanted to define such a radar as one with a power aperture of 1×10^6 watt-meters squared or more, and the Soviets favored a level of 1×10^{10}. A compromise level of 3×10^6 was accepted by both sides. This limitation on radars, combined with other restrictions, was to prevent a rapid expansion of the ABM system each side would be allowed under the ABM Treaty.

56. Nixon, *Memoirs*, pp. 609–12, 615–16; Kissinger, *White House Years*, pp. 1238–42; Newhouse, *Cold Dawn*, pp. 249–56.

57. Smith, *Doubletalk*, pp. 455–56; Powaski, *March to Armageddon*, pp. 142, 150; "Treaty between the United States of America and the Union of Soviet So-

cialist Republics on the Limitation of Anti-Ballistic Missile Systems," pp. 273–77, in Newhouse, *Cold Dawn*; ABM Treaty, "Agreed Interpretations, Common Understandings, and Unilateral Statements," pp. 494–95, in Smith, *Doubletalk*.

58. Jerome H. Kahan, *Security in the Nuclear Age: Developing U.S. Strategic Arms Policy* (Washington, D.C.: Brookings Institution, 1975), pp. 97, 187; "Interim Agreement between the United States of America and the Union of Soviet Socialist Republics on Certain Measures with Respect to the Limitations on Strategic Offensive Arms," 26 May 1972, Appendix 7, pp. 503–6, in Smith, *Doubletalk*. For another discussion of the treaty's provisions, see Powaski, *March to Armageddon*, p. 143. For the sake of simplicity, I have used the numbers for missile ceilings that are provided in Nitze, *Hiroshima to Glasnost*, pp. 330–331. Once the number of Soviet SLBMs went above 740, the added missiles were supposed to be replacements for older ICBMs and SLBMs that had been retired.

59. Newhouse, *Cold Dawn*, pp. 2–3, 260; Smith, *Doubletalk*, p. 455. See also Thomas W. Wolfe, *The SALT Experience* (Cambridge, Mass.: Ballinger, 1979), pp. 17–18, and Yanarella, *Missile Defense*, pp. 185–86. Strobe Talbott calls arms control "an attempt to codify MAD" (*Master of the Game*, p. 108).

CHAPTER FOUR. THE END OF THE SALT ERA: STRATEGIC CRISIS

1. Newhouse, *Cold Dawn*, p. 18.
2. Powaski, *March to Armageddon*, pp. 144, 156.
3. Spencer Rich, "Senate Approves Treaty to Limit ABM Defenses," *WP*, 4 August 1972, pp. A1, A18.
4. Ibid., p. A1. Talbott, *Master of the Game*, p. 135, claims that Senators Jackson and Thurmond also had reservations about the ABM Treaty but did not vote against it.
5. Rich, "Senate Approves Treaty," pp. A1, A18; Michael Getler, "SALT Support Seen Threatened in Senate," *WP*, 7 August 1972, p. A15; Spencer Rich, "A-Pact Change at Showdown," *WP*, 9 August 1972, p. A4; Spencer Rich, "Jackson A-Pact 'Elaborations' Are Shunned by White House," *WP*, 10 August 1972, p. A2.
6. For details on the passage of the Senate resolution, see Rich, "A-Pact Change," p. A4; Spencer Rich, "A-Arms Pact Voted, 23-1, by House Group," *WP*, 11 August 1972, p. A1; Bob Woodward and Carl Bernstein, "GOP Loses Bid to Delay Bugging Suit," *WP*, 12 August 1972, pp. A1, A10; Jack Fuller, "SALT Debate Foes Charged with Stalling," *WP*, 15 August 1972, p. A4; Jack Fuller, "Jackson Claims Russians Lied on Submarines," *WP*, 16 August 1972, p. A2; Jack Fuller, "SALT Pact Hits New Hill Snag," *WP*, 17 August 1972, p. A17; Jack Fuller, "5-Year Limit on Arms Wins Vote in House," *WP*, 19 August 1972, p. A1; Spencer Rich, "Senate Still Bickering on Missile 'Equality,'" *WP*, 8 September 1972, p. A12; Murrey Marder, "Arms Accord Voted with Tough Rider," *WP*, 15 September 1972, pp. A1, A8; Richard L. Lyons, "Congress Approves SALT Pact," *WP*, 26 September 1972, pp. A1, A10.
7. Robert G. Kaiser, "Soviet Union Ratifies Treaty Limiting ABMs," *WP*, 30 September 1972, p. A24; "Nixon Signs Treaty on Nuclear Weapons," *WP*, 1 October 1972, p. A5.

8. Talbott, *Master of the Game*, p. 136; Labrie, *SALT Hand Book*, pp. 161–62.

9. Labrie, *SALT Hand Book*, pp. 164–65; "New ABM Systems Banned in Soviet-American Protocol," *WP*, 4 July 1974, p. A7.

10. Kissinger, Press Conference, 3 July 1974, pp. 255–56.

11. Ibid., pp. 264–65.

12. Labrie, *SALT Hand Book*, pp. 166–67; Carroll Kilpatrick, "Summit Progress Noted: Kissinger Says Guidelines on SALT Near," *WP*, 24 November 1974, pp. A1, A8.

13. Wolfe, *SALT Experience*, pp. 211–16; Labrie, *SALT Hand Book*, pp. 167–68. For a discussion of the domestic political ramifications of the SALT negotiations in the election year of 1976, see Talbott, *Master of the Game*, p. 143.

14. Wolfe, *Salt Experience*, p. 219; Labrie, *SALT Hand Book*, pp. 381–82.

15. Labrie, *SALT Hand Book*, pp. 384–86.

16. Labrie, *SALT Hand Book*, pp. 384–87, 389, 393, 401, 410, 413, 417, 481.

17. Talbott, *Master of the Game*, p. 159; Murrey Marder, "Wrangling over SALT Illustrates U.S.-Soviet Gulf," *WP*, 2 January 1981, pp. A1, A14. Don Oberdorfer, *The Turn: From the Cold War to a New Era—The United States and the Soviet Union, 1983–1990* (New York: Poseidon Press, 1991), p. 235, called the Soviet invasion of Afghanistan "a world-changing event" that "demolished what was left of . . . détente." Oberdorfer further stated that the invasion "drastically affected the international climate of the 1980s, deepening fears that the Soviet Union was embarked on a course of expansion through force of arms" (ibid.).

18. Bernard Gwertzman, "Carter Seeks Treaty Delay; Recalls Envoy from Soviet [sic] over Moscow's Afghan Role," *NYT*, 3 January 1980, p. A1, A11; Talbott, *Master of the Game*, Chapter 10; Nitze, *Hiroshima to Glasnost*, pp. 423–24. There had long been serious doubts about the ability of the SALT II treaty to win Senate approval. Nitze expressed concern about the outcome of the SALT process in several places in the mid-1970s ("The Vladivostok Accord and SALT II," *Review of Politics* 37 (April 1975): 147–60, and "Assuring Strategic Stability in an Era of Détente," *Foreign Affairs* 54 (January 1976): pp. 207–8). Several other conservative strategic analysts expressed serious concerns also: Colin S. Gray, "SALT: Time to Quit," *Strategic Review* 4 (Fall 1976): 14–22; William R. Van Cleave, "SALT on the Eagle's Tail," *Strategic Review* 4, (Spring 1976), 44–55. Talbott saw in the Senate confirmation votes for Paul Warnke as director of ACDA and chief arms control negotiator a clear warning to the Carter administration that any agreement with the Soviets would be subject to close scrutiny by the Senate (*Master of the Game*, pp. 151–54). At the time of Carter's withdrawal of the treaty, the *New York Times* reported that the treaty would have experienced trouble in the Senate regardless of Soviet actions in other parts of the world (see Charles Mohr, "Arms Pact Outlook Called Dim Anyway," *NYT*, 4 January 1980, p. A6). The Soviets charged that the United States was using the Afghanistan "intervention" as a pretext for abandoning a treaty on which the United States had long been procrastinating (Craig R. Whitney, "Moscow Portrays Carter as 'Wicked,' " *NYT*, 4 January 1980, p. A1).

19. Robert L. Bartley, "SALT: A Bankrupt Process," *Wall Street Journal*, 15 June 1979, p. 16; Wolfe, *The SALT Experience*, pp. 117–18; Labrie, *SALT Hand Book*, pp. 387, 389, 412–13. Talbott, *Master of the Game*, p. 158, claims that without the freeze on MIRVs provided by SALT II, the Soviets could have placed as many as forty warheads on the SS-18. Talbott also quotes Paul Nitze as saying that the SALT II freeze on the number of warheads is a "much overplayed so-

called" asset of SALT II, but he does not give Nitze's rationale. The optimum number of warheads for the SS-18 is from ten to fourteen. It would make no sense for the Soviets to place forty warheads on each missile, since there are not twelve thousand hard targets to be attacked in the United States. Moreover, fractionating to forty warheads would significantly reduce the yield of the warheads, increase cross-targeting problems, and expand the foot-print of the SS-18 to the point where sufficient targets for the warheads could not be found within the footprint. For a positive view of the early SALT process, see: Jan M. Lodal, "Assuring Strategic Stability: An Alternative View," *Foreign Affairs* 54 (April 1976): 462–81.

20. "The Report of the Secretary of Defense James R. Schlesinger to the Congress on the FY 1975 Defense Budget and FY 1975-1979 Defense Program, March 4, 1974," quoted in "A Strategic Doctrine for the United States: Secretary Schlesinger's Report," *Strategic Review* 2 (Spring 1974): 4.

21. United States Congress, Senate, Committee on Foreign Affairs, Subcommittee on Arms Control, International Law and Organization, *Hearings on U.S. and Soviet Strategic Doctrine and Military Policies*, 91st Cong., 2d sess., 4 March 1974, pp. 5–6; and Mark B. Schneider, "SALT and the Strategic Balance: 1974," *Strategic Review* 2 (Fall 1974): 42. For a discussion of how the Soviets might profit from their tremendous throw-weight advantage, see Nitze, "Between Hope and Skepticism," p. 148.

22. Michael Getler, "Soviet SS-18 Believed Single-Warhead Type," *WP*, 28 January 1975, p. A4; "Soviets Test Huge Missile in Pacific," *WP*, 5 June 1975, p. A6; "Soviets Test SS-18, Largest MIRV Missile," *WP*, 10 June 1975, p. A5. Schneider, "SALT: 1974," p. 42, indicated that the Soviets had tested the SS-18 with five to eight warheads; Murrey Marder, "Schlesinger Sees Buildup in Soviet Arms," *WP*, 21 June 1975, pp. A1, A5.

23. Angus Deming, with Bruce van Voorst and Lloyd H. Norman, "Foreign Fallout," *NW*, 17 November 1975, p. 38; David M. Alpern, with Henry W. Hubbard, "The Countdown," *NW*, 17 November 1975, p. 28; Peter Goldman, with Thomas M. DeFrank, "Ford's Big Shuffle," *NW*, 17 November 1975, pp. 24–27. Regarding the possibility of excessive zeal for a SALT II agreement on Kissinger's part, see Nitze, *Hiroshima to Glasnost*, p. 339.

24. Alpern, "Countdown," pp. 28, 36.

25. Interview with Daniel O. Graham, High Frontier, Washington, D.C., 7 July 1987, p. 2.

26. Linda Charlton, "Groups Favoring Strong Defense Making Gains in Public Acceptance," *NYT*, 4 April 1977, p. 50. Lodal seeks to dismiss the size of Soviet boosters and the number of warheads they could carry as the result of imperatives in the Soviet technology base, but he does admit: "Clearly, the rate and scale of the present Soviet deployment of MIRVed land-based missiles are disappointing, if not outright suspicious" ("Assuring Strategic Stability," p. 463). For concern about political coercion, see U.S. Congress, Senate, Committee on Armed Services, *Fiscal Year 1977 Authorization for Military Procurement, Research and Development, and Active Duty, Selected Reserve, and Civilian Personnel Strengths, Hearings on S. 2965, Part 12, Research and Development*, 94th Cong., 2d sess., 1976, pp. 6725–26 (hereafter Senate, *Hearings on FY 77 Authorizations, Part 12, Research and Development*).

27. Bernard Brodie, "Implications for Military Power," in Frederick S. Dunn, Bernard Brodie, Arnold Wolfers, Percy E. Corbett, and William T. R.

Fox, *The Absolute Weapon: Atomic Power and World Order*, ed. by Brodie (New York: Harcourt, Brace, 1946), p. 76.

28. Drew Middleton, "World Military Situation Confronting Carter Shows Changes Have Favored Soviet," *NYT*, 4 January 1977, p. 8. Kissinger had similar misgivings about the significance of conventional military power. Specifically, he wondered about the value of Soviet and Cuban bases in Africa. American military officers feared these bases might be used to interdict transportation lines that carried oil and other materials between Europe and the Middle and Far East.

29. "The Real Paul Warnke," *New Republic*, 26 March 1977, pp. 22–23. Emphasis in original.

30. Ibid., p. 25; Paul C. Warnke, "Apes on a Treadmill," *Foreign Policy* (Spring 1975): 12–29. In "Apes on a Treadmill," Warnke comes across as one who believes military power is useless and that all international problems can be solved by diplomacy. He attacked DOD budgets as excessively large, disapproved of the role the United States had played in the world, criticized the American military force structure, and disparaged the Vietnam war.

31. Lodal, "Assuring Strategic Stability," p. 478. Lodal discounted the threat of a Soviet first strike because of the survivability of the other legs of the TRIAD. Information that came to light in 1987 about the spy ring headed by John A. Walker, Jr., suggests that Lodal may have been a little cavalier when he talked about the invulnerability of U.S. submarines. Walker's ring was active from 1968 to 1985. During that time, it is estimated that the Soviets were able to read over one million U.S. messages and gain a great deal of information about U.S. sensors, weapons, and naval tactics (Michael R. Gordon, "Weinberger Says the Walkers Gave Soviets Much Key Data," *NYT*, 17 April 1987, p. A9; George C. Wilson, "Soviet Submarines 'Have Closed the Gap': Lehman Says Walkers' Espionage Cut U.S. Technological Lead," *WP*, 3 April 1987, p. A5.)

32. Nitze, "Strategic Balance," especially pp. 136, 152–56.

33. Jerry W. Sanders, *Peddlers of Crisis: The Committee on the Present Danger and the Politics of Containment* (Boston: South End Press, 1983), p. 198. Talbott, *Master of the Game*, p. 146, claims that the "impetus" for this committee came from the President's Foreign Intelligence Advisory Board. For a report of General Keegan's criticism of United States intelligence work, see David Binder, "Air Force's Ex-Intelligence Chief Fears Soviet Has Military Edge," *NYT*, 3 January 1977, p. 2. Keegan was particularly worried by a major Soviet effort to harden installations and develop an extensive civil defense system, which indicated to Keegan that the Soviets were serious about being ready to fight and win a nuclear war.

34. Robert Scheer, *With Enough Shovels: Reagan, Bush and Nuclear War* (New York: Vintage Books, 1983), pp. 53–55.

35. Talbott, *Master of the Game*, p. 146.

36. Sanders, *Peddlers of Crisis*, p. 199.

37. Ibid., pp. 198–99, 285.

38. Richard Pipes, "Why the Soviet Union Thinks It Could Fight and Win a Nuclear War," *Commentary* 64 (July 1977): 21–34; see especially pp. 26–30, 34.

39. Ibid., pp. 21, 24–25, 29, 34. Pipes underestimates the casualties suffered by the United States in its wars. See Donald R. Baucom, "Technological War: Reality and the American Myth," *Air University Review* 32 (September-October 1981): 58–59. In the Civil War, 623,000 died; in World War I, 126,000 were

killed; and in World War II, about 307,000 were killed or died from other causes. For Brodie's statement on the utility of nuclear war, see Brodie, "Implications for Military Policy," p. 76.

40. "Bush Is Silent on Assessment of Soviet Aims," *NYT*, 3 January 1977, p. 2.

41. Sanders, *Peddlers of Crisis*, p. 203. Sanders is quoting from "Rumsfeld Says Russia Could Become Dominant Power," *San Francisco Chronicle*, 19 January 1977.

42. Sheer, *With Enough Shovels*, p. 58.

43. "Report on Soviet Nuclear Strategy Says Moscow Emphasizes Victory," *NYT*, 25 June 1977, p. 7.

44. See Jacquelyn K. Davis, "End of the Strategic TRIAD," *Strategic Review* 6 (Winter 1978): 38–40, and John Erickson, "The Chimera of Mutual Deterrence," *Strategic Review* 6 (Spring 1978): 11–17.

45. "The Real Paul Warnke," p. 23.

46. Pipes, "Why the Soviet Union Thinks It Could Fight and Win a Nuclear War," p. 21.

47. Ibid., 28–29, 34.

48. George W. Rathjens, "The Dynamics of the Arms Race," *Scientific American* 220 (April 1969): 19–20, 24. Rathjens suggests three ways in which the uncertainty underlying the arms race could be reduced (pp. 20–21). For another succinct statement of the arms race thesis, see Albert Wohlstetter, "Is There a Strategic Arms Race?" *Foreign Policy* (Summer 1974): 4. An almost identical version of this article is Wohlstetter's "Legends of the Strategic Arms Race, Part I: The Driving Engine," *Strategic Review* 2 (Fall 1974): p. 67 (hereafter Wohlstetter, "Legends, Part I"). For comments on the role of the action-reaction model of the arms race and how it related to the ABM debate of the late 1960s and early 1970s, see Geoffrey Till, "The Safeguard Debate: Image and Reality," *RUSI* 119 (December 1974): 45. A major source of this perception is Robert McNamara's speech of 18 September 1967 in which he announced his decision to deploy an ABM system.

49. Talbott, *Master of the Game*, p. 66; Wohlstetter, "Is There a Strategic Arms Race?" p. 4.

50. The articles on this topic published in *Foreign Policy* and *Strategic Review* were based upon *Competition or Race: Innovation and the Changing Size of Strategic Forces* by Wohlstetter, David McGarvey, Fred Hoffman, and Amoretta Hoeber. Wohlstetter's article in the fall 1974 edition of *Strategic Review* contains ten pages of charts and tables.

51. Albert Wohlstetter, "Rivals, But No Race," *Foreign Policy* (Fall 1974): 48–49, 50–52.

52. Ibid., pp. 79–81. For a summary of Wohlstetter's conclusions on the three main tenets of the arms race doctrine, see "Is There an Arms Race?" pp. 5–6. For another summary of Wohlstetter's main objections to the arms race thesis, see his "Optimal Ways to Confuse Ourselves," *Foreign Policy* (Autumn 1975): 170–71.

53. Editor's note at the bottom of page 170 of the autumn 1975 edition of *Foreign Policy*.

54. Warnke, "Apes on a Treadmill," pp. 12–29. Warnke's remarks about semantics are to some extent justified, since Wohlstetter raises the issue of semantics in his critique of the concept of an arms race (see Wohlstetter, "Is There a Strategic Arms Race?" p. 3).

55. Nitze, "Strategic Balance," p. 148.

56. Daniel Seligman, "Our ICBMs Are in Danger," *Fortune*, 2 July 1979, pp. 50, 52. The "cosmic roll of the dice" comment may be found in Strobe Talbott, *Endgame: The Inside Story of SALT II* (New York: Harper and Row, 1979), p. 52.

57. Robinson, "ABM System with MX," p. 23.

58. Davis, "Strategic TRIAD," pp. 36–39.

59. Bartley, "SALT: A Bankrupt Process," p. 16; Seligman, "Our ICBMs Are in Danger," pp. 50–51. Seligman explained why the United States could not afford to avoid the MINUTEMAN problem and rely on the other two legs of the TRIAD. For an argument against deploying MX, see Lodal, "Assuring Strategic Stability," pp. 474–75. Lodal argued that the vulnerability of the MINUTEMAN was largely "theoretical," that a multiple protective shelter system would be costly and its benefits unproven, and that ways of defending MINUTEMAN other than by ABM have been suggested (see below). Given the likely cost and probable technical problems associated with developing a mobile missile system, Lodal suggested that these systems be banned by a SALT II agreement to close off a new area of the strategic arms competition ("Assuring Strategic Stability," p. 476).

60. Bernard T. Feld and Kosta Tsipis, "Land-based Intercontinental Ballistic Missiles," *Scientific American* 241 (November 1979): 55–56.

PART THREE. AN AMERICAN PHOENIX

1. *The Book of Beasts*, ed. and trans. by T. H. White (New York: Dover Publications, 1984), p. 125.

CHAPTER FIVE. THE DEATH OF SAFEGUARD AND
THE REORIENTATION OF AMERICA'S ABM PROGRAM

1. Smith, *Doubletalk*, p. 204.

2. Ada Louise Huxtable, "A Bizarre Monument to Non-Architecture," *NYT*, 14 December 1975, Section II, p. D39. Huxtable noted that "the stark engineering composition of severely abstract forms, grimly silhouetted against open sky and flat land, upstages architecture totally. It is without doubt one of the most peculiarly impressive built [sic] groups of our time. Architects trying consciously for impact and meaning might just as well call it quits in the face of this kind of brute esthetic force." Huxtable saw the SAFEGUARD structures as symbolic of the death of the optimism of the engineer and technician: "All of that engineering elegance and efficiency born of rational, industrialized solutions that was [sic] to make a better world—led by the architect—did not bring a new dawn. It brought an era of more gigantic problems in the nature of life and survival than history has ever known." The structures are also symbolic of how the architect is being pushed out of his field by "engineers and investment builders." William K. Stevens, "Abandonment of Safeguard ABM System Stuns the Town of Langdon, N.D.," *NYT*, 25 November 1975, p. 74; "SAFEGUARD: What U.S. Got for $5.4 Billion," *U.S. News and World Report*, 30 June 1975, pp. 42–43; Clarence A. Robinson, Jr., "Army Spurs Missile Defense Technology," *AW*, 22 April 1974, pp. 12–13. Robinson pointed out that the perimeter acquisition radar located 25 miles northeast of the missile site radar was actually 110

feet high. However, the shape of this structure made it much less striking than that of the missile site radar. See also Bell Labs, *ABM Project History*, Part II, pp. 7-4–7-5 (for information on the perimeter acquisition radar, see Chapter 8).

3. Robinson, "Missile Defense Technology," p. 13.

4. Bell Labs, *ABM Project History*, Part II, pp. 3-8–3-9, 4-4–4-5; Robinson, "Missile Defense Technology," p. 14; "SAFEGUARD: What U.S. Got for $5.4 Billion," p. 42. In fact, the North Dakota SAFEGUARD site could also offer a limited degree of protection for MINUTEMAN missiles at Malmstrom Air Force Base in Montana, Minot Air Force Base in North Dakota, Francis E. Warren Air Force Base in Wyoming, and Ellsworth Air Force Base in South Dakota. It could not defend all sites simultaneously. For the ability of SAFEGUARD to protect other missile fields, see "Army Widens Ballistic Missile Research," *AW*, 8 December 1975, p. 17.

5. U.S. Congress, Senate, Committee on Appropriations, *Hearings before a Subcommittee on Department of Defense Appropriations For Fiscal Year 1975 on HR* [sic], *Part 2—Army*, 93d Cong., 2d sess., 1974, p. 31 (hereafter Senate, *Hearings on DOD Appropriations for FY 75*). In speaking of technological advances, J. Robert Oppenheimer once noted: "It is my judgment in these things that when you see something that is technically sweet you go ahead and do it and you argue about what to do about it only after you have had your technical success." Oppenheimer is quoted by Robert Jungk, *Brighter than a Thousand Suns: A Personal History of the Atomic Scientists*, trans. by James Cleugh (New York: Harcourt Brace Jovanovich, 1958), p. 296.

6. Robinson, "Missile Defense Technology," pp. 12, 14; Till, "Safeguard Debate," p. 41.

7. Robinson, "Missile Defense Technology," pp. 12, 14; Clarence A. Robinson, Jr., "Prototype Site Defense Construction Set," *AW*, 29 April 1974, p. 70; Benjamin M. Elson, "Kwajalein Range Plays Unique Role," *AW*, 16 June 1980, p. 227; Senate, *Hearings on DOD Appropriations for FY 75*, pp. 506–7, 538, 551, 609–10. See page 609 for a discussion of the modifications that transformed SPRINT I into SPRINT II.

8. Robinson, "Missile Defense Technology," p. 12; Robinson, "Site Defense Construction Set," p. 71.

9. Robinson, "Missile Defense Technology," p. 12; Robinson, "Site Defense Construction Set," p. 70; "Army Widens Ballistic Missile Research," p. 18.

10. Finlay Lewis, "ABM: Countdown to Oblivion," *WP*, 5 October 1975, p. A7; Walter Pincus, "Schlesinger Asks Fund for Safeguard Missile," *WP*, 15 October 1975, p. A2; Philip J. Klass, "Ballistic Missile Defense Tests Set," *AW*, 16 June 1980, p. 214. Major General Robert C. Marshall, BMD program manager for the army, would later admit that it would be virtually impossible to deploy a 100 percent effective missile defense against an attack using a large number of sophisticated warheads (Senate, *Hearings on FY 77 Authorizations, Part 12, Research and Development*, p. 6716).

11. Pincus, "Schlesinger," p. A2. DOD attached considerable importance to the experience that could be gained by operating a system with the complexity of SAFEGUARD. This experience would provide an important data base on personnel training and system maintainability. General Marshall in March 1976 told Congress that the failure to allow the army to operate SAFEGUARD for one year was detrimental to the army's ABM program. See Senate, *Hearings on DOD Appropriations for FY 75*, pp. 501–2; Robinson, "Missile Defense Technology," p. 13; Senate, *Hearings on FY 77 Authorizations, Part 12, Research and Devel-*

opment, p. 6727; U.S. Congress, Senate, Committee on Appropriations, *Department of Defense Appropriation Bill, 1976*, S.R. 94-446 to accompany H.R. 9861, 94th Cong., 1st sess., 6 November 1975, pp. 33–34.

12. Senate, *Hearings on FY 77 Authorizations, Part 12, Research and Development*, p. 6681.

13. John W. Finney, "Senate Approves Defense Spending of $90.7 Billion," *NYT*, 19 November 1975, p. 1; John W. Finney, "Safeguard ABM System to Shut Down; $5 Billion Spent in 6 Years since Debate," *NYT*, 25 November 1975, p. 74.

14. Finney, "Senate Approves Defense Spending," p. 12; U.S. Congress, Senate and House, *An Act Making Appropriations for the Department of Defense for the Fiscal Year Ending June 30, 1976, and the Period Beginning July 1, 1976, and Ending September 30, 1976, and for Other Purposes*, P.L. 94-212, 94th Cong., 1st sess., 1976, H.R. 9861, p. 3.

15. Senate, *Hearings on FY 77 Authorizations, Part 12, Research and Development*, p. 6684; Wolfe, *SALT Experience*, pp. 34–40. Wolfe claimed that the dismantling procedures were established by mid-1974 (*SALT Experience*, p. 35). For human interest stories about the site closing and its impact on the North Dakota communities around it, see Stevens, "Abandonment of Safeguard Stuns Langdon," p. 74; and Bill Richards, "Town Fears Chaos If ABM Site Shut," *WP*, 20 October 1975, pp. A1, A2. One-third of the people in Langdon lost their jobs when the ABM facility closed.

16. Finney, "Safeguard to Shut Down," pp. 1, 74.

17. Senate, *Hearings on DOD Appropriations for FY 75*, pp. 508, 538, 541, 549, 552, 555, 557, 575, 607. Page 607 provides a discussion of what it means to guard against technological surprise and how one does this. The cost of BMD to the army from FY 1956 through FY 1974 was about $10 billion; the appropriations for the approved SAFEGUARD program totaled $5.8 billion through FY 1974 (ibid., pp. 575, 608). About $906 million went for the Mickelsen complex ("SAFEGUARD: What United States Got for $5.4 Billion," p. 42).

18. Senate, *Hearings on FY 77 Authorizations, Part 12, Research and Development*, p. 6682.

19. Ibid., pp. 6679, 6682–84, 6686–87. This basic structure of the army's ABM program was continued even after the formation of the Strategic Defense Initiative Organization in 1984 (see Currie-McDaniel, *Army Strategic Defense Command*, Chapter 3).

20. Clarence A. Robinson, Jr., "DOD Presses for ABM Fund Restoration," *AW*, 7 June 1976, pp. 16–17 (hereafter Robinson, "ABM Fund Restoration").

21. Clarence A. Robinson, Jr., "U.S. Anti-Missile Work Stresses Optics," *AW*, 6 September 1976, p. 31.

22. Kenneth J. Stein, "New Missile Defense Systems Studied," *AW*, 11 October 1976, p. 34 (hereafter Stein, "New Defense Studied"); Clarence A. Robinson, Jr., "Soviets Grasping Strategic Lead," *AW*, 30 August 1976, pp. 14, 16; Robinson, "Anti-Missile Work Stresses Optics," pp. 30–31; "Strategic Defensive Systems Emphasized," *AW*, 20 September 1976, p. 49.

23. Clarence A. Robinson, Jr., "Missile Defense Radar System Tests Set," *AW*, 20 September 1976, p. 43 (hereafter Robinson, "Radar System Tests Set").

24. Stein, "New Defense Studied," pp. 34–35.

25. "Computer Proves Architecture Concept," *AW*, 11 October 1976, p. 35.

26. Bell Labs, *ABM Project History*, Part II, pp. 3–9, 4–6; Robinson, "Missile

Defense Technology," p. 13. Robinson reported that the software program that ran the SAFEGUARD system was the "most complex ever written."

27. Robinson, "Site Defense Construction," p. 71; Senate, *Hearings on FY 77 Authorizations, Part 12, Research and Development*, pp. 6686, 6734. This report claims that the SAFEGUARD computer could perform eighteen to twenty million operations per second.

28. Stein, "New Defense Studied," pp. 34–35.

29. "Processing of Data Key to Missile Defense," *AW*, 28 August 1978, pp. 12, 15; Clarence A. Robinson, Jr., "Missile Defense Gains Support," *AW*, 22 October 1979, p. 14.

30. Klass, "Missile Defense Tests Set," p. 218.

31. Ibid., pp. 214–16.

32. Ibid., p. 214; "Technology Milestone Met in Missile Defense Testing," *AW*, 29 September 1980, p. 25.

33. Klass, "Missile Defense Tests Set," p. 215.

34. Ibid., p. 214.

35. By this time, the army was talking of a layered defense composed of overlay and underlay systems. The former involved attacking warheads during and even before the midcourse portion of their flight, while the latter system would deal with targets that leaked through the overlay system and penetrated the atmosphere ("Technology Milestone Met in Missile Defense Testing," p. 25).

36. Klass, "Missile Defense Tests Set," p. 213. After partial successes in two test flights, the homing overlay experiment vehicle achieved a complete success on 10 June 1984 (Currie-McDaniel, *Army Strategic Defense Command*, pp. 30, 41–42). For a discussion of a different interceptor concept, see Craig Covault, "Antisatellite Weapon Design Advances," *AW*, 16 June 1980, pp. 244–45. Covault described the Vought antiballistic missile homing intercept weapon. Only one foot long, it was powered by fifty-six small rockets and carried a cryogenically cooled infra-red sensor that "saw" through eight telescopic eyes. Its "visual" signals were interpreted by an onboard microprocessor and used with signals from the vehicle's laser gyroscope to provide guidance instructions so the vehicle could home in on its target.

37. George Sarton, *A History of Science*, Vol. 2, *Hellenistic Science and Culture in the Last Three Centuries B.C.* (New York: W. W. Norton, 1959), p. 70.

38. H. G. Wells, *The War of the Worlds* (New York: Berkley Books, n.d.), p. 27; Jeff Hecht, *Beam Weapons: The Next Arms Race* (New York: Plenum Press, 1984), Chapter 2. In *War Stars: The Super-weapon and the American Imagination* (New York: Oxford University Press, 1988), pp. 21, 64, H. Bruce Franklin claimed that the "lunatics" or men from the moon in Washington Irving's *Mr. Knickerbocker's History of New York* wielded "directed-energy weapons." Two passages of this book would seem to support Franklin's claim. In one, Irving wrote of the moon men being armed with "concentrated sunbeams." In the second, he talked about how the lunatics "transfix us [earth men] with concentrated sunbeams." A considerable amount of imagination would seem to be required to find directed energy weapons in "concentrated sunbeams," for Irving gives no hint of how the beams were concentrated. See Washington Irving, *Mr. Knickerbocker's History of New York*, ed. by Michael L. Black and Nancy B. Black, vol. 7 in Richard Dilworth, general editor, *The Complete Works of Washington Irving*, (Boston: Twayne Publishers, 1984), pp. 48, 50.

39. "40 Americans Honored as Martyrs to Science," *NYT*, 5 April 1935, p. 1.

For samples of the stories dealing with radiation deaths and "death rays," see the following articles in the *New York Times*: "Blame Radium for Death," 9 June 1925, p. 14; "Abbé Tauleigne Gives His Life for Science; X-Ray Experiments in War Fatal to Frenchman," 7 June 1926, p. 3; "Warn of Ray Peril in Treating Cancer," 28 March 1929, p. 12; "Martyr to the X-Ray Will Lose Arm Today," 1 October 1930, p. 3.

40. "Tesla, at 78, Bares New 'Death-Beam,' " *NYT*, 11 July 1934, p. 18. For other stories about death rays, see "Says He Sold 'Death Ray': H. Grindell Matthews Declares It Goes to Americans," *NYT*, 2 March 1925, p. 4; and " 'Death Ray' Expert Scoffs at War Use," *NYT*, 2 May 1935, p. 22.

41. Robert Watson-Watt, *The Pulse of Radar: The Autobiography of Sir Robert Watson-Watt* (New York: Dial Press, 1959), pp. 43, 51–53; Henry Guerlac, "Early History of Radar," History of Division 14, Section A, Office of Scientific Research and Development, pp. VI9–VI13.

42. Edward Teller, *Better a Shield than a Sword: Perspectives on Defense and Technology* (New York: Free Press, 1987), p. 50; and Richard Rhodes, *The Making of the Atomic Bomb* (New York: Simon and Schuster, 1986), p. 315. This story is also recounted in Newhouse, *War and Peace*, p. 21.

43. Philip M. Boffey, William J. Board, Leslie H. Gelb, Charles Mohr, and Holcombe B. Noble, *Claiming the Heavens: The* New York Times *Complete Guide to the Star Wars Debate* (New York: Times Books, 1988), pp. 3–5.

44. John G. Trump to L. A. DuBridge, report, 20 January 1945, in folder marked A-1 RADAR—General—E.T.O., Box 14, Entry 60A, Record Group 18, National Archives, Washington, D.C. A scheme for using X-rays to kill engines by "quenching the spark of their motors" was announced in January 1933 ("X-Ray May Wreck Planes," *NYT*, 30 January 1933, p. 15).

45. Von Kármán, *Science, the Key to Air Supremacy*, p. 74.

46. Robert W. Seidel, "From Glow to Flow: A History of Military Laser Research and Development," *Historical Studies in the Physical Sciences*, 18, 1 (1987): 113–14; Hecht, *Beam Weapons*, pp. 22, 25; Teller, *Better a Shield*, pp. 31–32; Joan Lisa Bromberg, "The Birth of the Laser," *Physics Today* 41 [October 1988]: 26–33. Bromberg (p. 26) wrote that the development of the laser was more of a process than an act of invention. The process began in 1957 when Townes wrote in his notebook his idea for a "maser at optical frequencies."

47. As noted in the first chapter, the Advanced Research Projects Agency was started in 1958 and carried the name ARPA until 1972 when it became the Defense Advanced Research Projects Agency (DARPA).

48. Seidel, "From Glow to Flow," pp. 111, 113–16, 118–19.

49. Ibid., pp. 116, 118, 123–24, 126, 133–34. In all, some two thousand different varieties of lasing glass were examined. In addition to the problem with the commitment to ruby and glass lasers and the emphasis on finding the best lasing materials, Seidel has argued elsewhere ("How the Military Responded to the Laser," *Physics Today* 41 [October 1988]: pp. 36–43) that the American laser program shifted too quickly from "research and exploration to development and scaling-up." One thing that brought about this premature shift was "interservice competition to develop devices suited to the missions of each branch." Other factors included the "institutionalization of research programs in military as well as in contractor laboratories" and the "adoption of the Manhattan Project and the wartime program to develop radar as models for military laser development."

50. Seidel, "From Glow to Flow," pp. 132–35. The first gas laser used helium

as its lasing substance. Gas lasers had received some attention in programs run by the army and the air force. Jack Ruina, head of ARPA, had opposed these programs because DOD had assigned his office responsibility for laser development and he believed the other programs tended to dilute the overall effort. Hecht, *Beam Weapons*, p. 25, described one carbon dioxide laser with a 750-foot beam path and 8,800 watts of power.

51. Hecht, *Beam Weapons*, pp. 27, 58, 67–68. For another discussion of the GDL, see Philip J. Klass, "Power Boost Key to Feasibility," *AW*, 21 August 1972, pp. 32–35.

52. Philip J. Klass, "Research Nears Application Level," *AW*, 14 August 1972, pp. 12, 14, 15; Klass, "Power Boost," p. 40; U.S. Congress, Senate, Committee on Commerce, Science, and Transportation, "Laser Research and Applications," Committee Print, 96th Cong., 2d sess., November 1980, pp. 20–21 (hereafter Senate, "Laser Research and Applications"). See also "Technical Survey: U.S. Nears Laser Weapon Decisions," *AW*, 4 August 1980, pp. 48–49, 52–53.

53. Senate, "Laser Research and Applications," pp. 20–21; Clarence A. Robinson, Jr., "Army Pushes New Weapons Effort," *AW*, 16 October 1978, pp. 42–43 (hereafter Robinson, "New Weapons Effort"); "White Horse Concentrates on Neutral Particle Beam," *AW*, 4 August 1980, p. 63.

54. "Neutral Particle Programs Draw Focus," *AW*, 25 May 1981, p. 55; Robinson, "New Weapons Effort," p. 43.

55. Benjamin M. Elson, "USAF Weapons Lab Mission Expanded," *AW*, 29 January 1979, p. 213. This article contains information on the laser program at the Air Force Weapons Laboratory where the air force was working on a carbon dioxide gas dynamic laser for use aboard the airborne laser laboratory (pp. 212–13).

56. "U.S. Effort Redirected to High Energy Lasers," *AW*, 28 July 1980, pp. 50, 55–57; "Technology Eyed to Defend ICBMs, Spacecraft," *AW*, 28 July 1980, pp. 32–34, 39–42. Brown's decision in this case seems to have been surrounded with controversy. A Defense Science Board (DSB) task force examining high energy lasers had prepared a report recommending emphasis on near-term applications such as shipboard defense. According to some sources, this report was misrepresented to Brown by the DSB chairman, Eugene G. Fubini, who believed high energy lasers in space should be emphasized. For additional information on this controversy, see "Laser Applications in Space Emphasized," *AW*, 28 July 1980, p. 62. For the remarks concerning laser battle stations, see "Pentagon Studying Laser Battle Stations in Space," *AW*, 28 July 1980, p. 57 (hereafter "Laser Battle Stations in Space"). Regarding the lasers themselves, two of the more promising types that DARPA was pursuing at this time were the excimer ("excited dimer") and free-electron lasers. These are described in the article on pages 58–59. Concerning the expression "battle station," aerospace engineer Maxwell W. Hunter II was certainly one of the first to use it (see his 31 October 1977 paper "Strategic Dynamics and Space-Laser Weaponry"; Hunter provided me with a copy during an October 1987 interview). Hunter's use of this expression was publicized in Clarence Robinson's 16 October 1978 article in *AW*, "Army Pushes New Weapons Effort," passim, especially p. 48. More will be said about Hunter in the next chapter. On DARPA's increasing role, see "Army Beam Programs Moving to DARPA," *AW*, 4 August 1980, p. 51.

57. "Army Beam Programs Moving to DARPA," p. 51; "Technology to Defend

ICBMs," pp. 34–35, 40; "White Horse Concentrates on Neutral Particle Beam," pp. 63, 65.

58. "White Horse Concentrates on Neutral Particle Beam," p. 63; "High-Intensity Electron Beams Pushed," *AW*, 4 August 1980, p. 67.

59. "Technology to Defend ICBMs," pp. 40–41; "Laser Battle Stations in Space," pp. 57–58, 61; "Laser Applications," p. 62.

60. Robinson, "Missile Defense Gains Support," pp. 15–16.

61. "Laser Battle Station Mirror Proposed," *AW*, 25 May 1981, p. 64. DARPA's LODE program had determined that a "segmented, deformable surface design" was the preferred form for large mirrors such as the United Technologies device. United Technologies' estimate that it would take four and a half years to complete the 10-meter mirror was based on its experience in fabricating a 2.5-meter mirror for NASA's space telescope.

62. "Laser Applications," p. 63; "Senate Directs Air Force to Formulate Laser Plan," *AW*, 25 May 1981, p. 53.

63. "Directed-Energy Effort Shifted," *AW*, 4 August 1980, p. 44; "Technology to Defend ICBMs," p. 42; "White Horse Concentrates on Neutral Particle Beam," p. 65.

64. Clarence A. Robinson, Jr., "Laser Technology Demonstration Proposed," *AW*, 23 February 1981, pp. 16–18.

65. Clarence A. Robinson, Jr., "Advance Made on High-Energy Laser," *AW*, 23 February 1981, pp. 25–27; "High-Intensity Electron Beams Pushed," pp. 67–68. The entire lasing device is itself destroyed within a millisecond by the detonation of the nuclear bomb that provides the pumping energy.

66. Clarence A. Robinson, Jr., "Beam Weapons Technology Expanding," *AW*, 25 May 1981, p. 41.

67. "Technology to Defend ICBMs," pp. 41–42.

68. Robinson, "Beam Weapons Technology," p. 42.

CHAPTER SIX. THE REEMERGENCE OF BALLISTIC MISSILE
DEFENSE AS A NATIONAL ISSUE: 1977–1981

1. Hunter Interview, p. 45.

2. Lodal, "Assuring Strategic Stability," p. 475. For another discussion of defense schemes originated by Garwin, see Feld and Tsipis, "Land-Based Intercontinental Ballistic Missiles," p. 56 (hereafter Feld and Tsipis, "Land-Based ICBMs").

3. Feld and Tsipis, "Land-Based ICBMs," p. 56.

4. Klass, "Ballistic Missile Defense Tests Set," p. 218.

5. Robinson, "Missile Defense Gains Support," p. 15. "U.S. Funds Killer Satellite Effort," *AW*, 6 February 1978, p. 18, describes the homing interceptor vehicle.

6. Robinson, "Anti-Missile Work Stresses Optics," p. 32; Robinson, "Soviets Grasping Strategic Lead," pp. 14, 16–17; Robinson, "Radar System Tests Set," pp. 42, 47.

7. Robinson, "Missile Defense Gains Support," p. 16; Robinson, "ABM System with MX," p. 23.

8. Robinson, "ABM System with MX," pp. 23–24; "Technology Milestone Met in Missile Defense Testing," p. 26. For a discussion of the technical challenges of LOADS, see: "Demonstration Planned for MX Defense System," *AW*, 16 June

1980, pp. 220–21. Among these challenges were achieving sufficient hardening to survive in a hostile nuclear environment that included explosions of incoming ICBM warheads and the nuclear warheads of ABMs; being able to sit dormant for long periods and then come on line and operate (its radar cannot be on before an attack, as the radar might indicate to the Soviets the location of the MX missile being defended in the MPS mode); and bulk filtering, which the army believed it had solved to some extent.

9. Robinson, "ABM System with MX," pp. 23–24; "Demonstration Planned for MX Defense System," p. 220.

10. Robinson, "Anti-Missile Work Stresses Optics," p. 30; Clarence A. Robinson, Jr., "ICBM Intercept in Boost Phase Pushed," *AW*, 17 July 1978, pp. 47–48; Robinson, "Radar System Tests Set," pp. 43, 46–47; Clarence A. Robinson, Jr., "Technology Program Spurs Missile Intercept Advances," *AW*, 5 June 1978, pp. 108–11.

11. Robinson, "Missile Defense Gains Support," pp. 14, 16; Robinson, "New Weapons Effort," pp. 42–43, 45, 48–49, 51–52.

12. Robinson, "New Weapons Effort," pp. 43, 48. Robinson quoted his anonymous source as saying that basing directed energy weapons in space "is the only new strategic concept to present itself in a number of decades, and the only one which merits the words . . . potentially decisive. It should be implemented with all due haste."

13. Ibid., p. 48.

14. Ibid., p. 49.

15. Hunter, "Strategic Dynamics," circulated by the author. Hunter's paper is ten pages long and includes a series of appendixes that add another seven pages. Hunter provided me with a copy during an interview in October 1987. In what is an apparent reference to Hunter's paper, Robinson, "New Weapons Effort," p. 43, stated that the study was done for the army. Hunter left me with the impression that he had completed the study more or less on his own initiative. When Robinson's article indicates that the Lockheed official is speaking, this is also a reference to Hunter's paper. To see how extensively Robinson relied on Hunter's paper, compáre pages 48–49 of Robinson, "New Weapons Effort," with pages 4–6 and A-7 of Hunter's study. What is perhaps the first use of the expression "battle station" comes on page 5 of Hunter's paper and on page 48 of Robinson's article.

16. "Biographical Data: Maxwell W. Hunter II," supplied to me by Hunter; Bell Labs, *ABM Project History*, Part I, p. I-1, points out Hunter's participation in the NIKE II project.

17. Hunter, "Great Zeus!" p. 6. Hunter provided me with a copy of this memoir during an interview on 29 October 1987. Hunter named Arthur Kantrowitz as the first person to make the connection between space-based lasers and the BMD mission.

18. Ibid.

19. Hunter Interview, pp. 44–45.

20. Hunter, "Strategic Dynamics," p. 1.

21. Ibid., pp. 3–4.

22. Ibid., pp. 5–6; Teller, *Better a Shield than a Sword*, p. 31, also comments on the revolutionary nature of laser weapons.

23. Interview with Malcolm Wallop, U.S. Senate, 16 December 1987, pp. 1–2.

24. Ibid., pp. 1–2, 7, 17; Angelo Codevilla, *While Others Build: The Com-*

monsense Approach to the Strategic Defense Initiative (New York: Free Press, 1988), pp. 59, 60–63.

25. Hunter Interview, pp. 9–11.

26. Wallop Interview, p. 3; Hunter Interview, p. 12; Codevilla, *While Others Build*, pp. 63–65. For more on the tendency of the different armed forces to favor certain types of weapons systems, see Carl H. Builder, *The Masks of War: American Military Styles in Strategy and Analysis*, RAND Corporation Research Study (Baltimore: Johns Hopkins University Press, 1989).

27. Codevilla, *While Others Build*, p. 66.

28. Ibid., p. 68.

29. Ibid., Hunter Interview, p. 13.

30. Hunter Interview, pp. 13, 15; Codevilla, *While Others Build*, p. 68.

31. "Defense Dept. Experts Confirm Efficacy of Space-Based Lasers," *AW*, 28 July 1980, p. 65; Codevilla, *While Others Build*, p. 69.

32. "Experts Confirm Efficacy of Space-Based Lasers," p. 65. For other details on the gang of four briefing, see Codevilla, *While Others Build*, p. 69.

33. "Experts Confirm Efficacy of Space-Based Lasers," p. 66. According to Codevilla, *While Others Build*, p. 69, Miller briefed on the process of upscaling a chemical laser to the point where it would develop 10 megawatts of power by burning 50 kilograms of hydrogen and fluorine per second. This device would have been 3 feet in diameter and 15 feet long.

34. "Experts Confirm Efficacy of Space-Based Lasers," p. 66.

35. M[axwell] Hunter to R. Capiaux, memorandum, "Weekly Activity Report for W[eek]/E[nding] 12 Oct. 1979," 15 October 1979 (copy provided by Hunter); and Codevilla, *While Others Build*, p. 68.

36. M[axwell] Hunter to R. Capiaux, memorandum, "Weekly Activity Report/Strategic Weaponry for W[eek]/E[nding] 30 Nov. 1979," 4 December 1979 (copy provided by Hunter).

37. M[axwell] Hunter to R. Capiaux, memorandum "Weekly Activity Report/Strategic Weaponry for W[eek]/E[nding] 7 Dec. 1979," 10 December 1979 (copy provided by Hunter).

38. "Experts Confirm Efficacy of Space-Based Lasers," p. 65.

39. Ibid., pp. 65–66; Codevilla, *While Others Build*, p. 73. Wallop's amendment was defeated 51 to 39. For further details on efforts to undermine the gang of four briefing, see Codevilla, *While Others Build*, pp. 70–73. Hunter claimed that two staffers had lunch with DARPA representatives Tanimoto and Pike on 3 December and secured from DARPA an agreement to work for an immediate increase in the funding request. Also, Codevilla was scheduled to meet with Dr. Hans Mark, secretary of the air force, on 18 December to "discuss how the USAF would organize to handle such a [missile defense?] program" (Hunter to Capiaux, 10 December 1979).

40. Wallop Interview, p. 7.

41. Hunter Interview, p. 14; Telephone Interview with Angelo Codevilla, 15 July 1987, p. 2; Wallop Interview, pp. 4–5.

42. Malcolm Wallop, "Opportunities and Imperatives of Ballistic Missile Defense," *Strategic Review* 7 (Fall 1979): 13–15.

43. Ibid., pp. 18–19.

44. Ibid., p. 14, 20–21.

45. Wallop Interview, pp. 6–7; Senator Paul Laxalt to Donald R. Baucom, letter, 12 January 1988.

46. Interview with Edward Teller, Washington, D.C., 6 July 1987, pp. 1–2.

For information on the nuclear tests, see Lawrence E. Davies, "Underground Nuclear Test Set at Aleutian Site," *NYT*, 29 May 1967, p. 51; Gladwin Hill, "Larger A-Blasts Likely in Nevada," *NYT*, 5 April 1969, p. 7; Wallace Turner, "Amchitka Girding for Atomic Blasts; Test Plan Attacked," 14 July 1969, *NYT*, pp. 1, 38; and Wallace Turner, "Aleutian H-Bomb Is Fired without Setting Off Quake," *NYT*, 3 October 1969, pp. 1, 26.

47. Graham Interview, pp. 2–3. George Keyworth noted that in an August 1981 meeting with Reagan and Meese, the president expressed discomfort with "the 'nakedness' of deterrence without defense, without any control over what had to be done should a nuclear war be initiated" (Interview with George A. Keyworth, Keyworth Company, Washington, D.C., 28 September 1987, p. 1).

48. Interview with Martin Anderson, Hoover Institution, Stanford, California, 3 August 1987, p. 1. Martin Anderson, Reagan for President Committee, Policy Memorandum Number 3, Foreign Policy and National Security, August 1979, p. 6; copy provided to me by Anderson (hereafter Anderson, Policy Memorandum 3). For a more accessible account of the visit to Cheyenne Mountain, see Martin Anderson, *Revolution* (New York: Harcourt Brace Jovanovich, 1988), pp. 80–83.

49. Anderson, Policy Memorandum 3, pp. 2, 6–7; Anderson, *Revolution*, pp. 85–86.

50. Daniel O. Graham, *Shall America Be Defended? SALT II and Beyond* (New Rochelle, N.Y.: Arlington House Publishers, 1979), especially pp. 6–7, 9, 13–15, 51, 84–85, 106, 151–52, 157, 244–45.

51. Graham Interview, p. 2; Graham, *Shall America Be Defended?*, pp. 93–95, 105, 122, 124, 128, 131, 134, 146, 240–41, 243, 245.

52. Graham Interview, pp. 3–4, 6; Interview with Arnold Kramish, Washington, D.C., 25 May 1988.

53. "Nashua, N.H., Shrugs at a High Compliment," *NYT*, 2 August 1987, p. Y13.

54. Lou Cannon, *Reagan* (New York: G. P. Putnam's Sons, 1982), pp. 250–53.

55. Graham Interview, pp. 4–5. Herken, *Counsels of War*, p. 337, reported that Graham was the first to speak with Reagan on ballistic missile defense, having discussed it with him in 1976 and 1979. I found no evidence of the 1976 discussions. Indeed, judging from the way Graham viewed strategic defenses as late as 1979 (see *Shall America Be Defended?*), I think it unlikely that such discussions took place.

56. National Committee on Resolutions to the Republican National Convention, *Republican Platform: Family, Neighborhood, Work, Peace, Freedom*, Detroit, 14 July 1980, pp. 55–56. A copy was provided to me by Martin Anderson.

57. Anderson, *Revolution*, p. 86; Codevilla, *While Others Build*, p. 67. Codevilla also named William Van Cleave as a supporter of a new BMD effort.

58. Talbott, *Master of the Game*, p. 3.

59. Robert Dallek, *Ronald Reagan: The Politics of Symbolism* (Cambridge, Mass.: Harvard Unversity Press, 1984), p. 63.

60. Anderson Interview, p. 4.

61. Anderson, *Revolution*, pp. 88–92.

62. Ibid., pp. 90–92.

63. Robinson, "Beam Weapons Technology," p. 41; for a discussion of conflicting technical reports, see pp. 42–43. Evidently, after a DARPA report presented a fairly optimistic picture of the future of laser weapons, a DOD study was undertaken to counter it.

64. Quoted in "Laser Weaponry Technology Advances," *AW*, 25 May 1981, p. 65.

65. Hedrick Smith, "U.S. Might Consider Reviving the ABMs," *NYT*, 16 January 1981, p. 11.

66. Weinberger is quoted in "Senate Discussing ABM Need to Guard Multiple Shelter MX," *AW*, 9 February 1981, p. 91.

67. Robinson, "Beam Weapons Technology," p. 40.

68. For a report of Pentagon opposition to expanding ABM efforts in the four years before Reagan's March 1983 speech, see Codevilla, *While Others Build*, pp. 70–73, 77–82.

69. "Senate Directs Air Force to Formulate Laser Plan," p. 52.

70. Ibid., p. 53.

71. Ibid., p. 52.

72. Ibid., p. 53.

73. Robinson, "Beam Weapons Technology," pp. 40, 43; "Senate Directs Air Force to Formulate Laser Plan," p. 52. Wallop had wanted to add $152.5 million to DARPA's budget and $97.5 million to the air force's budget for laser R&D; but, according to Wallop, foot dragging by high-level Pentagon officials revealed that the required backing for these measures was lacking, so he had to settle for a $50 million addition (the $30 million mentioned above plus $20 million for DARPA). For a discussion of the way conflicting reports, delays, and testimonies were used to defeat Wallop's bill, see Robinson, "Beam Weapons Technology," pp. 42–43. For another account of the effort to establish a space-based laser program office in the air force, see Codevilla, *While Others Build*, pp. 77–92. According to Codevilla, Wallop was opposed in this undertaking by Warner and Tower, who used various parliamentary maneuvers to delay the passage of the measure that required the air force to establish the program office. Furthermore, Codevilla claimed that the air force emasculated the new office by staffing it with officers who had failed to earn promotions. This would have made the office a professional graveyard that could not attract dynamic, effective officers. Again, for the tendency of the military services to favor the development of certain traditional weapon systems, see Builder, *Masks of War*.

PART FOUR. STRATEGIC CRISIS, PRESIDENTIAL RESPONSE

1. William S. Cohen, "Presidential Paradoxes," *NYT*, 19 December 1982, p. E17.

CHAPTER SEVEN. THE HIGH FRONTIER

1. Henry A. Kissinger, *A World Restored* (Gloucester, Mass.: Peter Smith, 1957), p. 327.

2. Graham Interview, p. 6; John M. Fisher to Daniel O. Graham, letter, 8 September 1981, Karl R. Bendetsen Papers on High Frontier (hereafter Bendetsen Papers on High Frontier).

3. "Haig Seeks Space-Based Weapons Report," *AW*, 25 May 1981, pp. 42–43; Daniel O. Graham to Joseph Coors, letter, 18 May 1981, and Alexander M. Haig, Jr., to Daniel O. Graham, letter, 26 September 1981, both in Bendetsen Papers on High Frontier.

4. Daniel O. Graham, "Toward a New Strategy: Bold Strokes Rather than Increments," *Strategic Review* 9 (Spring 1981): 9–16.

5. Ibid., pp. 9–12.

6. Ibid., p. 12.

7. Ibid., pp. 11–12.

8. Ibid., p. 13.

9. Ibid., pp. 13, 15.

10. Ibid., p. 13.

11. Daniel O. Graham, "Bold Strokes for a Strategic Nuclear Balance," *Signal* 35 (May-June 1981): 57–60, 63–64, and "New Strategy on the High Frontier of Space," *Officer* 57 (November 1981): 26–27.

12. Interview with Frank Barnett, National Strategy Information Center, New York, 1 October 1986. Barnett was interviewed by Stanley A. Blumberg.

13. Ibid., pp. 6–7.

14. Graham Interview, p. 7. John M. Fisher to Daniel O. Graham, letter, 29 July 1981, Daniel O. Graham to Richard Scaife, letter, 16 July 1981, Daniel O. Graham to Joseph Coors, letter, 18 May 1981, Karl R. Bendetsen to Edwin Meese III, letter, 30 July 1981, and memorandum to Flo Randolph, hand dated 29 July 1981, all in Bendetsen Papers on High Frontier. Flo Randolph is listed on another memorandum in Bendetsen's papers as Meese's secretary.

15. Fisher to Graham, 29 July 1981.

16. Barnett Interview; Graham Interview, pp. 6–8, 14. The Bendetsen Papers on High Frontier contain letters dated 12 August 1981 from Bendetsen to Joseph Coors, Jaquelin Hume, and William Wilson indicating they had agreed to serve on the panel.

17. Interview with Joseph Coors, Adolph Coors Company, Golden, Colorado, 31 July 1987, pp. 1–2, 5–6; and a personal biographical sketch provided by Coors's office. Coors stated in his interview that he was introduced to the issue of strategic defense through his service on the board of directors of the Heritage Foundation, which eventually became the sponsor of Graham's High Frontier organization.

18. Interview with Jaquelin Hume, Washington, D.C., 28 October 1987, pp. 1–2. The Bohemian Club was founded in 1870 with its headquarters in San Francisco. Soon after its beginning, club members (including novelist Jack London) started holding an annual encampment at Meeker's Grove on the Russian River near Monte Rio, California. The club still owns 2,750 acres of redwood trees at the grove and among these trees has 128 camps. Each year, for three weeks at the end of July, club members participate in an encampment that features entertainment and speeches by national leaders. Speakers have included NSC adviser Henry Kissinger, Senator Barry Goldwater, Secretary of Defense Melvin Laird, General Motors president Edward Cole, and astronaut Neil Armstrong. The encampments give these leaders an opportunity to meet, exchange views, and establish connections. This information on the Bohemian Club was found in Wallace Turner, "At the Bohemian Club; Men Join, Women Serve," *NYT*, 12 January 1981, p. A16.

19. Hume Interview, pp. 1–2.

20. Interview with William A. Wilson, Washington, D.C., 7 December 1987, pp. 6–7; *Who's Who in American Politics: 1987–88*, 11th Ed., p. 154; *The World Almanac and Book of Facts*, 1986 ed., p. 616.

21. Teller, *Better a Shield*, pp. 121–23; and William J. Broad, *Star Warriors* (New York: Simon and Schuster, 1985), pp. 15, 52–54.

22. Robinson, "Advance Made on High-Energy Laser," pp. 25–27; William J. Broad, "X-Ray Laser Weapon Gains Favor," *NYT*, 15 November 1983, pp. C1-C2; Broad, *Star Warriors*, pp. 16, 117, 122; Interview with Admiral James D. Watkins, United States Navy Historical Center, Washington Navy Yard, 29 September 1987, p. 16; Coors Interview, p. 6.

23. Broad, *Star Warriors*, pp. 122–23; G[eorge] A. Keyworth to Karl Bendetsen, letter, 10 November 1981, Bendetsen Papers on High Frontier; Keyworth Interview, pp. 8, 11–12. Keyworth stated that Meese assigned him to serve as liaison between the White House and the High Frontier Panel.

24. "High Frontier Panel Members," roster dated 30 September 1981, in Bendetsen Papers on High Frontier.

25. Karl R. Bendetsen for John M. Fisher, memorandum, 4 March 1982, and Karl R. Bendetsen to Edwin Meese III, letter, 30 July 1981, both in Bendetsen Papers on High Frontier.

26. The particulars of this dispute are detailed in the following correspondence: John M. Fisher to Daniel O. Graham, letter, 8 September 1981; "Agenda [for] 5 September High Frontier Panel Meeting," n.d.; list of meeting attendees dated 5 September [1981]; Fisher to Graham, letter, 8 September 1981; Fisher to Graham, memorandum, 31 August 1981; Fisher to Graham, memorandum, 29 July 1981; R[obert] C. Richardson to Karl [R.] Bendetsen, aide memoire, n.d.; Graham to Bendetsen, memorandum, 4 September 1981. For an example of the detailed management style of Fisher, see Fisher to Graham, letter, 12 June 1981. All of these documents are in Bendetsen Papers on High Frontier. The issues dividing the two sides in this dispute are very complex and resulted in long letters between those involved in the disagreement. No effort has been made here to exhaust the details in the conflict that spread beyond the High Frontier area into several conservative defense organizations. Other documents in Bendetsen's High Frontier Papers dealing with this dispute include Fisher to Graham, 8 September 1981 (a letter more than four pages long giving Fisher's side of the dispute); Fisher to Bendetsen, 30 September 1981 (Fisher resigns from High Frontier Panel and gives "official" and "unofficial" reasons for his resignation); Bendetsen to Fisher, letter, 5 October 1981; Graham to Fisher, 28 October 1981; Fisher to Bendetsen, letter, 13 November 1981 (another letter more than four pages long with Fisher's side of the disagreement); and Bendetsen to Fisher, letter, 20 November 1981. For sources on the shift from the American Security Council Foundation to the Heritage Foundation, see Graham Interview, pp. 4, 7–8; Daniel O. Graham, *High Frontier: A New National Strategy* (Washington, D.C.: High Frontier, 1982), p. ix; Ed[win J.] Feulner, [Jr.], Dan[iel O.] Graham, Karl [R.] Bendetsen, memorandum of understanding, 14 September 1981; and Fisher to Bendetsen, letter, 30 September 1981. The last two documents are in Bendetsen Papers on High Frontier.

27. "High Frontier Meeting: Attendees," 9 September 1981; "High Frontier: The Program," 14 September 1981; Dan[iel] Graham, "Panel Meetings," memorandum to Project High Frontier Panel members, 15 September 1981. All documents are contained in Bendetsen Papers on High Frontier.

28. Anderson, *Revolution*, pp. 94–95.

29. Ibid., p. 95.

30. "Agenda for High Frontier Panel, November 2 and 3, 1981"; Karl R. Bendetsen to William A. Wilson, letter, 6 November 1981; and Currie-McDan-

iel, *Strategic Defense Command*, p. 17. The agenda and letter are in Bendetsen Papers on High Frontier.

31. Karl R. Bendetsen to the High Frontier Panel, memorandum, "Summary of Our Principal Conclusions," 4 November 1981, in Bendetsen Papers on High Frontier.

32. Jaquelin H. Hume to Karl R. Bendetsen, letter, 9 September 1981; Daniel O. Graham to Jaquelin H. Hume, letter, 16 September 1981; Jaquelin H. Hume to Karl R. Bendetsen, letter, 28 September 1981; and Karl R. Bendetsen to Jaquelin H. Hume, letter, 5 October 1981. All letters are in Bendetsen Papers on High Frontier.

33. Karl R. Bendetsen to Caspar Weinberger, letter, 27 November 1981; Karl R. Bendetsen to Ed[win] Meese, memorandum, 2 December 1981; Karl R. Bendetsen to High Frontier Panel members, Memorandum, "Situation Report," 20 December 1981 (hereafter referred to as Bendetsen, "Situation Report"); draft of "Proposed Memorandum for the President," 2 December 1981, p. 5. All documents are in Bendetsen Papers on High Frontier.

34. Bendetsen, "Situation Report."

35. Ibid.

36. Ibid.

37. Karl [R. Bendetsen], "Report to the Members of the High Frontier Project Panel," 9 January 1982, in Bendetsen Papers on High Frontier (hereafter Bendetsen, 9 Jan. 82 Report); Hume Interview, p. 3. Hume stated that he arranged the meeting.

38. Presidential Schedule for Friday, 8 January 1982 (revised update), supplied by Martin Anderson; Bendetsen, 9 Jan. 82 Report. Most published accounts of this meeting place Wilson at the meeting. See, for example, Herken, *Counsels of War*, p. 337. Herken also claimed that Bendetsen's group met four times with the president and his top advisers. I found evidence of only one meeting before the president's speech of March 1983.

39. Karl R. Bendetsen, memorandum for the president, "Conclusions and Recommendations of the High Frontier Panel," 18 December 1981, in Bendetsen Papers on High Frontier.

40. Bendetsen, 9 Jan. 82 Report.

41. Ibid.

42. Martin Anderson, minutes of management meeting, 8:30 A.M., 11 January 1982. Anderson provided me two copies of these minutes, one typed and the other in his own hand. The comments about opposition to the concepts of the High Frontier Panel are from the handwritten version of the minutes. In *Revolution*, p. 91, Anderson indicated reservations about Keyworth's attitude toward BMD, saying that Keyworth was "generally supportive of missile defense."

43. Keyworth Interview, pp. 17–18.

44. Herken, *Counsels of War*, p. 336. According to Herken, the evidence for this account of Keyworth's position is a 13 November 1981 letter from Wallop to Baker that was made available to him (ibid., p. 396 n23). For a very unfavorable appraisal of Keyworth's attitudes toward ABM and his role in this story, see Codevilla, *While Others Build*, pp. 83–84. According to Codevilla, Keyworth was a strong opponent of expanded support for ABM lasers. Keyworth supposedly was afraid that BMD would be oversold and would fail to live up to expectations. As a result, the public would become disillusioned with the idea of BMD, and it would lose necessary public support.

45. "Laser ABM and Shuttle to Be Reviewed by Administration, Keyworth Says," *Aerospace Daily*, 8 September 1981, p. 35.

46. Coors Interview, p. 2; Graham Interview, p. 10; Keyworth Interview, pp. 8–9; Karl R. Bendetsen to William A. Wilson, letter, 6 November 1981, in Bendetsen Papers on High Frontier.

47. Graham, *High Frontier*, especially pp. 6, 33–34, 92.

48. [Daniel O. Graham], untitled concept paper, 9 July 1981; Edward Teller to Karl R. Bendetsen, telegram, 3 September 1981; Dan[iel O. Graham] to Karl [R. Bendetsen], letter, 28 October 1981; [Karl R. Bendetsen] to William A. Wilson, letter, 6 November 1981. All documents are in Bendetsen Papers on High Frontier.

49. Wilson Interview, p. 10.

50. Ibid., p. 11; Graham Interview, pp. 8–10.

51. Karl R. Bendetsen, memorandum for panel members, "Some Ground Rules for Participants," 26 August 1981, in Bendetsen Papers on High Frontier. Graham's typed name appears at the end of this document.

52. The sources here are two letters: Daniel O. Graham to Karl R. Bendetsen, 4 December 1981, and Daniel O. Graham to Karl R. Bendetsen, 10 December 1981, both in Bendetsen Papers on High Frontier. The two letters say virtually the same thing regarding why Graham felt compelled to publish a High Frontier study. In the 10 December letter, Graham described some details of the imminent separation of High Frontier from the Heritage Foundation, a separation that seems to have been mutually agreeable to Feulner and Graham, and discussed the use of letterhead stationery with the names of George Keyworth and Albert C. Wedemeyer. The first letter has a line drawn across it and contains a note in the upper left-hand corner: "Superceded 12/10/81."

53. Graham to Bendetsen, letters, 4 and 10 December 1981.

54. Karl R. Bendetsen to Daniel O. Graham, letter, 11 December 1981, and Jaquelin H. Hume to Karl R. Bendetsen, 11 December 1981, both in Bendetsen Papers on High Frontier.

55. Bendetsen to Graham, letter, 11 December 1981.

56. Daniel O. Graham to Jaquelin H. Hume, letter, 28 December 1981, in Bendetsen Papers on High Frontier.

57. Daniel O. Graham to Karl R. Bendetsen, letter, 5 January 1982; Karl R. Bendetsen to Daniel O. Graham, letters, 8 and 9 January 1982; Edward Teller to Daniel O. Graham, letter, 9 January 1982; Jaquelin H. Hume to Daniel O. Graham, letter, 18 January 1982; William A. Wilson to Daniel O. Graham, letter, 26 January 1982. All letters in Bendetsen Papers on High Frontier.

58. Bendetsen to Fisher, memorandum, 4 March 1982.

59. "Washington Observations," *Air Force Magazine* (February 1982): 21. Graham had already stolen a march on the panel. By 7 January he had completed the summary of his High Frontier concept that would appear in the published report. Apparently, he had succeeded somehow in getting a copy of this to the White House staff before the panel's 8 January meeting with the president. Bendetsen said he saw the summary at the White House on 8 January (presumably while he and the panel were there to meet with the president), although he did not know what the document was until a later meeting the same day with Graham and Graham's staff during which Bendetsen described the outcome of the meeting with the president. (Karl R. Bendetsen to Daniel O. Graham, letter, 9 January 1982, in Bendetsen Papers on High Frontier. The comments about the summary are found in this letter's postscript.) The quota-

tion from the *Air Force* article in a sense confirms one of the major concerns of High Frontier supporters. They were afraid that the advocates of established programs (for example, program managers) would kill the space initiatives of High Frontier to protect their own programs.

60. Graham Interview, pp. 11–12; Daniel O. Graham to Karl R. Bendetsen, letter, 8 February 1982, in Bendetsen Papers on High Frontier.

61. Graham, "New Strategy," pp. 26–27.

62. Leon Wynter and Peter Perl, "Cold Eases; Snow in Forecast," *WP*, 13 January 1982, pp. C1, C4; Lawrence Meyer and Howie Kurtz, "71 Feared Dead as Plane Hits Bridge, Smashes Cars, Plunges into Potomac," *WP*, 14 January 1982, pp. A1, A6; Stephen J. Lynton and Tom Vesey, "Metro Train Derails; 3 Die," *WP*, 14 January 1982, pp. A1, A16; and Ron Shaffer and Peter Perl, "Series of Disasters Paralyzes Capital Area at Rush Hour," *WP*, 14 January 1982, pp. A1, A17.

63. Graham Interview, pp. 16–18. He would later comment that the Boeing study was "like the cavalry riding over the hill. . . . [W]e had been getting so much flak out of the Pentagon that even some of my own people were saying: 'General, we have so many opponents, I don't know how we'll make it.' "

64. Graham Interview, pp. 17–18. According to Wallop (Interview, pp. 11, 23–24), DeLauer remained a strong opponent of missile defense and in the fall of 1982 directed a study that cast doubts on Graham's concept. When the general complained about the study to the secretary of defense, Weinberger reportedly responded that though he and DeLauer agreed that a missile defense would enhance the nation's security, they did not share Graham's optimism about the state of the technologies that would be involved. (Don Oberdorfer, "A New Age of Uncertainty Is Born," *WP*, 4 January 1985, p. A20.) Where Keyworth is concerned, we have noted previously that though he was already involved with the High Frontier Panel and was participating in meetings with members of the White House staff on the matter of ballistic missile defense, he seems to have been lukewarm at best about pursuing a new ABM initiative. The actual time of his conversion to ABM supporter is difficult to ascertain. According to Arnold Kramish (in a discussion with me on 7 June 1988), Goldie briefed Keyworth on 14 January, not 13 January as Graham recalled. Kramish considered this a very important meeting, since he dates Keyworth's conversion to strategic defense supporter from this time. As will be seen later, McFarlane and Keyworth fix the time of Keyworth's conversion as the week before the president's 23 March 1983 speech (Interview with Robert C. McFarlane, Center for Strategic and International Studies, Washington, D.C., 15 September 1987, p. 12; Keyworth Interview, pp. 17–22). Senator Wallop's memories would seem to support a later conversion for Keyworth. In fact, Wallop thinks that Keyworth's opposition may have continued beyond the president's speech (Interview, pp. 14–15).

65. Phil Truluck to Ed Feulner, memorandum, 19 February 1982, in Bendetsen Papers on High Frontier. Truluck does not fully identify Jenkins. Anderson's minutes of management meeting, 11 January 1982, lists Jim Jenkins as a participant.

66. Graham, *High Frontier*. At Graham's request, Bendetsen provided the vague statement about Bendetsen's role in High Frontier that appears in the published report (compare the statement on page xi of the report with the statement in Karl R. Bendetsen to Daniel O. Graham, letter, 16 February 1982, Bendetsen Papers on High Frontier).

67. Graham, *High Frontier*, pp. 1–3, 6, 17–18, 92–94. For a recent discussion

of the tie between economic and military power, see Paul Kennedy, *The Decline and Fall of the Great Powers* (New York: Random House, 1987).

68. Graham, *High Frontier*, pp. 3, 6, 31–32, 35, 83, 92–98.

69. Ibid., pp. 32, 34, 92.

70. Ibid., pp. 4, 7–8, 115–17. "Multitiered" refers to the fact that this BMD system would attack approaching ICBMs in more than one phase of their flight trajectory. The flight of an ICBM is divided into four phases: boost, postboost, midcourse, and terminal.

71. Ibid., pp. 4, 8, 68, 121–28; for a diagram of Graham's missile defense system, see p. 24.

72. Ibid., Appendix E. See especially pp. 68, 71, 135–36.

73. Ibid., pp. 1–3, 6, 21–22, 31. One is reminded here of the competitive-strategies concept that came to be espoused in DOD while Weinberger was secretary of defense.

74. Graham, *High Frontier*, pp. 1, 21–22, 81–83, 87–88.

75. Michael Getler, "Major Shift in Strategy Proposed: Use of Weapons on Space Satellites to Kill Incoming Missiles Suggested," *WP*, 5 March 1982, p. A8. Bendetsen sent copies of this article to High Frontier Panel members by means of a 5 March memorandum that stated: "I had been convinced that I had a clear understanding with Dan Graham that he would not go public in a manner which seized the initiative that The President might otherwise have had on his own for a switch away from the doctrine of Mutual Assured Destruction."

76. Daniel O. Graham, "The High Frontier: Summary of a New National Strategy," *Defense Science 2000*[+] 1, 2 (1982): 20–21, 66–79.

77. Daniel O. Graham, "Preventing World War III—How to Neutralize the Numbers by Exploiting Defense in the 'High Frontier,' " *Government Executive* 14 (July 1982): 16, 18–19.

78. "Selling the High Frontier Defense Strategy," Interview with General Daniel O. Graham, *Defense Electronics* (October 1982): 169–70, 172, 174–75.

79. Ron[ald Reagan] to Karl [R. Bendetsen], letter, 20 January 1982, in Bendetsen Papers on High Frontier.

80. Jaquelin H. Hume to Karl R. Bendetsen, letter, 16 February 1982, in Bendetsen Papers on High Frontier.

81. Truluck to Feulner, 19 February 1982. Keyworth's charge to develop his own program may be a reference to the direction he received from Meese during the 11 January staff meeting noted above.

82. William A. Wilson to Karl R. Bendetsen, letter, 15 March 1982; Daniel O. Graham to William A. Wilson, letter, 29 March 1982. Bendetsen asked Wilson to send a copy of his 15 March letter to Graham (Karl [R. Bendetsen] to William A. Wilson, mailgram, 19 March 1982), and he apparently did. All documents in Bendetsen Papers on High Frontier.

83. J[aquelin] H. Hume to Karl R. Bendetsen, letter, 21 April 1982, and Karl R. Bendetsen to Jaquelin H. Hume, 29 April 1982, both in Bendetsen Papers on High Frontier.

84. G[eorge] A. Keyworth to Karl [R. Bendetsen], letter, 3 May 1982, in Bendetsen Papers on High Frontier. Hume sent Bendetsen a copy of his letter from Keyworth (Jaquelin H. Hume to Karl R. Bendetsen, 10 May 1982, in Bendetsen Papers on High Frontier).

85. Keyworth Interview, pp. 16–17; U.S. Department of Defense, Director of the Strategic Defense Initiative Organization, "*SDI: A Technical Progress Report*," April 1987, pp. 28–29, submitted to the secretary of defense. An early ex-

perimental version of the adjustable beam-directing mirror was composed of sixty-nine compensating actuators. Programs were under way in 1987 to produce mirrors with between ten thousand and one hundred thousand actuators.

86. Keyworth Interview, pp. 18–19.

87. Karl R. Bendetsen to Frank Barnett et al. memorandum, 7 December 1982, and Jaquelin H. Hume to Karl R. Bendetsen, letter, 10 May 1982, both in Bendetsen Papers on High Frontier.

88. Karl R. Bendetsen to Jaquelin H. Hume, letter, 4 October 1982, in Bendetsen Papers on High Frontier; "Launching a Space Policy," editorial, *Washington Times*, 4 October 1982. Keyworth was one White House staffer with whom Bendetsen maintained contact. During the summer, both Bendetsen and Coors met with Keyworth, who apparently discussed with them some of the technical developments uncovered through the work of the Frieman Committee. See Joseph Coors to Karl R. Bendetsen, letter, 18 October 1982; Karl R. Bendetsen to Joseph Coors, letter, 25 October 1982; Karl R. Bendetsen to William A. Wilson, letter, 16 November 1982; and Frank R. Barnett to Karl R. Bendetsen, letter, 3 November 1982. These letters are in Bendetsen Papers on High Frontier. In his 3 November letter, which responds to a 4 October letter from Bendetsen, Barnett stated that he favored another meeting of the panel to see if it would be possible to "make another effort to 'prod' the Government into action."

89. Karl R. Bendetsen to Frank Barnett et al., memorandum, 7 December 1982; Geraldine Pugh to Didi Berry, memorandum, 10 December 1982; and Karl R. Bendetsen to George A. Keyworth, letter, 13 December 1982, all in Bendetsen Papers on High Frontier.

90. Karl R. Bendetsen, "Proposal for Inclusion in the President's State of the Union Address," 27 December 1982, in Bendetsen Papers on High Frontier.

91. Edward Teller to Karl R. Bendetsen, letter, 29 December 1982, in Bendetsen Papers on High Frontier.

92. Gerry [Geraldine] Pugh to George A. Keyworth, memorandum, 28 December 1982, and Gerry Pugh to Anthony Dolan, memorandum, 28 December 1982, both in Bendetsen Papers on High Frontier. The memoranda forwarded to each individual a slightly modified version of the panel's proposed insert for the State of the Union Address. Joseph Coors to Karl R. Bendetsen, letter, 24 February 1983. Coors gave me a copy of this letter.

CHAPTER EIGHT. THE PRESIDENTIAL DECISION

1. I give here the common version of Hugo's famous statement. It is found in John Bartlett, *Familiar Quotations: A Collection of Passages, Phrases, and Proverbs Traced to Their Sources in Ancient and Modern Literature*, ed. by Emily Morison Beck and the editorial staff of Little, Brown, and Company, 15th and 125th anniversary edition, revised and enlarged (Boston: Little, Brown, 1980), p. 491. An 1888 translation renders this passage as: "An invasion of armies can be resisted, but there is no resistance to an invasion of ideas" (see Victor Hugo, *History of a Crime: Deposition of a Witness*, 2 vols., trans. by Huntington Smith [New York: Thomas Y. Crowell, 1888], 237).

2. McFarlane Interview, p. 11.

3. Thomas S. Kuhn, *The Structure of Scientific Revolutions*, International Encyclopedia of Unified Science, *Foundations of the Unity of Science*, vol. 2, no.

2 (Chicago: University of Chicago Press, 1970), Chapters 6–11. According to Kuhn, scientists operate within a structural paradigm that is composed of concepts that are embodied in textbooks and procedures. This paradigm governs the way scientists view their world and dictates the research questions they pursue. The pursuit of these questions is "normal science." At some point an anomaly develops that cannot be explained within the confines of the paradigm, creating a paradigm crisis that eventually leads to the development of a new theory that becomes part of a new paradigm.

4. Keyworth Interview, p. 3.

5. Lauren H. Holland and Robert A. Hoover, *The MX Decision: A New Direction in U.S. Weapons Procurement Policy?* (Boulder, Colo.: Westview Press, 1985), pp. 70–73, 220; U.S. Air Force Ballistic Missile Office, Official History for Fiscal Years 1980 and 1981, pp. 25–27, 29–30, 37–38 (hereafter BMO History, 1980–1981). Raymond L. Puffer, historian of the Air Force Ballistic Missile Office, Norton Air Force Base, California, provided extracts of this unpublished official history.

6. BMO History, 1980-1981, pp. 39, 136, 151–55; Holland and Hoover, *MX Decision*, p. 139, 142–45; Desmond Ball, "The MX Basing Decision," *Survival* 22 (March–April 1980): 58.

7. BMO History, 1980-1981, p. 165.

8. Ibid., p. 166.

9. Ibid., p. 41; Holland and Hoover, *MX Decision*, pp. 165-68.

10. BMO History, 1980-1981, pp. 166–68. For a story on the opposition effort, see Joyce Wadler, "Great Basin States Joyously Bubbling," *WP*, 3 October 1981, pp. A1, A12.

11. BMO History, 1980-1981, pp. 168–70.

12. Ibid., pp. 171–72.

13. Ibid., pp. 172–73. Information on the size and cost of the air force EIS is from page 173.

14. Ibid., 174–75; U.S. Air Force Ballistic Missile Office, Official History for Fiscal Years 1982 and 1983, p. 32 (hereafter BMO History, 1982-1983) (an extract of this unpublished official history was provided by Raymond L. Puffer, historian of the Air Force Ballistic Missile Office, Norton Air Force Base, California); Holland and Hoover, *MX Decision*, pp. 171–73. Schriever and Scowcroft had both retired from the United States Air Force.

15. BMO History, 1980-1981, p. 175; BMO History, 1982-1983, p. 32.

16. BMO History, 1982-1983, pp. 32–33; Richard Halloran, "Reagan Drops Mobile MX Plan, Urges Basing Missiles in Silos; Proposed Building B-1 Bomber," *NYT*, 3 October 1981, pp. 1, 13.

17. "Background Statement from White House on MX Missile and B-1 Bomber," *NYT*, 3 October 1981, p. 12.

18. Lee Lescaze and George C. Wilson, "Reagan Asks for 100 MXs, 100 B1 Bombers," *WP*, 3 October 1981, p. A12; Phil Gailey, "Future Steps for Program," *NYT*, 3 October 1981, p. 13. Weinberger's comment was reported by Leslie H. Gelb, "Silos and Vulnerability," *NYT*, 3 October 1981, p. 13.

19. Michael Getler, "President Exchanges Political Problems," *WP*, 3 October 1981, p. A9.

20. BMO History, 1982-1983, pp. 34, 102.

21. Holland and Hoover, *MX Decision*, p. 182.

22. Ibid., pp. 180–84.

23. Ibid., p. 188.

24. BMO History, 1982-1983, p. 103.

25. Currie-McDaniel, *Army Strategic Defense Command*, pp. 20–21.

26. Holland and Hoover, *MX Decision*, pp. 216–21.

27. "Text of Reagan and Pentagon Statements on MX Missile Basing Proposal," *NYT*, 23 November 1982, p. A14; "Transcript of President's Address on Nuclear Strategy toward Soviet Union," *NYT*, 23 November 1982, p. A12; " 'Peacemaker' Loses Missile Name Game," *NYT*, 23 November 1982, p. A14; Holland and Hoover, *MX Decision*, p. 224.

28. "Text of Reagan and Pentagon Statements," p. A14.

29. Holland and Hoover, *MX Decision*, p. 225.

30. "Texts of Reagan and Pentagon Statements" p. A14.

31. Holland and Hoover, *MX Decision*, p. 225.

32. Ibid., pp. 225–26.

33. Richard Halloran, "House, 245-176, Votes Down $988 Million for MX Missile; Setback for Reagan Policy," *NYT*, 8 December 1982, p. A1; Richard Halloran, "3 of 5 Chiefs Asked Delay on MX," *NYT*, 9 December 1982, p. A1; Holland and Hoover, *MX Decision*, pp. 222, 227. Hedrick Smith reported that Vessey's announcement of the JCS split contributed to the spread of a "mood of revolt" in Congress (Smith, "Defeat on MX Puts Reagan in a Defensive Mode: Politically Unprepared, the Administration Now Seeks to Buy More Time," *NYT*, 12 December 1982, Section IV, p. 1). According to Linton Brooks, Admiral James Watkins was the person principally responsible for having the JCS consider the matter of the dense pack basing mode. The air force initially held that the details of this basing mode were technical matters with which the JCS need not be concerned. Brooks and others advised Watkins that the JCS had to consider the issues surrounding dense pack, for Congress was sure to ask the Joint Chiefs for their opinions (Brooks to Donald R. Baucom, letter, 24 July 1989).

34. For an excellent summary of where things stood in mid-December 1982, see Smith, "Defeat on MX Puts Reagan in a Defense Mode," and Leslie Gelb, "Defeat on MX Puts Reagan in a Defense Mode: New Deployment Needed, Maybe New Strategy Too," *NYT* 12 December 1982, Section IV, p. 1; George C. Wilson, "*MX*: How a Missile Got a Life of Its Own," *WP*, 12 December 1982, pp. A1, A9. The Goldwater quotation is from John Newhouse, "Annals of Diplomacy: The Abolitionist—I," *New Yorker*, 2 January 1989, p. 52 (hereafter Newhouse, "Abolitionist—I"). Newhouse's article is the first of two articles. It contains a superb discussion of the chaotic situation that prevailed in the area of nuclear strategy on the eve of President Reagan's March 1983 speech on strategic defense. See especially pp. 47–50. See also Cohen, "Presidential Paradoxes," p. E17.

35. BMO History, 1982-1983, p. 35. The commission stated that strategic force modernization and arms control negotiations were the cornerstones of strategic stability. According to the recommendations of the commission, the United States should deploy the MX in existing MINUTEMAN silos while developing a small, single-warhead missile that would have greater flexibility in its basing mode. Furthermore, the United States should continue arms negotiations with the Soviet Union (ibid., pp. 35, 37).

36. McFarlane Interview, pp. 2–3.

37. Ibid., p. 2.

38. David S. Yost, "The Delegitimization of Nuclear Deterrence?" *Armed Forces and Society* 16 (Summer 1990): 489.

39. Ibid.

40. Ibid., pp. 489–90; John Herbers, "Widespread Vote Urges Nuclear Freeze," *NYT*, 4 November 1982, p. A22; David S. Yost, "Public Opinion, Political Culture, and Nuclear Weapons in the Western Alliance," 31 May 1989 (draft paper provided to me by Yost), pp. 24–25. In both the draft and published papers, Yost pointed out the paradox of an American people who would support the freeze movement while still indicating in polls taken at the time that they continued to support U.S. deterrence policies and still distrusted the Soviet Union. Yost quoted the work of Everett Carll Ladd ("Things a Pollster Can Count On," *Christian Science Monitor*, 21 September 1988, p. 11), who argued that the high vote for a nuclear freeze was not really a manifestation of support for the goals of the freeze movement but rather an effort to signal the government to "do what is possible to draw the world back from the possibility of nuclear war." In his "Public Opinion" draft paper, Yost presented these statistics: although freeze leaders claimed 70 percent of Americans supported their goals, a CBS-*NYT* poll showed that 80 percent of the people would oppose a freeze if the Soviets could cheat, 67 percent would oppose it if the Soviets were left in a stronger position, and 72 percent would oppose a unilateral freeze by the United States. Other polls from this period suggest, according to Yost, "that no more than 57% of the public ever heard or read about the freeze movement."

41. McFarlane Interview, p. 5. For another comment on the impact of the freeze movement, see Herken, *Counsels of War*, p. 340.

42. McFarlane Interview, pp. 1–4. With regard to Reagan's attitude toward nuclear weapons, John Newhouse has referred to Reagan as an abolitionist who "wanted to have the advantage in nuclear weapons or else to rid the world of them" (Newhouse, "Abolitionist—I," p. 39). For a similar account of McFarlane's role in these events and the thinking of Reagan and McFarlane on arms reductions, see Lou Cannon, *President Reagan: The Role of a Lifetime* (New York: Simon & Schuster, 1991), pp. 325–27 (hereafter Cannon, *Role of a Lifetime*). Cannon believed that had the Reagan administration not "bungled" the effort to secure support for MX deployment, "it is doubtful if the Strategic Defense Initiative would have ever come into being" (p. 323). For more information on how arms control was viewed in the Reagan administration, see Oberdorfer, *The Turn*, passim. An abbreviated version of Oberdorfer's views is "Reagan and the Russians: Revising History's 'First Draft,'" *WP*, 29 September 1991, p. C5.

43. McFarlane Interview, p. 4. Once again, this is a common thread among those who favored a new BMD program for the United States. High technology was America's forte. It would be sound strategy for the United States to push the strategic competition into a realm where the United States has the advantage. This line of thinking is to be found in the writings of Graham especially. It is in consonance with the idea of competitive strategy that became important in the Pentagon under Caspar Weinberger.

44. Ibid., p. 6.

45. Interview with John M. Poindexter, Rockville, Maryland, 28 January 1988, pp. 1–2.

46. Ibid., pp. 2–4.

47. Holland and Hoover, *MX Decision*, p. 220.

48. Watkins Interview, pp. 1–2, 5.

49. Discussion with Admiral James D. Watkins USN (Ret.), Department of Energy, 25 October 1989 (I refer to this meeting as a "discussion" rather than an "interview," for no transcript was made of the admiral's remarks; the only

record of our discussion is my notes); Watkins Interview, pp. 1–3; Interview with Captain Linton F. Brooks, USN, National Security Council Staff, Old Executive Office Building, Washington, D.C., 21 December 1987, pp. 1–3. Brooks was known as "the smartest man in the Navy" (conversation with Captain John Byron, USN, at the National Defense University on 26 January 1989).

50. Watkins Interview, pp. 1–5; Brooks Interview, p. 6. Brooks said of Watkins: "He's got tremendous faith in technology—future technology. He's been to sea enough to understand present technology is flawed. But he's got this tremendous faith in future technology." Watkins elaborated on the meaning of his "strategic valley of death" metaphor in his discussion with me on 25 October 1989. He actually visualized the basing mode effort in two ways. In addition to the valley of death analogy described above, he conceptualized the situation posed by the basing mode effort in terms of a grand strategic chess game in which the United States would spend billions on each basing mode program only to have each of these "moves" easily checked by Soviet countermoves made possible by their superiority in heavy ICBMs. The outcome of this strategic chess game would be disastrous for the United States. After spending exorbitant sums on a series of ineffective basing modes, America would inevitably face a Soviet checkmate. The United States had to break out of the basing mode paradigm and look for effective alternatives such as hardening command and control facilities, developing and deploying the D-5 missile, and so on.

51. Watkins Discussion; Brooks Interview, pp. 6–7; Poindexter Interview, pp. 18–19.

52. William A. Au, *The Cross, the Flag, and the Bomb: American Catholics Debate War and Peace, 1960–1983*, Contributions to the Study of Religion, No. 12, ed. by Henry W. Bowden (Westport, Conn.: Greenwood Press, 1985), pp. xiv–xv, 201–2 (hereafter Au, *Catholics Debate War and Peace*). A copy of the complete pastoral letter was printed in the 19 May 1983 edition of *Origins*. It was also printed in book form by the National Conference of Catholic Bishops.

53. Au, *Catholics Debate War and Peace*, pp. 202–3.

54. Ibid., pp. 203–4; George Weigel, *Tranquillitas Ordinis: The Present Failure and Future Promise of American Catholic Thought on War and Peace* (New York: Oxford University Press, 1987), pp. 267–68.

55. Au, *Catholics Debate War and Peace*, pp. 203–4. For specific information on linkages between the freeze movement and the thinking of Catholic leaders on nuclear weapons, see Weigel, *Tranquillitas Ordinis*, pp. 262, 265–66.

56. Watkins Discussion. The importance Watkins attached to the activities of the bishops was apparent during our discussion. Although it had been over five years since he was involved with this issue, he still had an extensive grasp of the contents of the pastoral on war and peace. He ticked down through the different versions of the letter, stating how each version had been changed until the final edition appeared, an edition the admiral considered a definite improvement over the first version.

57. The admiral's address was reprinted in James D. Watkins, "The Moral Man in the Modern Military," *Sea Power* (December 1982): 17–18, 20. This quotation is on page 17 (emphasis in original). The date of the admiral's address is not given in this reprint. However, the Public Affairs Office of Marymount College provided the date of 22 August 1982 for the speech. In 1986 Marymount College became coeducational and was renamed Marymount University.

58. Watkins, "Moral Man," p. 20.

59. Ibid. (emphasis in original). Watkins expressed similar views a few

months later in a message to the class of 1983 at Annapolis (Watkins, "We Are a Moral People: A Message to the Class of 1983," *Shipmate* [January-February 1983]: 19–20.) Two years after this speech, Robert C. Toth of the *Los Angeles Times* would report on the religious views and activities of United States military leaders. His article is antagonistic and contentious. Although he quotes Watkins as saying in "speech*es*" that he "is a moral man," Toth does not specify the speeches nor does he say anything about their context, which included the proceedings of the Catholic bishops that raised questions about the morality of military service and caused some to leave the navy. See Robert C. Toth, "Role of Religious Faith at Pentagon Raises Questions, Doubts," *Los Angeles Times*, 30 December 1984, p. 4. Watkins answered Toth's article (Watkins, "Role of Religious Faith at Pentagon," *Los Angeles Times*, 18 May 1985, Section II, p. 2). Because the *Times* delayed publication of Watkins's answer for over four months, his letter was seen by the newspaper's readers as outside the context established by the contentious tone of the Toth article. On 2 June, the *Times* printed six responses to the admiral's letter. Aside from the mere mention of Toth's article in two of these letters, the focus of comment was on the content of the Watkins letter. For another perspective on Watkins and his response to the pastoral letter, see Cannon, *Role of a Lifetime*, p. 327.

60. Watkins Discussion; Watkins Interview, pp. 3, 5.

61. The principal source for this meeting is Anderson, *Revolution*, p. 97. I am skeptical of Anderson's account for the following reasons. Anderson did not identify the source of his information about the meeting, which he dates only to the month of December 1982 (he did not list a specific day). Since Anderson had left the White House staff about a year before the December meeting, he could not have had first-hand knowledge of the events he described. Furthermore, neither McFarlane nor Watkins, both of whom probably would have attended this meeting, mentioned it in my interviews with them. Nor does Caspar Weinberger mention a December meeting in his *Fighting for Peace: Seven Critical Years in the Pentagon* (New York: Warner Books, 1990). This makes the quotation Anderson attributes to Reagan, the quotation given in the text, problematical. Is it based on a transcript of the meeting or on a later recollection? Was it reported by someone who actually attended the meeting? In spite of these difficulties, I decided to include an account of this meeting because I was able to find two other bits of corroborating information for its occurrence, although I have found no substantial evidence as to what actually was said during the meeting. One piece of corroborating evidence came from Dr. Willard J. Webb, historian for the Joint Chiefs of Staff (Telephone Conversation, 12 September 1990). Vessey's appointment calendars are maintained at Fort Ritchie, Maryland. Webb had personnel at Fort Ritchie check to see if a meeting with the president was listed during December 1982. A meeting was *scheduled* for 22 December to discuss strategic issues. I have found one piece of evidence that suggests this meeting may have been canceled. On 20 December Secretary of Defense Weinberger provided William Clark with an agenda for a meeting between Reagan, the secretary of defense, and the Joint Chiefs of Staff that was scheduled on 22 December (Cap [Caspar Weinberger], memorandum for the assistant to the president for national security affairs, "JCS Meeting with the President," 20 December 1982). Weinberger's memorandum is attached to a JCS Document Processing Record that is initialed twice by the air force member of the Chairman's Staff Group. The first set of initials are dated 20 December 1982. The second set of initials comes below a handwritten message: "Return

to Files. OBE [overtaken by events]." This second set of initials shows the time and date of this comment as "0113 [1:13A.M.], 22 Dec. 82." If this means the meeting was canceled, it would explain why people like Weinberger and Watkins have never mentioned it.

On the other hand, those who believe there was a December meeting could be confusing a meeting that was canceled in December with a meeting that actually occurred in February. President Reagan's 1990 memoir is of little help here. Although he does claim to have discussed missile defenses with the Joint Chiefs before the 11 February meeting, his discussion is sketchy and anecdotal and gives no date for the discussion (Reagan, *An American Life* [New York: Simon and Schuster, 1990], pp. 547–48, 571). On page 547, Reagan tells us that he suggested a possible missile defense program to the Joint Chiefs, who huddled briefly (evidently in Reagan's presence) and then agreed that Reagan's suggestion was worth exploring. Reagan then said: "Let's do it." On page 571, Reagan said the Joint Chiefs came back "two weeks after the 'Evil Empire' speech" and stated that it might be feasible to develop "a shield against nuclear missiles." At least one recent account of the origins of the Strategic Defense Initiative has uncritically incorporated Anderson's account of the December meeting (see John Prados, *Keepers of the Keys: A History of the National Security Council from Truman to Bush* [New York: William Morrow, 1991], p. 484). Lou Cannon, who interviewed virtually all of the major participants in these events, including Vessey, Watkins, and Clark, and who cited Anderson's *Revolution* in several places, does not mention a December 1982 meeting in *Role of a Lifetime*.

62. [Linton Brooks], "CNO and the Strategic Defense Initiative," n.d., copy supplied by Watkins, p. 4 (hereafter Brooks, "CNO and SDI"). Watkins advised me that Brooks was the author of this summary of the admiral's activities relating to strategic defense, and Brooks confirmed this point.

63. Watkins Discussion; Brooks Interview, pp. 4–6; Brooks, "CNO and SDI," p. 4. According to Brooks, for about fifteen years, Teller had been making occasional calls on the CNOs. Brooks stated that in addition to visiting Watkins, Teller had called on Admirals Elmo Zumwalt and Thomas B. Hayward.

64. In a note he penned on a draft of this chapter, Watkins wrote that he "found his [Teller's] responses to be in reasonable consonance with a number of highly classified briefings on a variety of sensors and other programs being investigated at the leading edge of future technological possibilities."

65. Watkins Interview, pp. 13–14, 17; Watkins Discussion; Brooks, "CNO and SDI," p. 4; Brooks Interview, p. 6. The story of the reed was first told to the author during his interview with Watkins on 29 September 1987. Unfortunately, this story was part of a chat that preceded the formal interview and was not on the tape recording of the interview. As a result, it is not in the formal interview transcript. However, in his 25 October 1989 discussion with me, Watkins confirmed the story and elaborated on this episode.

66. Watkins Discussion.

67. Brooks, "CNO and SDI," pp. 4–5; Brooks Interview, pp. 7–9. Brooks used the jargon of the Pentagon to describe the iterative process Watkins used to work out his position—this was a "bring-me-another-rock" process. The idea here, of course, is that rocks do not look alike, but you can hardly describe how they are different in a definitive way. This jargon emphasizes the intuitive nature of Watkins's search for an answer to America's strategic conundrum. What this process essentially does is force the staff to devise a number of alter-

natives and keep presenting them until they hit upon one which the senior officer intuitively believes will work.

68. Brooks Interview, p. 2; Watkins Interview, pp. 7–8.

69. Watkins Interview, pp. 7–8.

70. Ibid., pp. 8–9. The information on the attitudes of Gabriel and Vessey
comes from Cannon, *Role of a Lifetime*, p. 328. At least part of Cannon's material here was based on a 26 January 1990 interview with Vessey.

71. Watkins Interview, pp. 10–11, 31. Watkins believed that Weinberger
may have taken this position because he knew that Reagan already favored
some form of strategic defense program.

72. The way in which the meeting with the president was scheduled and
how the agenda was set is unclear, since Watkins, Poindexter, McFarlane, and
Brooks present accounts that are lacking in details and somewhat conflicting.
According to McFarlane, Watkins and Poindexter had been talking informally
for some time about the fact that the United States was approaching a dead
end with offensive deterrence. From Poindexter, McFarlane understood that
Watkins was optimistic about directed energy weapons technology and the possibility that missile defense might help solve America's strategic problems. Mc-
Farlane claimed to have met Watkins and Poindexter at a January luncheon at
Tingy House (the CNO's residence at the Washington Navy Yard) and encouraged Watkins to work for a JCS consensus supporting a role in U.S. strategy for
missile defense. (McFarlane Interview, pp. 4, 6–7.)

Watkins denied that he specifically coordinated his efforts with Poindexter
or McFarlane. Nevertheless, Watkins did indicate that he remembered Mc-
Farlane from the time of McFarlane's "days on the Hill," presumably a reference to McFarlane's 1979-1981 stint on the staff of the Senate Armed Services
Committee. Furthermore, Watkins stated that McFarlane was one of his two
principal contacts in the White House, George Keyworth being the other.
Watkins also indicated that he felt responsible for assuring that the Joint
Chiefs presented a unanimous position in support of a new strategic defense effort at the 11 February meeting with the president. Moreover, Watkins said
that he may also have sent some general papers on strategic issues through the
NSC staff as a matter of routine coordination and probably kept the NSC staff informally advised of the work he was doing. (Watkins Interview, pp. 13, 16–17,
21–22, 31–32.) Linton Brooks has the impression that there were discussions
between Watkins and McFarlane on strategic defense, but he could not remember exactly when they occurred. With regard to the transmission to the NSC of
papers on strategic issues, Brooks could remember no such episodes *before*
Reagan's March 1983 speech. After the speech, Brooks recalled, Watkins sent
over a white paper on missile defense and perhaps some other papers. Overall,
Brooks believes it is more likely that Watkins influenced McFarlane than the
other way around. (Brooks Interview, pp. 12–13, and Brooks to Baucom, 24 July
1989.)

Admiral John Poindexter claimed that he and McFarlane were working on
ideas for strategic defense independently of the JCS. He denied McFarlane's
claim that Watkins was coordinating his efforts with Poindexter. According to
Poindexter, McFarlane discovered that the Joint Chiefs were involved in their
own serious reappraisal of America's strategic situation when he met General
Paul Gorman, assistant to the chairman of the JCS, in January to arrange for
the JCS's February meeting with the president. Gorman and McFarlane then
agreed on an agenda that would surface the issue of strategic defense. (Poindex-

ter Interview, pp. 2–4.) All of this points toward the likelihood of some form of coordination between Watkins and McFarlane before the 11 February 1983 meeting with the president.

73. Oberdorfer, "New Age of Uncertainty," p. A20; Brooks, "CNO and SDI," p. 7; Watkins Interview, p. 10; Poindexter Interview, p. 6.

74. McFarlane Interview, p. 8; Watkins Interview, pp. 10–11, 30–32; Brooks, "CNO and SDI," p. 7.

75. Brooks, "CNO and SDI" p. 7; Watkins Interview, pp. 10, 28; McFarlane Interview, pp. 8–9. Oberdorfer reported in the *Washington Post* that "one participant [in the 11 February 1983 meeting of the JCS with the president] told a friend later that, as the discussion proceeded, Reagan asked those around the table, 'Would it not be better to defend lives than to avenge them?' To this observer, familiar with the president's ways, the ring of that rhetoric signified a policy change whose time had come" ("New Age of Uncertainty," p. A20). Similar language was used by Senator Wallop when arguing for the rapid deployment of space-based laser systems. He talked about these systems as "weapons whose only real role in the world is to kill the things that kill people" (*Congressional Record*, 97th Cong., 1st sess., 13 May 1981, 127:9613. See also *Congressional Record*, 96th Cong., 2d sess., 1 July 1980, 126:18114.) The actual statement, "Wouldn't it be better to protect the American people rather than avenge them," comes from the briefing that Brooks and Holland prepared with Watkins before his 5 February meeting with the JCS. (Brooks to Baucom, 24 July 1989, and Brooks, "CNO and SDI," TAB A, "CNO Presentation to JCS of 5 February 1983," p. 8). There would seem to be little doubt at this time that the critical point in Reagan's decision process was the 11 February 1983 meeting with the JCS. Of this meeting Weinberger wrote: "My own feeling is that the issue [of starting a new missile defense program] was finally and completely decided in the President's mind after a meeting in the Cabinet room that he and I had with the Joint Chiefs of Staff on February 11, 1983" (Weinberger, *Fighting for Peace*, p. 304). Watkins and McFarlane also point to this meeting as the critical one. Cannon, *Role of a Lifetime*, pp. 324–330, gives an account very similar to the one offered in this study. Still, Martin Anderson has argued that the 22 December meeting was the critical one because, he claims, Reagan *"ordered* [italics in original] the Chiefs to proceed" with missile defenses (Anderson, "Joint Chiefs Not Fathers of SDI," letter to the editor, *Policy Review* [Winter 1991]: 96.) Anderson's letter is in response to my own article "Hail to the Chiefs: The Untold History of Reagan's SDI Decision," *Policy Review* (Summer 1990): 66–73. In spite of his claim for the 22 December meeting, Anderson himself wrote in *Revolution*, p. 97, that on 11 February the JCS "recommended to him [Reagan] that the United States . . . move ahead with the research and development of a missile defense system." If Reagan "ordered" the Joint Chiefs to start a missile defense program in December 1982, why would they recommend the same thing to him in February 1983? This leaves unaddressed the matter of a president ordering the Joint Chiefs to take an action contrary to their military judgment and what might have happened to the president's new missile defense program had the Joint Chiefs been called to testify before Congress on this issue, just as they had been called to testify on the dense pack basing mode about two weeks before the 22 December meeting.

76. McFarlane Interview, p. 9. For a broader discussion of McFarlane's role in the Reagan government, see Brock Brower, "Bud McFarlane: Semper Fi," *New York Times Magazine*, 22 January 1989, pp. 26–29, 32, 38. Brower ac-

cepted uncritically McFarlane's account of his role in the decision process that led to Reagan's March 1983 speech. For a rebuttal of some of the critical remarks in Brower's article, see Leonard Garment, letter to the editor, *New York Times Magazine*, 12 February 1989, p. 8.

77. McFarlane Interview, pp. 9–10.

78. Ibid., p. 10.

79. Ibid., pp. 10–11. Herken, *Counsels of War*, p. 342, says that Reagan supposedly told Clark and McFarlane "that he was reluctant to repeat the same litany of bad news in the 'threat' speech that was scheduled for later in the month without also offering a more positive and compensating vision of the future."

80. McFarlane Interview, p. 11.

81. Keyworth Interview, p. 3.

82. Ibid., pp. 19–20; McFarlane Interview, p. 12.

83. McFarlane Interview, p. 12; Keyworth Interview, p. 20. McFarlane and Keyworth agreed on few details of the events that occurred during the last few days before the president's speech. For example, Keyworth claimed to have been informed of the pending presidential policy statement on Saturday, 19 March. McFarlane stated that this did not occur until Tuesday, 22 March. McFarlane recalled that the speech insert was largely his work. Keyworth said that he essentially took over the drafting of the insert after his meeting with McFarlane and even coordinated it with Vessey. McFarlane remembered working on the insert for a considerable time that Tuesday before sending it to the Pentagon for review by Secretary Weinberger and General Colin Powell, who was then Weinberger's military assistant. The service chiefs were also shown a copy. In another account, Vessey and Watkins approved a draft of the speech insert on 20 March aboard an aircraft at Andrews Air Force Base, right outside of Washington, just before departing on official travel (Brooks, "CNO and SDI," p. 7). The account presented in the text is an attempt to reconcile, to the extent possible, the conflicting remembrances of those involved in the events.

84. Keyworth Interview, pp. 21–22. According to Codevilla, *While Others Build*, pp. 69, 76, 83, Reis and Seymour Zeiberg, deputy under secretary of defense for research and engineering during the Carter administration, had written a report designed to undermine support for the use of space-based lasers against ICBMs. Codevilla claimed that this report was embarrassingly bad. The ambiguous role of Keyworth in these events was noted also in Boffey et al., *Claiming the Heavens*, p. 21. Here, Boffey and his co-authors quote a "former White House official" as saying that Keyworth "clearly went through a conversion. . . . He felt very strongly about the need to support the president on things the president felt strongly about, and he worked hard those few days to ensure the program would be directed toward research."

85. McFarlane Interview, pp. 12–14; Poindexter Interview, pp. 10–12; Keyworth Interview, pp. 23, 25. Keyworth refers to McFarlane fielding the "unbelievable opposition that emerged in the next three days." Keyworth claimed that Secretary of State George Shultz was very upset by the president's initiative; called Keyworth a "lunatic" in front of the president; and charged that BMD was the "idea of a blooming madman," would not work, and would destroy the NATO alliance. Keyworth also recalled that Richard Perle telephoned from Portugal and "suggested strongly that I fall on my sword. I should tell the president that I would oppose the new idea publicly, do anything to get it stopped." With regard to Keyworth's recollection of Shultz's "lunatic" and "madman"

comments, Richard Burt and Linton Brooks advised that such remarks are not in keeping with the style followed by Shultz when dealing with the president (Linton F. Brooks to Donald R. Baucom, letter, 31 July 1989). Poindexter presented a run-down of those who favored and those who opposed the new defense program. Those favoring the announcement, according to Poindexter, were Vice President Bush, Secretary Weinberger, and General Vessey. Opposed were Richard Perle, Richard Burt, and Fred Ikle. Poindexter claimed that Perle "burned up the telephone lines creating friction all over the United States calling everybody he could think of trying to kill the idea." Furthermore, Poindexter recalled that although Shultz opposed the missile defense idea, Burt was the opponent most heard from in the State Department. Burt claimed that he did not learn of Reagan's pending speech until the morning of 23 March while he was in Canada with the party of Vice President Bush. Burt said that his vocal opposition to SDI came after the president's speech. (Brooks to Baucom, 31 July 1989).

86. McFarlane Interview, p. 12. I here accept McFarlane's account of the final preparation of the speech insert in spite of conflicts between his recollections and those of Keyworth. All accounts I have seen agree that McFarlane was the focal point of the staff work leading to the president's decision and announcement of the decision. I find it difficult to believe that McFarlane would abdicate the crucial responsibility for the final draft of the president's comments to anyone else, especially since he was the person fielding objections from key government agencies and officials. Furthermore, at one point in his interview, Keyworth stated that McFarlane selected elements of the opposition he considered valid criticisms, and "we tried to accommodate them in the speech." Keyworth further claimed that there were two versions of the speech sent to the president: the "wimp" version and the "real" version. The president picked the "real" version. (Keyworth Interview, p. 27.) In *An American Life*, p. 571, Reagan indicated that he played an active role in writing the speech insert and that there was considerable "bureaucratese" in the draft. He also stated that this speech was the "one hassled over by N.S.C., State and Defense." For a recent account of these events that also sees McFarlane as the central player, see Cannon, *Role of a Lifetime*, pp. 323–33; Cannon called McFarlane the "principal creator" of SDI (p. 323).

87. McFarlane Interview, p. 14.

88. Ibid., p. 13; Keyworth Interview, pp. 29–30. Keyworth recalled being asked to assemble a group of scientists who would provide a consensus of favorable opinion on the president's new program. His reaction was that "you couldn't get a consensus in the scientific community on the benefits of motherhood and certainly not on an issue of national security because of the pacifism of the community." Earlier in his interview Keyworth had traced this strain of pacifism to the reaction of the scientific community to the development and use of the atomic bomb in World War II (p. 21). Keyworth also stated that Shultz had asked Teller if there was any way a defensive system could stop 99 percent of an attacking force. Keyworth said that neither he, McFarlane, nor the president had any such illusions that the effectiveness of a strategic defense system could be that high.

89. Ronald W. Reagan, transcript of 23 March 1983 speech, in "President's Speech on Military Spending and a New Defense," *NYT*, 24 March 1983, p. A20. Keyworth provided me with a copy of a 22 March version of the missile defense portion of the speech with Reagan's hand-written emendations (Ronald

W. Reagan, "A Call for a Bold Defense," 22 March 1983 draft of speech insert). Two key sentences were added by Reagan himself: "Would it not be better to save lives than to avenge them?" and "I call upon the scientific community which gave us nuclear weapons to turn their great talents to the cause of mankind and world peace; to give us the means of rendering these weapons impotent and obsolete."

EPILOGUE: TRIUMPH AND TRANSITION

1. Paul H. Nitze, "On the Road to a More Stable Peace," in *Department of State Bulletin* 85 (April 1985): 27. This is the text of an address Nitze delivered to the World Affairs Council in Philadelphia.

2. NSC 162/2, 30 October 1953, in William Z. Slany, ed., *Foreign Relations of the United States, 1952–1954*, Vol. 2: *National Security Affairs*, Part I (Washington, D.C.: Government Printing Office, 1984), p. 582.

3. For Weinberger's view, see *Fighting for Peace*, p. 302.

4. Senator Albert Gore, Jr., quoted in George C. Wilson, "Air Force Acts to Break ICBM Impasse," *WP*, 24 March 1989, p. A1.

5. For a discussion of early opposition to SDI in the scientific community, see Charles Mohr, "Scientists Dubious over Missile Plan," *NYT*, 25 March 1983, p. A8. For assessments of the arms control achievements of the Reagan presidency, see Ronald F. Lehman II, "The Arms Control Legacy of the Reagan Administration: A Focus on START," *Strategic Review* 16 (Fall 1988): pp. 13–20; Thomas E. Mann, "Thinking about the Reagan Years," in Larry Berman, ed., *Looking Back on the Reagan Presidency* (Baltimore: Johns Hopkins University Press, 1990), p. 25 (hereafter Berman, ed., *Reagan Presidency*). In his study of the Reagan presidency, Lou Cannon stated that SDI was "useful in prodding them [the Soviets] to return to the arms-control bargaining table" (*Role of a Lifetime*, pp. 741–42). Similar views on the role of SDI in arms control are found in Oberdorfer, *The Turn*, pp. 22–25, 127–30, 145–50, 157, 191–92, 197–200, 216–17, 253–54, 267.

6. Condoleezza Rice, "U.S.-Soviet Relations," in Berman, ed., *Reagan Presidency*, pp. 82–85; MacKubin Thomas Owens, "How Much Is Enough? Defense Spending for an Era of Uncertainty," *Strategic Review* 19 (Fall 1991): 7–8. For a discussion of how SDI apparently stressed the Soviet system, see James M. McConnell, "SDI, the Soviet Investment Debate, and Soviet Military Policy," *Strategic Review* 16 (Winter 1988): 47–62; see especially pp. 48, 57. In August 1990, Prime Minister Margaret Thatcher credited the SDI program with convincing the Soviets that they "could never, never, never achieve their aim by military might." This contributed to Soviet recognition of the "poverty of their own system" (speech given at the Strategic Defense Initiative Organization's National Test Facility, Colorado Springs, Colorado, 3 August 1990). That the Soviets were aware of their technological backwardness and their inability to compete with the United States in the realm of high technology weaponry is indicated in Oberdorfer, *The Turn*, pp. 214–16, 407.

Most recently, Francis Fukuyama (*The End of History and the Last Man* [New York: Free Press, 1992], pp. 75–76) declared: "In particular, President Reagan's Strategic Defense Initiative (SDI) posed a severe challenge because it threatened to make obsolete an entire generation of Soviet nuclear weapons, and shifted the superpower competition into areas like microelectronics and other innovative technologies where the Soviet Union had serious disadvantages. Soviet leaders, including many in the military, understood that the corrupt economic system inherited from Brezhnev would be unable to keep up in an SDI-dominated world, and were willing to accept short-run retrenchment for the sake of long-run survival."

7. Francis Fukuyama, "The End of History?" *National Interest* (Summer 1989): 3–18. Fukuyama's thesis is that "the century that began full of self-confidence in the ultimate triumph of Western liberal democracy seems at its close to be returning full circle to where it started: not to an 'end of ideology' or a convergence between capitalism and socialism, as earlier predicted, but to an unabashed victory of economic and political liberalism." For articles related to the Fukuyama phenomenon, see Allan Bloom, Gertrude Himmelfarb, Irving Kristol, Daniel Patrick Moynihan, and Stephen Sestanovich, "Response to Fukuyama," *National Interest* (Summer 1989): 19–35; James Atlas, "What Is Fukuyama Saying and to Whom Is He Saying It?" *New York Times Magazine*, 22 October 1989, pp. 38–40, 42, 54–55; Harvey J. Kaye, "The Concept of the 'End of History' Constitutes a Challenge to the Liberal Consensus in Scholarship and in Public Life," *Chronicle of Higher Education*, 25 October 1989, p. A48; Richard Bernstein, "The End of History, Explained for the Second Time: Fukuyama Replies," *NYT*, 10 December 1989, p. E6; Francis Fuyukama, "Beyond the End of History: Still the Best Theory for the Bizarre Events of '89," *WP*, 10 December 1989, pp. C1, C4; and Haynes Johnson, "The Reappearance of History," *WP*, 29 December 1989, p. 2A.

8. Melissa Healy, "High-Tech Missile Hits Bull's-Eye," *Los Angeles Times*, 22 January 1991, p. 1.

9. Oberdorfer, *The Turn*, p. 29, stated that Reagan's 1983 SDI speech "brought forth fierce opposition" in Moscow. After detailing Mikhail Gorbachev's opposition to SDI and his efforts to secure restrictions on this program (pp. 101, 144–50, 155–56, 186), Oberdorfer stated that by the time Gorbachev arrived for the 1987 Washington summit, "he had left behind most of the demands for curbing Reagan's Star Wars plans." For Reagan's offers to share SDI technology with the Soviets, see "Question-and-Answer Session with Reporters on Domestic and Foreign Policy Issues," 29 March 1983, in *Public Papers of the Presidents of the United States: Ronald Reagan, 1983 (Book 1, 1 January to 1 July)* (Washington, D.C.: Government Printing Office, 1984), p. 465, and Oberdorfer, *The Turn*, pp. 146, 149, 204.

10. Mikhail Gorbachev, Personal Message to Heads of State or Government Attending the G7 Meeting in London, Appendix, p. 6. My copy of this document, secured through the Congressional Research Service, is undated; the approximate date of the document is 10 July 1991. According to newspaper accounts, Gorbachev's letter, which outlined his agenda for conferring with the G7 leaders, was carried to London by a Soviet advance team headed by Vladimir Shcherbakov and Yvgeny Primakov; this team began pushing Gorbachev's agenda in London on Friday, 12 July. The letter is twenty-three pages long and has an appendix of forty pages (the appendix of my copy includes only thirty-one pages). For information on the letter, see Steven Greenhouse, "Gorbachev Note to Group of 7 Said to Fall Short of Reform," *NYT*, 16 July 1991, p. A8; Glenn Frankel, "Soviet Advance Team Presses Gorbachev's Economic Program," *WP*, 16 July 1991, p. A15. For other discussions of possible East-West cooperation on missile defenses see "Another Russian Official Has Come Out

in Favor of U.S.-Soviet Cooperation on Strategic Defense," *SDI Monitor* 6 (November 1991): 279; Vincent Kiernan, "Soviets Warm to Joint Missile Defenses," *Space News* 2 (14–20 October 1991): 1, 20; and Henry F. Cooper, "From Confrontation to Cooperation on Ballistic Missile Defense," *Armed Forces Journal* 129 (January 1992): 16–17.

SELECTED BIBLIOGRAPHY

INTERVIEWS

Anderson, Martin. Hoover Institution, Stanford, California. Interview, 3 August 1987.

Barnett, Frank. National Strategy Information Center, New York. Interview by Stanley A. Blumberg, 1 October 1986.

Brooks, Linton F. Old Executive Office Building, Washington, D.C. Interview, 21 December 1987.

Codevilla, Angelo. Telephone interview, 15 July 1987.

Coors, Joseph. Adolph Coors Company, Golden, Colorado. Interview, 31 July 1987.

Graham, Daniel O. Offices of High Frontier, Inc., Washington, D.C. Interview, 7 July 1987.

Hume, Jaquelin. Madison Hotel, Washington, D.C. Interview, 28 October 1987.

Hunter, Maxwell W., II. Ramada Renaissance Hotel, Washington, D.C. Interview, 29 October 1987.

Keyworth, George A. Keyworth Company, Washington, D.C. Interview, 28 September 1987.

Kramish, Arnold. Offices of the Strategic Defense Initiative Organization, Washington, D.C. Interview, 25 May 1988.

McFarlane, Robert C. Center for Strategic and International Studies, Washington, D.C. Interview, 15 September 1987.

Poindexter, John M. Poindexter home, Rockville, Maryland. Interview, 28 January 1988.

Teller, Edward. Cosmos Club, Washington, D.C. Interview, 6 July 1987.

Wallop, Malcolm. U.S. Senate, Washington, D.C. Interview, 16 December 1987.

Watkins, James D. U.S. Department of Energy, Washington, D.C. Discussion, 25 October 1989. (No formal transcript was produced.)

_____. U.S. Navy Historical Center, Washington Navy Yard. Interview, 29 September 1987.

Wilson, William A. Jefferson Hotel, Washington, D.C. Interview, 7 December 1987.

DOCUMENTS AND REPORTS

Anderson, Martin. Reagan for President Committee. Policy Memorandum Number 3: Foreign Policy and National Security, August 1979.

"Background Statement from White House on MX Missile and B-1 Bomber." *New York Times*, 3 October 1981, p. 12.

Bell Laboratories. *ABM Research and Development at Bell Laboratories: Project History, October 1975*. Study completed for the U.S. Army Ballistic Missile Defense Systems Command under contract DAHC60-71-C-0005.

Bendetsen, Karl R. Papers on High Frontier. When used by me, these papers were kept in Mr. Bendetsen's office at 1850 K Street, N.W., Washington, D.C. Since then, Mr. Bendetsen's papers have been shipped to the Hoover Institution at Stanford, California.

[Brooks, Linton F.]. "CNO and the Strategic Defense Initiative." N.d.

General Board, United States Forces, European Theater, Antiaircraft Artillery Section. "V-2 Rocket Attacks and Defense," Study 42. N.d. [late 1945 or early 1946]. Document 502.101-42 in the Air Force Historical Research Center, Maxwell Air Force Base, Alabama.

Hunter, Maxwell W., II. "Strategic Dynamics and Space-Laser Weaponry." 31 October 1977. Paper circulated privately by Hunter.

McNamara, Robert S. "Text of McNamara Speech on Anti-China Missile Defense and U.S. Nuclear Strategy." *New York Times*, 19 September 1967, pp. 18–19.

Mark, W[illia]m S., Jr.; Joseph P. D'Arezzo; R. A. Ranson; and G. D. Bagley. "Detection and Plotting of the V-2 (Big Ben) Missile as Developed in ETO." 4 July 1945. Document 142.0423-16 Jul.-Sep. 1945 in the Air Force Historical Research Center, Maxwell Air Force Base, Alabama.

National Committee on Resolutions to the Republican National Convention. *Republican Platform: Family, Neighborhood, Work, Peace, Freedom*. 14 July 1980. Detroit, Michigan.

Nitze, Paul H. "On the Road to a More Stable Peace." In *Department of State Bulletin* 85 (April 1985): 27–29.

Nixon, Richard M. Inaugural Address. 20 January 1969. Transcript in *New York Times*, 21 January 1969, p. 21.

————. "The President's News Conference of March 14, 1969." Document 108. In *Public Papers of the Presidents of the United States, Containing the Public Messages, Speeches, and Statements of the President: Richard Nixon, 1969*, pp. 208–16. Washington, D.C.: Government Printing Office, 1971.

————. "Statement on Deployment of the Antiballistic Missile System, March 14, 1969." Document 109. In *Public Papers of the Presidents of the United States, Containing the Public Messages, Speeches, and Statements of the President: Richard Nixon, 1969*, pp. 216–19. Washington, D.C.: Government Printing Office, 1971.

NSC 162/2, 30 October 1953. In William Z. Slany, ed. *Foreign Relations of the United States, 1952–1954*. Vol. 2: *National Security Affairs*, Part I. Washington, D.C.: Government Printing Office, 1984.

Reagan, Ronald. "Text of Reagan and Pentagon Statement on MX Missile Basing Proposal." *New York Times*, 23 November 1982, p. A14.

――――――. "Transcript of President's Address on Nuclear Strategy toward Soviet Union." *New York Times*, 23 November 1982, p. A12.

――――――. Transcript of 23 March 1983 speech. In "President's Speech on Military Spending and a New Defense," *New York Times*, 24 March 1983, p. A20.

Tennant, T. C. *Survey of Guidance Systems.* Part 1: United States Missiles. 31 March 1957. This document is also known as the Gilfillan Report after Gilfillan Brothers of Los Angeles, the company that contracted with the U.S. Army to complete the survey. This report may be found in the Redstone Scientific Information Center, Redstone Arsenal, Alabama.

Thatcher, Margaret. Speech given at the Strategic Defense Initiative Organization's National Test Facility, Colorado Springs, Colorado. 3 August 1990.

Trump, John G., to L. A. DuBridge. Report, 20 January 1945. In folder marked A-1 RADAR—General—ETO, Box 14, Entry 60A, Record Group 18, National Archives, Washington, D.C.

U.S. Army Air Forces. Scientific Advisory Group. *Toward New Horizons: A Report to General of the Army H[enry] H. Arnold.* 12 vols. Washington, D.C.: Headquarters Army Air Forces, December 1945. Vol. 1: *Science, the Key to Air Supremacy*, by Th[eodore] von Kármán.

U.S. Congress. House, Committee on Armed Services. *Investigation of National Defense Missiles: Hearings before the Committee Pursuant to H. Res. 67.* 85th Cong., 2d sess., 1958.

――――――. Committee on Science and Technology. *United States Civilian Space Programs, 1958–1978: A Report Prepared for the Subcommittee on Space Science and Applications of the Committee on Science and Technology by the Science Policy Research Division of the Congressional Research Service of the Library of Congress.* Serial D., vol. 1, 97th Cong., 1st sess., January 1981.

――――――. Senate. Committee on Appropriations. *Department of Defense Appropriations Bill, 1976.* S.R. 94-446 to accompany H.R. 9861, 94th Cong., 1st sess., 6 November 1975.

――――――. Committee on Appropriations. *Hearings before a Subcommittee on Department of Defense Appropriations for Fiscal Year 1975 on H.R.* [sic], *Part 2—Army.* 93d Cong., 2d sess., 1974.

――――――. Committee on Armed Services. *Fiscal Year 1977 Authorization for Military Procurement, Research and Development, and Active Duty, Select Reserve, and Civilian Personnel Strengths, Hearings on S. 2965, Part 12, Research and Development.* 94th Cong., 2d sess., 1976.

――――――. Committee on Commerce, Science, and Transportation. "Laser Research and Applications." Committee Print, 96th Cong., 2d sess., November 1980.

――――――. Committee on Foreign Affairs. Subcommittee on Arms Control, International Law and Organization. *Hearings on U.S. and Soviet Strategic Doctrine and Military Policies.* 91st Cong., 2d sess., 4 March 1974.

――――――. Senate and House. *An Act Making Appropriations for the Department of Defense for the Fiscal Year Ending June 30, 1976, and the Period Beginning July 1, 1976, and Ending September 30, 1976, and for Other Purposes.* P.L. 94-212, 94th Cong., 1st sess., 1976, H.R. 9861.

U.S. Department of Defense. Director of the Strategic Defense Initiative Organization. *SDI: A Technical Progress Report.* April 1987.

U.S. Department of the Air Force. Headquarters United States Air Force. Air

Force Technical Committee. *Semi-Annual Progress Report of the Guided Missiles Program, Department of the Air Force (31 October 1949).* Case No. 13-2, Report No. 10. Wright-Patterson Air Force Base, Dayton, Ohio. This document may be found in the Redstone Scientific Information Center, Redstone Arsenal, Alabama.

U.S. Executive Office of the President. Office of Defense Mobilization. Security Resources Panel of the Science Advisory Committee. *Deterrence and Survival in the Nuclear Age: Report to the President* (Gaither Report). 7 November 1957.

"Visions of Star Wars: A NOVA/Frontline Special Report." Report No. 5008. Boston: WGBH Foundation, 1986. This is a transcript of a NOVA program that was originally broadcast on 22 April 1986.

ARTICLES AND SPEECHES

"ABM: Winning Isn't Everything." *Newsweek,* 18 August 1969, pp. 20–22.

"After the Pentagon Papers: Talk with Kistiakowsky, Wiesner." *Science* 174 (November 1971): 923–28.

Alpern, David M., with Henry W. Hubbard. "The Countdown." *Newsweek,* 17 November 1975, pp. 27–28, 33–34, 36.

Anderson, Martin. "Joint Chiefs Not Fathers of SDI." Letter to the Editor. *Policy Review* (Winter 1991): 96.

"Another Russian Official Has Come Out in Favor of U.S.-Soviet Cooperation on Strategic Defense." *SDI Monitor* 6 (November 1991): 279.

"Armaments: Plea for an Extra Button." *Newsweek,* 28 July 1969, p. 39.

"Army Beam Programs Moving to DARPA." *Aviation Week,* 4 August 1980, p. 51.

"Army Widens Ballistic Missile Research." *Aviation Week,* 8 December 1975, pp. 17–18.

Atlas, James. "What Is Fukuyama Saying and to Whom Is He Saying It?" *New York Times Magazine,* 22 October 1989, pp. 38–40, 42, 54–55.

Baldwin, Hanson W. "Slow-Down in the Pentagon." *Foreign Affairs* 17 (January 1965): 262–80.

Ball, Desmond. "The MX Basing Decision." *Survival* 22 (March-April 1980): 58–65.

Baucom, Donald R. "Hail to the Chiefs: The Untold History of Reagan's SDI Decision." *Policy Review* (Summer 1990): 66–73.

———. "Technological War: Reality and the American Myth." *Air University Review* 32 (September-October 1981): 56–66.

Bloom, Allan; Gertrude Himmelfarb; Irving Kristol; Daniel Patrick Moynihan; and Stephen Sestanovich. "Response to Fukuyama." *National Interest* (Summer 1989): 19–35.

Bosma, John. "Space and Strategic-Defense Reorientation: Project Defender." *Defense Science and Electronics* (September 1983): 58–65.

Brodie, Bernard. "Implications for Military Policy." In Frederick S. Dunn, Bernard Brodie, Arnold Wolfers, Percy E. Corbett, and William T. R. Fox, *The Absolute Weapon: Atomic Power and World Order,* pp. 71–107. Ed. by Bernard Brodie. New York: Harcourt, Brace, 1946.

Bromberg, Joan Lisa. "The Birth of the Laser." *Physics Today* 41 (October 1988): 26–33.

Brower, Brock. "Bud McFarlane: Semper Fi." *New York Times Magazine*, 22 January 1989, pp. 26–29, 32, 38.

Cahn, Anne Hessing. "American Scientists and the ABM: A Case Study in Controversy." In *Scientists and Public Affairs*, ed. by Albert Teich, pp. 41–120. Cambridge, Mass.: MIT Press, 1974.

"Computer Proves Architecture Concept." *Aviation Week*, 11 October 1976, p. 35.

Covault, Craig. "Antisatellite Weapon Design Advances." *Aviation Week*, 16 June 1980, pp. 243–47.

Davis, Jacquelyn K. "End of the Strategic Triad." *Strategic Review* 6 (Winter 1978): 36–44.

"Defense Dept. Experts Confirm Efficacy of Space-Based Lasers." *Aviation Week*, 28 July 1980, pp. 65–66.

Deming, Angus, with Bruce van Voorst and Lloyd H. Norman. "Foreign Fallout." *Newsweek*, 17 November 1975, pp. 36, 38.

"Demonstration Planned for MX Defense System." *Aviation Week*, 16 June 1980, pp. 220–21.

"Directed-Energy Effort Shifted." *Aviation Week*, 4 August 1980, pp. 44–47.

Elson, Benjamin M. "Kwajalein Range Plays Unique Role." *Aviation Week*, 16 June 1980, pp. 223, 226–28.

————. "USAF Weapons Lab Mission Expanded." *Aviation Week*, 29 January 1979, pp. 212–16.

Erickson, John. "The Chimera of Mutual Deterrence." *Strategic Review* 6 (Spring 1978): 11–17.

Feld, Bernard T., and Kosta Tsipis. "Land-Based Intercontinental Ballistic Missiles." *Scientific American* 241 (November 1979): 51–61.

Fukuyama, Francis. "The End of History?" *National Interest* (Summer 1989): 3–18.

Garment, Leonard. Letter to the Editor. *New York Times Magazine*, 12 February 1989, p. 8.

Getler, Michael. "Chinese Missile Shot Forcing Nike Choice." *Technology Week*, 7 November 1966, pp. 13–14.

Goldman, Peter, with Thomas M. DeFrank. "Ford's Big Shuffle." *Newsweek*, 17 November 1975, pp. 24–27.

Graham, Daniel O. "Bold Strokes for a Strategic Nuclear Balance." *Signal* 35 (May-June 1981): 57–60, 63–64.

————. "The High Frontier: Summary of a New National Strategy." *Defense Science 2000*+ 1, 2 (1982): 20–21, 66–79.

————. "New Strategy on the High Frontier of Space," *Officer* 57 (November 1981): 26–27.

————. "Preventing World War III—How to Neutralize the Numbers by Exploiting Defense in the 'High Frontier.'" *Government Executive* 14 (July 1982) 16, 18–19.

————. "Selling the High Frontier Defense Strategy." Interview with General Daniel O. Graham. *Defense Electronics* (October 1982): 169–70, 172, 174–75.

————. "Toward a New Strategy: Bold Strokes Rather Than Increments." *Strategic Review* 9 (Spring 1981): 9–16.

Gray, Colin S. "The MX Debate." *Survival* 20 (May-June 1978): 105–12.

————. "SALT and the American Mood." *Strategic Review* 3 (Summer 1975): 41–51.

————. "SALT: Time to Quit." *Strategic Review* 4 (Fall 1976): 14–22.

"Haig Seeks Space-Based Weapons Report." *Aviation Week*, 25 May 1981, pp. 42–43.

Halperin, Morton H. "The Decision to Deploy the ABM: Bureaucratic and Domestic Politics in the Johnson Administration." *World Politics* 25 (October 1972): 62–95.

"High-Intensity Electron Beams Pushed." *Aviation Week*, 4 August 1980, pp. 67–68.

Kiernan, Vincent. "Soviets Warm to Joint Missile Defenses." *Space News* 2 (October 1991): 1, 20.

"Kissinger Assesses the Moscow Summit and the Arms Race," 3 July 1974. In *SALT Hand Book: Key Documents and Issues, 1972–1979*, ed. by Roger P. Labrie, pp. 264–65. Washington, D.C.: American Enterprise Institute for Public Policy Research, 1979.

Klass, Philip J. "Ballistic Missile Defense Tests Set." *Aviation Week*, 16 June 1980, pp. 213–18.

———. "Power Boost Key to Feasibility." *Aviation Week*, 21 August 1972, pp. 32–40.

———. "Research Nears Application Level." *Aviation Week*, 14 August 1972, pp. 12–15.

"Laser Applications in Space Emphasized." *Aviation Week*, 28 July 1980, pp. 62–64.

"Laser Battle Station Mirror Proposed." *Aviation Week*, 25 May 1981, p. 64.

"Laser Weaponry Technology Advances." *Aviation Week*, 25 May 1981, pp. 65, 68–71.

Lehman, Ronald F., II. "The Arms Control Legacy of the Reagan Administration: A Focus on START." *Strategic Review* 16 (Fall 1988): 13–20.

Lodal, Jan M. "Assuring Strategic Stability: An Alternative View." *Foreign Affairs* (April 1976): 462–81.

McConnell, James M. "SDI, the Soviet Investment Debate, and Soviet Military Policy." *Strategic Review* 16 (Winter 1988): 47–62.

Mann, Thomas E. "Thinking about the Reagan Years." In *Looking Back on the Reagan Presidency*, ed. by Larry Berman, pp. 18–29. Baltimore: Johns Hopkins University Press, 1990.

"The Nation: Moving Ahead, Nixon Style." *Time*, 15 August 1969, p. 12.

"Neutral Particle Programs Draw Focus." *Aviation Week*, 25 May 1981, pp. 55, 57, 59–60.

Newhouse, John. "Annals of Diplomacy: The Abolitionist—I." *New Yorker*, 2 January 1989, pp. 37–52.

———. "Annals of Diplomacy: The Abolitionist—II." *New Yorker*, 9 January 1989, pp. 51–62, 64–70, 72.

Nitze, Paul H. "Assuring Strategic Stability in an Era of Détente." *Foreign Affairs* 54 (January 1976): 207–32.

———. "The Strategic Balance: Between Hope and Skepticism." *Foreign Policy* (Winter 1974-75): 136–56.

———. "The Vladivostok Accord and SALT II." *Review of Politics* 37 (April 1975): 147–60.

Owens, MacKubin Thomas. "How Much Is Enough? Defense Spending for an Era of Uncertainty." *Strategic Review* 19 (Fall 1991): 7–8.

"Pentagon Studying Laser Battle Stations in Space." *Aviation Week*, 28 July 1980, pp. 57–59, 61–62.

Pipes, Richard. "Why the Soviet Union Thinks It Could Fight and Win a Nuclear War." *Commentary* 64 (July 1977): 26–34.

"Processing of Data Key to Missile Defense." *Aviation Week*, 28 August 1978, pp. 12–15.

Rathjens, George W. "The Dynamics of the Arms Race." *Scientific American* 220 (April 1969): 15–25.

"The Real Paul Warnke." *New Republic*, 26 March 1977, pp. 22–25.

"Report on Soviet Nuclear Strategy Says Moscow Emphasizes Victory." *New York Times*, 25 June 1977, p. 7.

Rice, Condoleezza. "U.S.-Soviet Relations." In *Looking Back on the Reagan Presidency*, ed. by Larry Berman, pp. 71–89. Baltimore: Johns Hopkins University Press, 1990.

Robinson, Clarence A., Jr. "Advance Made on High-Energy Laser." *Aviation Week*, 23 February 1981, pp. 25–27.

_____. "Army Pushes New Weapons Effort." *Aviation Week*, 16 October 1978, pp. 42–43, 45, 48–49, 51–52.

_____. "Army Spurs Missile Defense Technology." *Aviation Week*, 22 April 1974, pp. 12–15.

_____. "Beam Weapons Technology Expanding." *Aviation Week*, 25 May 1981, pp. 40–43, 46–47.

_____. "DOD Presses for ABM Fund Restoration." *Aviation Week*, 7 June 1976, pp. 16–17.

_____. "ICBM Intercept in Boost Phase Pushed." *Aviation Week*, 17 July 1978, pp. 47, 49–50.

_____. "Laser Technology Demonstration Proposed." *Aviation Week*, 23 February 1981, pp. 16–19.

_____. "Layered Defense System Pushed to Protect ICBMs." *Aviation Week*, 9 February 1981, pp. 83, 85–86.

_____. "Missile Defense Gains Support." *Aviation Week*, 22 October 1979, pp. 14–17.

_____. "Missile Defense Radar System Tests Set." *Aviation Week*, 20 September 1976, pp. 42–43, 46–47, 49, 51.

_____. "Prototype Site Defense Construction Set." *Aviation Week*, 29 April 1974, pp. 70–71, 73, 75–76.

_____. "Soviets Grasping Strategic Lead." *Aviation Week*, 30 August 1976, pp. 14–18.

_____. "Space-Based Laser Battle Stations Seen." *Aviation Week*, 8 December 1980, pp. 36–37, 40.

_____. "Technology Program Spurs Missile Intercept Advances." *Aviation Week*, 5 June 1978, pp. 108–11.

_____. "U.S. Anti-Missile Work Stresses Optics." *Aviation Week*, 6 September 1976, pp. 30–34.

_____. "U.S. to Test ABM System with MX." *Aviation Week*, 19 March 1979, pp. 23–26.

Rosen, Stephen P. "Safeguarding Deterrence." *Foreign Policy* (Summer 1979): 109–23.

"Safeguard: Pro and Con." *Newsweek*, 21 July 1969, pp. 26–27.

"Safeguard: What U.S. Got for $5.4 Billion." *U.S. News and World Report*, 30 June 1975, pp. 42–43.

"The Scale Tips against the ABM." *Newsweek*, 21 July 1969, pp. 25–26, 28.

Schlesinger, Arthur, Jr. "The Historian and History." *Foreign Affairs* 41 (April 1963): 491–97.

Schneider, Mark B. "SALT and the Strategic Balance: 1974." *Strategic Review* 2 (Fall 1974): 41–47.

Seidel, Robert W. "From Glow to Flow: A History of Military Laser Research and Development." *Historical Studies in the Physical Sciences* 18, 1 (1987): 111–47.

————. "How the Military Responded to the Laser." *Physics Today* 41 (October 1988): 36–43.

Seligman, Daniel. "Our ICBMs Are in Danger." *Fortune*, 2 July 1979, pp. 50–56.

"Senate Directs Air Force to Formulate Laser Plan." *Aviation Week*, 25 May 1981, pp. 52–53.

"Senate Discussing ABM Need to Guard Multiple Shelter MX." *Aviation Week*, 9 February 1981, p. 91.

Stein, Kenneth J. "New Missile Defense Systems Studied." *Aviation Week*, 11 October 1976, pp. 34–36.

"Strategic Defensive Systems Emphasized." *Aviation Week*, 20 September 1976, p. 49.

"A Strategic Doctrine for the United States: Secretary Schlesinger's Report." *Strategic Review* 2 (Spring 1974): 4–6.

"The Surprising Lady from Maine." *Newsweek*, 18 August 1969, p. 21.

"Technology Eyed to Defend ICBMs, Spacecraft." *Aviation Week*, 28 July 1980, pp. 32–34, 39–42.

"Technology Milestone Met in Missile Defense Testing." *Aviation Week*, 29 September 1980, pp. 25–26.

Till, Geoffrey. "The Safeguard Debate: Image and Reality." *RUSI* 119 (December 1974): 40–46.

"U.S. Effort Redirected to High Energy Lasers." *Aviation Week*, 28 July 1980, pp. 50, 55–57.

"U.S. Funds Killer Satellite Effort." *Aviation Week*, 6 February 1978, pp. 18–19.

Van Cleave, William R. "SALT on the Eagle's Tail." *Strategic Review* 4 (Spring 1976): 44–55.

Wallop, Malcolm. "Opportunities and Imperatives of Ballistic Missile Defense." *Strategic Review* 7 (Fall 1979): 13–21.

Warnke, Paul C. "Apes on a Treadmill." *Foreign Policy* (Spring 1975): 12–29.

"Washington Observations." *Air Force Magazine* (February 1982): 21.

Watkins, James D. "The Moral Man in the Modern Military." *Sea Power* (December 1982): 17–18, 20.

————. "We Are a Moral People: A Message to the Class of 1983." *Shipmate* (January-February 1983): 19–20.

"White House Concentrates on Neutral Particle Beam." *Aviation Week*, 4 August 1980, pp. 63–66.

Wiesner, Jerome B., and Herbert F. York. "National Security and the Nuclear-Test Ban." *Scientific American* 211 (October 1964): 27–35.

Wilson, George C. "President, Dr. Bethe Differ over Usefulness of AntiMissile Missile." *Aviation Week*, 19 February 1962, p. 29.

Wohlstetter, Albert. "Is There a Strategic Arms Race?" *Foreign Policy* (Summer 1974): 3–20.

————. "Legends of the Strategic Arms Race, Part I: The Driving Engine." *Strategic Review* 2 (Fall 1974): 67–92.

_____. "Legends of the Strategic Arms Race, Part II: The Uncontrolled Upward Spiral." *Strategic Review* 3 (Winter 1975): 71–86.

_____. "Optimal Ways to Confuse Ourselves." *Foreign Policy* (Autumn 1975): 170–98.

_____. "Rivals, But No Race." *Foreign Policy* (Fall 1974): 48–81

Yost, David S. "The Delegitimization of Nuclear Deterrence?" *Armed Forces and Society* 16 (Summer 1990): 489–90.

_____. "Public Opinion, Political Culture, and Nuclear Weapons in the Western Alliance." Draft paper, 31 May 1989.

MEMOIRS

Anderson, Martin. *Revolution.* New York: Harcourt Brace Jovanovich, 1988.

Hunter, Maxwell W., II. "Great Zeus!" Personal paper, 4 July 1987.

Killian, James R. *Sputnik, Scientists, and Eisenhower: A Memoir of the First Special Assistant to the President for Science and Technology.* Cambridge, Mass.: MIT Press, 1977.

Kissinger, Henry. *White House Years.* Boston: Little, Brown, 1979.

Nitze, Paul H., with Ann M. Smith and Steven L. Rearden. *From Hiroshima to Glasnost: At the Center of Decision—A Memoir.* New York: Grove Weidenfeld, 1989.

Nixon, Richard. *Memoirs of Richard Nixon.* New York: Grosset and Dunlap, 1978.

Reagan, Ronald. *An American Life.* New York: Simon and Schuster, 1990.

Smith, Gerard. *Doubletalk: The Story of the First Strategic Arms Limitations Talks.* Garden City, N.Y.: Doubleday, 1980.

Teller, Edward. *Better a Shield than a Sword: Perspectives on Defense and Technology.* New York: Free Press, 1987.

Watson-Watt, Robert. *The Pulse of Radar: The Autobiography of Sir Robert Watson-Watt.* New York: Dial Press, 1959.

Weinberger, Caspar. *Fighting for Peace: Seven Critical Years in the Pentagon.* New York: Warner Books, 1990.

York, Herbert F. *Making Weapons, Talking Peace: A Physicist's Odyssey from Hiroshima to Geneva.* New York: Basic Books, 1987.

_____. *Race to Oblivion: A Participant's View of the Arms Race.* New York: Simon and Schuster, 1970.

BOOKS — ~~33~~ 30 ↓ totaL

Adams, Benson D. *Ballistic Missile Defense.* New York: American Elsevier Publishing Company, 1971.

Armacost, Michael H. *The Politics of Weapons Innovation: The Thor-Jupiter Controversy.* New York: Columbia University Press, 1969.

Au, William A. *The Cross, the Flag, and the Bomb: American Catholics Debate War and Peace, 1960–1983.* Contributions to the Study of Religion, No. 12, ed. by Henry W. Bowden. Westport, Conn.: Greenwood Press, 1985.

Boffey, Philip M.; William J. Broad; Leslie H. Gelb; Charles Mohr; and Holcombe B. Noble. *Claiming the Heavens: The* New York Times *Complete Guide to the Star Wars Debate.* New York: Times Books, 1988.

† "FROM CROSSBOW to H-BOMB' BY BERNARD BRODIE Y FAWN BRODIE INDIANA U. Press 1973.

Broad, William J. *Star Warriors.* New York: Simon and Schuster, 1985.

Brodie, Bernard. *Strategy in the Missile Age.* Princeton, N.J.: Princeton University Press, 1959.

Builder, Carl H. *The Masks of War: American Military Styles in Strategy and Analysis.* RAND Corporation Research Study. Baltimore: Johns Hopkins University Press, 1989.

Cannon, Lou. *President Reagan: The Role of a Lifetime.* New York: Simon and Schuster, 1991.

————. *Reagan.* New York: G. P. Putnam's Sons, 1982.

Charlton, Michael. *The Star Wars History—From Deterrence to Defence: The American Strategic Debate.* London: BBC Publications, 1986.

Churchill, Winston S. *The Second World War.* Vol. 6: *Triumph and Tragedy.* New York: Bantam Books, 1953.

Clark, Ronald W. *War Winners.* London: Sidgwick and Jackson, 1979.

Codevilla, Angelo. *While Others Build: The Commonsense Approach to the Strategic Defense Initiative.* New York: Free Press, 1988.

Dallek, Robert. *Ronald Reagan: The Politics of Symbolism.* Cambridge Mass.: Harvard University Press, 1984.

Franklin, H. Bruce. *War Stars: The Superweapon and the American Imagination.* New York: Oxford University Press, 1988.

Freedman, Lawrence. *The Evolution of Nuclear Strategy.* New York: St. Martin's Press, 1983.

Graham, Daniel O. *High Frontier: A New National Strategy.* Washington, D.C.: High Frontier, 1982.

————. *Shall America Be Defended? SALT II and Beyond.* New Rochelle, N.Y.: Arlington House, 1979.

Hecht, Jeff. *Beam Weapons: The Next Arms Race.* New York: Plenum Press, 1984.

Herken, Gregg. *Counsels of War.* Expanded ed. New York: Oxford University Press, 1987.

Holland, Lauren H., and Robert A. Hoover. *The MX Decision: A New Direction in U.S. Weapons Procurement Policy?* Boulder, Colo.: Westview Press, 1985.

Irving, David. *The Mare's Nest.* Boston: Little, Brown, 1965.

Jungk, Robert. *Brighter than a Thousand Suns: A Personal History of the Atomic Scientists.* Trans. by James Cleugh. New York: Harcourt Brace Jovanovich, 1958.

Kahan, Jerome H. *Security in the Nuclear Age: Developing U.S. Strategic Arms Policy.* Washington, D.C.: Brookings Institution, 1975.

Kaplan, Fred. *Wizards of Armageddon.* New York: Simon and Schuster, 1983.

Kennedy, Paul. *The Decline and Fall of the Great Powers.* New York: Random House, 1987.

Kevles, Daniel J. *The Physicists: The History of a Scientific Community in Modern America.* New York: Vintage Books, 1977.

Kissinger, Henry. *A World Restored.* Gloucester, Mass.: Peter Smith, 1957.

Kuhn, Thomas S. *The Structure of Scientific Revolutions.* International Encyclopedia of Unified Science. *Foundations of the Unity of Science,* vol. 2, no. 2. Chicago: University of Chicago Press, 1970.

Labrie, Roger P., ed. *SALT Hand Book: Key Documents and Issues, 1972–1979.* Washington, D.C.: American Enterprise Institute for Public Policy Research, 1979.

McGovern, James. *Crossbow and Overcast.* New York: William Morrow, 1964.

Newhouse, John. *Cold Dawn: The Story of SALT.* New York: Holt, Rinehart, and Winston, 1973.

————. *War and Peace in the Nuclear Age.* New York: Alfred A. Knopf, 1989.

Oberdorfer, Don. *The Turn: From the Cold War to a New Era—The United States and the Soviet Union, 1983–1990.* New York: Poseidon Press, 1991.

Powaski, Ronald E. *March to Armageddon: The United States and the Nuclear Arms Race, 1939 to the Present.* New York: Oxford University Press, 1987.

Prados, John. *Keepers of the Keys: A History of the National Security Council from Truman to Bush.* New York: William Morrow, 1991.

Ralegh [sic], Sir Walter. *The History of the World Treating of the Beginning and First Ages of the Same from the Creation unto . . . the Romans (Prevailing over All) Made Conquest of Asia and Macedon.* Edinburgh: Archibald Constable, 1820.

Rhodes, Richard. *The Making of the Atomic Bomb.* New York: Simon and Schuster, 1986.

Sanders, Jerry W. *Peddlers of Crisis: The Committee on the Present Danger and the Politics of Containment.* Boston: South End Press, 1983.

Sarton, George. *A History of Science.* Vol. 2: *Hellenistic Science and Culture in the Last Three Centuries B.C.* New York: W. W. Norton, 1959.

Scheer, Robert. *With Enough Shovels: Reagan, Bush, and Nuclear War.* New York: Vintage Books, 1983.

Talbott, Strobe. *Endgame: The Inside Story of SALT II.* New York: Harper and Row, 1979.

————. *The Master of the Game: Paul Nitze and the Nuclear Peace.* New York: Alfred A. Knopf, 1988.

Teich, Albert, ed. *Scientists and Public Affairs.* Cambridge, Mass.: MIT Press, 1974.

Wells, H. G. *The War of the Worlds.* New York: Berkley Books, n.d.

Weigel, George. *Tranquillitas Ordinis: The Present Failure and Future Promise of American Catholic Thought on War and Peace.* New York: Oxford University Press, 1987.

Wolfe, Thomas W. *The SALT Experience.* Cambridge, Mass.: Ballinger, 1979.

Yanarella, Ernest J. *The Missile Defense Controversy: Strategy, Technology, and Politics, 1955–1972.* Lexington: University of Kentucky Press, 1977.

Yost, David S. *Soviet Ballistic Missile Defense and the Western Alliance.* Cambridge, Mass.: Harvard University Press, 1988.

OFFICIAL HISTORIES

Anderson, Mary D. *Annual Historical Summary of SAFEGUARD System Command* (1 July 1968–30 June 1969). Vol. 1. Narrative, 31 October 1968. This study was found in the Office of the Historian, U.S. Army Strategic Defense Command, Huntsville, Alabama.

Currie-McDaniel, Ruth. *The U.S. Army Strategic Defense Command: Its History and Role in the Strategic Defense Initiative.* 2d ed. Huntsville, Ala.: U.S. Army Strategic Defense Command, January 1987.

Guerlac, Henry. *Early History of Radar.* History of Division 14, Section A, Office of Scientific Research and Development. Edward L. Bowles, professor emeritus at MIT, provided me a xeroxed copy of an original hextograph copy of this study. A copy is available in Box 4111, Record Group 277, National Archives, Washington, D.C.

Jarrell, Ruth, and Mary T. Cagle. *History of the Plato Antimissile Missile System: 1952–1960*. Redstone Arsenal, Ala.: U.S. Army Ordnance Missile Command, 23 June 1961.

Reed, Sidney G.; Richard H. Van Atta; and Seymour J. Deitchman. *DARPA Technical Accomplishments: An Historical Review of Selected DARPA Projects*. Vol. 1, IDA Paper P-2192. Alexandria, Va.: Institute for Defense Analyses, February 1990.

Rosenberg, Max. *The Air Force and the National Guided Missile Program, 1944–1950*. Washington, D.C.: Headquarters United States Air Force, Historical Division Liaison Office, June 1964.

Sturm, Thomas A. *The USAF Scientific Advisory Board: Its First Twenty Years, 1944–1964*. Office of Air Force History Special Studies. Washington, D.C.: Government Printing Office, 1986; reprint of 1967 edition.

U.S. Air Force Ballistic Missile Office. Official History for Fiscal Years 1980 and 1981. Extracts were provided me by Raymond L. Puffer, historian of the Air Force Ballistic Missile Office, Norton Air Force Base, California.

————. Official History for Fiscal Years 1982 and 1983. Extracts were provided me by Raymond L. Puffer, historian of the Air Force Ballistic Missile Office, Norton Air Force Base, California.

INDEX